Death Valley SUV Trails

A guide to 40 four-wheeling excursions
in the backcountry in and around
Death Valley National Park

Roger Mitchell

Two roads diverged in the woods, and I-
I took the one less traveled by,
And that has made all the difference.

Robert Frost

Death Valley SUV Trails

A guide to 40 four-wheeling excursions in the backcountry in and around Death Valley National Park

Roger Mitchell

All photos by the author except as noted

Track & Trail Publications
Oakhurst California

Track & Trail Publications
P.O. Box 1247
Oakhurst CA 93644

Printed in the United States of America

Second and Revised Edition 2006

Front Cover: The Hanaupah Canyon Road
Rear Cover: The start of the Titus Canyon Road

Other current Track & Trail Publications:

Inyo-Mono SUV Trails
High Sierra SUV Trails, Volume I – The East Side
High Sierra SUV Trails, Volume II – The Western Slope
High Sierra SUV Trails, Volume III – The Far North Country
Southern California SUV Trails, Volume I – The Western Mojave Desert
Southern California SUV Trails, Volume II – The Eastern Mojave Desert
Great Basin SUV Trails, Volume I – Southern Nevada
Great Basin SUV Trails, Volume II – Southwestern Nevada
Exploring the Sierra Vista National Scenic Byway

Maps, book design and layout by Track & Trail Publications

Library of Congress Cataloging-in-Publication data:

Mitchell, Roger, 1938-
Death Valley SUV Trails, 2nd ed.
Bibliographic references (p.) and index
ISBN number 0-9707115-9-X
(1) Death Valley National Park (Calif. and Nev.) – Guidebook (2) Death Valley National Park (Calif. and Nev.) – History (3) Death Valley National Park (Calif. and Nev.) Mines and mining

This book is dedicated to the memory of Burton Frasher, Sr.
(1888-1955) whose early photographic postcards of Death
Valley did so much to whet the public's interest in the region.
(photo courtesy Pomona Public Library)

The author and publisher of this guide make no representations as to the condition, degree of difficulty, or safety of any of the routes described in this publication. At the time of this printing, all route descriptions were reasonably up to date, as far as is known to the author. Keep in mind, however, that conditions can and do change, sometimes in a matter of minutes. Backroad travelers should enter the mountains and deserts with their vehicles in good mechanical condition, carrying extra clothing, water, and food, should a breakdown or other emergency occur. It is recommended that each vehicle carry a detailed map of the area to be visited, and that drivers first inquire about road conditions at the office of the appropriate land management agency before attempting any of these routes.

It should also be noted that administrative actions by the National Park Service and the Bureau of Land Management, can limit and otherwise impact the visitor's use of roads without any prior notice. Roads that are open one day may be closed the next.

Finally, unknown to the author, some of the routes described herein may cross unmarked private property. Please respect the owner's rights, and obey any NO TRESPASSING signs that may be lawfully posted.

Contents

Frasher photo from the author's collection

Excursion Map

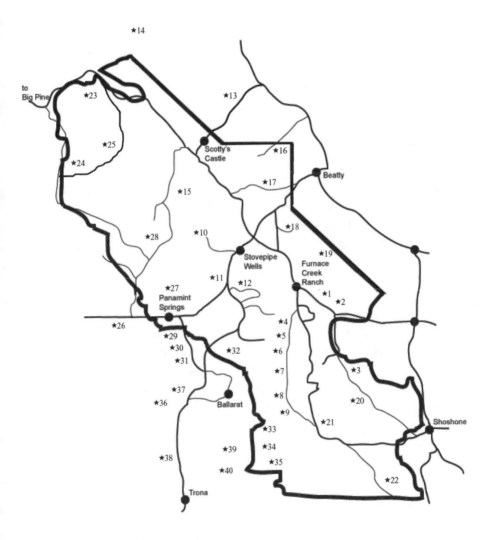

to
Big Pine

★14

★23

★13

★25

Scotty's
Castle

★16

★24

★17

Beatty

★15

★28

★10

★18

★19

Stovepipe
Wells

Furnace
Creek
Ranch

★27
Panamint
Springs

★11

★12

★1
★2

★26

★4

★29

★5

★30

★32

★6

★31

★7

★3

★37

★8

★20

★36

Ballarat

★9

★21

Shoshone

★33

★38

★39

★34

★40

★35

★22

Trona

The Death Valley Country

Acknowledgments

First, I would like to thank my long-suffering wife, Loris, who has been my traveling companion, my scribe, my proofreader, my literary critic and in more recent publications my co-author. Without her assistance and support this book would not have been possible. Likewise, publication would not have been possible without the technical support of Glenn Harmelin.

Thanks, too, go to Blair Davenport, of the Death Valley Museum, and to Beth Porter of the Eastern California Museum. They were very helpful in providing some of the historic photos. National Park Service personnel who assisted in this publication were Ranger-Naturalist, Charlie Callagan, whose time, advice, and suggestions were invaluable, and Corky Hayes, the Chief of Interpretation, and her assistant, Terri Baldino.

My research for this guide was greatly aided by the patient staffs at the county libraries in Beatty, Bishop, Independence, Trona, and Ridgecrest. I am also indebted to the very professional assistance provided at the Henry Madden Library, California State University at Fresno, the Nevada State Library in Carson City, the California Room of the California State Library in Sacramento, the California Division of Mines and Geology Library in Sacramento, and the library of the U.S. Geological Survey in Menlo Park CA.

At the Searles Valley Historical Society in Trona, Sharon Hartley, Margaret "Lit" Brush, and Ruth Payton graciously opened their files for my research. It was Lit who brought to my attention the presence of W.D. Clair's diary, which provided great insights into life at Clair's Camp in the year 1942.

The W.D. Clair story was further augmented and enhanced by W.D.'s grandson Earl Clair, and his daughter-in-law Margaret Clair, who graciously allowed me into their homes to conduct recorded interviews with them about their personal recollections of living at Clair's Camp. (My research into "The Life and Times of W.D. Clair" can be found in the *Proceedings of the Sixth Death Valley Conference on History and Prehistory.*)

I particularly appreciate the help of Remi Nadeau IV, author and noted historian who reviewed the portions of my manuscript involving his great great grandfather's "shotgun road" to Lookout, and who kindly provided the photograph of Mr. Nadeau and his freight team.

Finally, recognition should also go to the staff and volunteers, and the hundreds of people who financially support the Maturango Museum in Ridgecrest and the Eastern California Museum in Independence. These institutions perform a valuable service in preserving the history of the western side of the greater Death Valley region.

RM

Introduction

This is a guidebook to the back roads and jeep trails of the greater Death Valley region. If you are one who simply likes to take his four-wheel drive rig out to push it to the limit, this guide may not be for you. If, however, you are interested in broadening your knowledge and experience of the desert, while enjoying wholesome outdoor activity, then hopefully this guide may be of some assistance. It was not my intent to simply make this an inventory of poorly maintained back roads. Most of the outings I describe have some interesting scenic or other unique feature. Most of the excursions are not really difficult, providing you have a high clearance vehicle and exercise prudence and caution.

Death Valley National Park contains 3.4 million acres, much of it accessible only on foot or by semi-improved dirt roads

I grew up in the shadow of Death Valley, and came to have an intimate knowledge of its mountains, hidden canyons, and broad valleys. I have never outgrown the enjoyment of exploring some back road for the first time, or of climbing to the summit of a new peak.

In 1968 I wrote the first edition of *Death Valley Jeep Trails,* followed by *Inyo Mono Jeep Trails* in 1969 and *Western Nevada Jeep Trails* in 1973. All three books covered the region in and surrounding what was then Death Valley National Monument. But a lot has happened in the last third of a century. I feared that many of the trails I described in the 1960s had been closed for one reason or another. Some were; however, I was pleasantly surprised to find many of my favorite routes were not only still open, but also virtually unchanged over the last thirty-five years.

At the time these roads were rechecked, the trail information was current. Conditions can vary, however, so the reader must use common sense and adapt to post-publication changes. Trails may wash out and become virtually impassable.

Sometimes backcountry roads are upgraded to higher standards, as has been the case in Titus Canyon. Interestingly enough, with the 1976 closure of Death Valley to mining, some roads which had good graded surfaces are no longer being maintained. They are deteriorating to the status of jeep trails once again. Obviously, it would be prudent to inquire about current road conditions at the Death Valley Visitor Center or NPS offices in Stovepipe Wells, Scotty's Castle, or Beatty before actually going out to try them. For adjoining areas outside the park, inquiries can be made at the BLM office in Ridgecrest (Tonopah for Nevada areas) and the Interagency Visitor Center in Lone Pine.

Readers of the 2001 First Edition may notice that while it contained 46 backcountry excursions, this 2006 revised edition describes only 40. I have dropped eight of those routes, because several have been expanded and included in other volumes of the SUV Trails series. A few others were dropped, because the routes were of little interest. The excursion up Surprise Canyon to the site of Panamint City was deleted, because of litigation and its ultimate closure by the BLM. However, I have also added two new excursions in BLM areas outside the national park: Bonnie Claire Playa and the Escape Trail over the Slate Range. Based on reader comments, I have expanded the historical content and added many more old photographs. In keeping with our newer books in this series, GPS coordinates have also been added at key points. I hope our readers will find this revised edition even more informative than the first.

(Death Valley Museum photo)

Backcountry Regulations
Within the National Park

The following regulations are applicable within Death Valley National Park:

Off-Road Driving: The routes described in this guide are open to travel by street-legal off-road vehicles. Driving off these routes is not permitted.

Camping: Camping is not allowed along the Grotto Canyon Road, Titus Canyon Road, the West Side Road, the Racetrack Road between Teakettle Junction and Homestake Dry Camp, or the first eight miles of the Cottonwood Canyon Road. Camping is not allowed at the Inyo Mine, the Lost Burro Mine, or the Ubehebe Lead Mine. Finally, camping is not permitted within two hundred yards of any water source, or one hundred feet from any flowing stream. (These regulations are subject to revision, so check with the rangers.)

Fires: Campfires are not permitted, except in fire pits in the developed campgrounds. The gathering of any wood, alive or dead, is prohibited.

Firearms: Firearms are not permitted in Death Valley National Park.

Pets: Pets must be on a leash and restrained at all times. They are not allowed off the roads, on the trails, or in wilderness areas.

Collecting: The collecting of plants, wildflowers, animals, rocks, minerals, fossils and artifacts, and use of metal detectors is strictly prohibited.

Wildlife: The feeding of wild animals is illegal. It encourages them to depend on an unnatural food source, rather than forage for their natural diet. They can lose their natural fear of humans, and become dangerously aggressive.

Mining: Mining took place in Death Valley long before it became a national park. Even with its national monument status between 1933 and 1994, Death Valley was one of only two units in our National Park System where mining was permitted. That all changed in 1976 when a new law, the *Mining in Parks Act*, was enacted. This legislation permitted existing mining to continue until its validity could be evaluated, but prohibited the staking of new claims, and required an evaluation of nearly 50,000 mining claims. By 1980, mining was allowed to continue on 2,000 of the 50,000 evaluated claims. In 1989, many of the talc mines in Warm Springs Canyon were bought and the land transferred to the National Park Service. Then in 1994 passage of the California Desert Protection Act prohibited the filing of new claims in the newly established Death Valley National Park. Valid existing claims could continue to be worked. Currently only about one hundred valid mining claims remain in the park.

Private Property: Although new mining claims can no longer be located within the national park, there is still private property, including many patented mining claims. Respect the rights of the owners.

Backcountry Regulations
Outside the Park

In general the lands surrounding Death Valley National Park are federally owned public lands administered by the Department of Interior's Bureau of Land Management. On the western and southern sides of Death Valley, jurisdiction lies with the Ridgecrest Resource Office (part of the Desert Conservation District). BLM lands on the Nevada side of Death Valley are the responsibility of the Tonopah BLM office.

The U.S. Forest Service and the BLM have a mission that is clearly different from that of the National Park Service. The major emphasis of the NPS is resource preservation first and foremost, with recreation secondary. The responsibility of USFS and the BLM is resource management in a broader sense, which may include preservation in places, but also provides for a wide variety of multiple uses, of which recreation is only one.

Off-Road Driving: In recent years, the BLM and the Forest Service have done a pretty good job of posting their lands relative to vehicle use. Essentially, these agencies classify ORV use on their lands in one of three ways: Closed, Restricted Use, or Open.

Closed areas are generally those areas formally designated as *Wilderness*, or less formally as *Wilderness Study Areas*. There are many such areas surrounding Death Valley National Park, including the Piper Mountain, Sylvania Mountains, Funeral Mountains, Resting Spring Range, Ibex, Manly Peak, Argus and Malpais Wilderness Areas. In addition, vehicle use may be prohibited in small areas because of some local resource that might be damaged.

Restricted Use generally means that motor vehicle travel is permitted, but limited to designated roadways. The vast majority of BLM administered land is in this category.

Open areas are generally open to all types of vehicles with no restrictions of any kind. The nearest such places to Death Valley are the Spangler Hills south of Trona, the Dumont Dunes, and the Olancha Dunes.

Camping: Generally camping is permitted anywhere on public lands administered by the Bureau of Land Management and the U.S. Forest Service, unless it is specifically prohibited.

Fires: Campfires at undeveloped campsites are permitted. A California Campfire Permit should be in the possession of the person having the fire. These are available at no charge from any state (CDF) fire station, U.S. Forest Service Ranger Station, or BLM office.

Firearms: Generally the safe discharge of firearms for hunting or recreational purposes is permitted on public land, unless posted or near habitation sites, as specified by state law.

Pets: Generally there are no federal restrictions on pets on USFS or BLM lands.

Mining: Outside the national park boundaries, public lands under USFS and BLM administration are generally open to mineral entry, unless they lie within designated *Wilderness Areas*. In the last few years many new regulations have been added that apply to the staking of mining claims. Contact the nearest BLM office for the details.

Collecting: The collecting of Indian arrowheads, pots, grinding stones, petroglyphs, pictographs, and any other artifact is prohibited on public lands by the National Antiquities Act of 1906 and the Archaeological Resource Protection Act of 1979. The collecting of rocks and mineral specimens for home use and personal collections is generally permitted on lands administered by the BLM.

BLM regulations prohibit the taking of plant or invertebrate fossils for commercial purposes; however, reasonable quantities may be picked up for personal collections.

Dead wood for campfires may be gathered. The taking of a wildflower specimen, while discouraged, is nevertheless permitted as long as it is not a rare, endangered, or otherwise protected species.

Archaeological Sites

Death Valley, Panamint Valley and the Saline Valley are rich in archaeological sites, many of them unmapped, and still unknown to archaeologists. Of those that are known, only a handful have been systematically excavated and studied. Unfortunately over the years, and in spite of the National Antiquities Act of 1906 and the Archeological Resources Protection Act of 1979 which outlaw private collecting and the looting of archaeological sites, arrowhead collectors and pot hunters have made their way along the ancient shorelines and into the canyons, plundering these irreplaceable resources. Without any harmful intentions, many citizens have deprived science of answers to the questions of anthropologists and archaeologists about where we came from and when we got here.

The debate as to when man came over the Bering land bridge into North America has been going on for nearly a century. The answers are slow to come. Some like Ruth Simpson and her African protegé, the late Dr. L.S.B. Leaky, believe they have uncovered in the Calico Hills, near Barstow, evidence that man was in North America 50,000 years ago. (For more about this site, see *Southern California SUV Trails, Volume I - The Western Mojave Desert.*) Others in the field have been very skeptical about the Calico "stone tools", arguing that they are products of nature, not man. Until recently many scientists believed that man has only been in the New World since the last glaciers retreated some 10,000 to 12,000 years ago. The argument goes on; however, there have been some startling new finds in recent years in some very unlikely places. A cave in Pennsylvania has yielded man-made artifacts with a reasonably accurate date of about 15,000 years ago. Radiocarbon dates from a site in central Mexico have revealed that man killed mammoths there 20,000 years ago. A cave in Peru strongly suggests human occupation 24,000 years ago.

So what does all this have to do with back roads and jeep trails in the Death Valley country? As you take many of these routes, you will pass through, or very near, a number of archaeological sites. Most park visitors will not recognize them as such, but you may, if you have a keen eye. I would urge that anyone reading this guide not disturb any artifacts or sites that you might come upon. If you find an arrowhead, please leave it where you find it. It might have been made, and lost, by a Timbisha Shoshone just a few generations ago. It may have no particular significance. On the other hand it might be an early Archaic fluted point of the San Dieguito Culture from 9,000 to 11,000 years ago and thus extremely important. Stone tools from these people have been found in Death Valley, Panamint Valley, Owens Valley and at China Lake. It seems likely to assume that many more artifacts are out there waiting to be found. Please let their discovery help unlock the secrets of the past. They are of no scientific use to anyone if you take them home and put them in a drawer.

With these thoughts in mind, I will not point the way to petroglyphs, pictographs, chipping sites, house rings, cave sites, or other archaeological features, except in general terms. Unfortunately, too much vandalism has occurred already.

If, in your backcountry wanderings, you find something you think is unusual or significant, do not disturb it. Take a photo or two, carefully diagram its position, and report it to National Park Headquarters behind the Visitor Center at Furnace Creek. The National Park Service has staff archaeologists trained to evaluate and follow-up on such citizen reports. If your find is outside the park, notify the Bureau of Land Management's Ridgecrest Resource Office at (760) 384-5400, or write to the BLM's Desert District Office at 6221 Box Springs Blvd., Riverside CA 92507, (909) 697-5200.

A Word of Warning

Although many of the roads and trails described herein have been used by the author for the last thirty or more years, they were, nevertheless, all re-scouted prior to the printing of this book. The route descriptions were accurate at the time they were last rechecked. Conditions change, however, sometimes in a matter of minutes. Bad roads become graded, and good roads can become flooded, washed out, or buried by landslides. A section of trail that has been Class I or II for the last fifty years may deteriorate to Class V very suddenly. A single thunderstorm may make a road suddenly dangerous or impassable. **The reader must exercise great caution and use common sense when traveling any of these routes. Never drive anyplace where you cannot see ahead. When in doubt always stop and scout the route ahead on foot. If possible, have a passenger slowly guide you through difficult places. Stream crossings warrant particular attention for water depth, current, and bottom conditions. Remember, the Death Valley country is a very lonely land. If your vehicle gets stuck or breaks down, you are on your own. Help may be a very long distance away.**

Be very watchful of changing weather conditions, particularly in the summer when moist tropical air can be drawn northward over the hot southwest deserts. Violent thunderstorms can develop quickly, and under these conditions, torrents of heavy rain can instantly turn a usually dry wash into a raging river. **Do not camp in any wash if the weather is at all unsettled, and be sure to stay out of narrow canyons during these periods.**

The number one rule in backcountry exploration is to let someone know where you are going, when you expect to return, and then to check in when you do return. This simple procedure could save your life. Of course, two vehicles are safer than one. **Go prepared!** Always carry plenty of extra water, food, gasoline, and a few simple mechanics' tools. Every backcountry rig should be permanently equipped with a toolbox, wire, electrical tape, tire repair kit, and an assortment of nuts and bolts. Vehicles larger than a motorcycle should also carry a shovel, a tire pump, and a tow chain. Other survival essentials include matches, an adequate first aid kit, canteens of water, flashlights, and warm jackets for all. If you should become stuck, stalled, or otherwise stranded, be calm. Analyze your situation. If somebody knows where you are, and you are prepared, there will be little to worry about. You will survive!

Be aware, too, that public land managing agencies such as the Bureau of Land Management and the National Park Service can administratively close a road or area with little or no advance notice. One must always heed the signs placed by these agencies.

In summary then: **be vigilant, be cautious, and be safe. Remember: no guarantee is made that the reader will find the trail as described.**

Acronyms

In order to economize in the use of words, I have sometimes resorted to the use of acronyms in certain frequently used word groups. Hopefully, these initials will not sound foreign to the reader. We tend to use them this way in everyday speech.

ARPA   Archaeological Resources Preservation Act, a federal law enacted by Congress in 1979 that carries stiff penalties for disturbing and taking of archaeological artifacts.

BIA   Bureau of Indian Affairs, a federal agency under the Department of the Interior responsible for matters relating to Native Americans.

BLM   Bureau of Land Management, a federal agency under the Department of the Interior responsible for the multiple use management of millions of acres of federal land outside of our national parks, national forests, and national wildlife preserves.

CDPA   California Desert Protection Act, legislation passed by the Congress in 1994 which changed Death Valley from a national monument to a national park, greatly expanding its size in the process, and designating 93% of the new park as Wilderness.

DFG   Department of Fish and Game, a State of California agency responsible for managing the state's wildlife.

MPA   Mining in the Parks Act, legislation passed by Congress in 1976 that started the process of phasing out mining in Death Valley National Monument.

NAWS   Naval Air Weapons Station (at China Lake), formerly NOTS.

NOTS   Naval Ordnance Test Station (at China Lake) now NAWS, Naval Air Weapons Station.

NPS   National Park Service, a federal agency under the Department of the Interior.

SUV   Sport utility vehicle.

USFS   United States Forest Service, a federal agency under the Department of Agriculture responsible for the multiple use management of millions of acres of federally owned forest lands.

USGS   United States Geological Survey, a federal agency under the Department of the Interior responsible for mapping and geological studies.

Maps

A good map is one of those essential items every backroad explorer should have before leaving home. Maps are always a compromise between scale and detail. The more area a map covers, the less detail it can show. If you are out in the boondocks, looking for some specific feature such as an old mine or spring, you are likely to need all the detail a map can provide. On the other hand, the 7½-minute series of topographic maps cover only 61 square miles, and when you start buying them by the dozen, the cost quickly adds up.

Some folks like to carry the DeLorme State Atlas, because it is relatively inexpensive and covers an entire state. At a scale of 1:250,000, however, by necessity it lacks a lot of detail. While it is better than nothing, I feel the largest area a useful map should cover is the 910 square miles provided by the 1:100,000 topographic sheets. Even then, it takes seven of these maps to cover just the Death Valley National Park. These maps show topographic features, such as mountains, canyons, and even major washes. In this series, roads are shown as a red line; the thicker the line, the better the road. It is sometimes difficult to distinguish between a paved road, a road with an all weather gravel surface, a bladed road, and a pair of tracks in the sand. Further, some, but not all, jeep trails are depicted. Many other cultural features such as cabin sites, mine shafts, and foot trails are not shown at all. These 1:100,000 maps come in two standard formats, the straight topo map published by the USGS, or the BLM version that is based on the USGS map, but includes a lot of additional data such as land ownership, restricted areas, and often even road number designations. Curiously, the BLM editions cost less than the USGS versions, and show more detail.

At one time the basic map published by the U.S. Geological Survey was the 15-minute quadrangle. At a scale of 1:62,500 these maps were an ideal compromise between scale and detail. Alas however, the USGS discontinued this series about forty years ago, in favor of the 7½-minute series. Thus today, you must buy four of the new quadrangles to cover the same area as a single 15-minute sheet. If you are going to need minute detail about a relatively small area, you are simply going to have to suck it up, and pay the current rate for a 7½-minute map. At the heading of each backcountry excursion, I will give you the names of both the 1:100,000 map sheets, as well as the 1:24,000 quadrangles.

GPS Coordinates

As most folks are aware, there are 24 specialized satellites circling the earth, transmitting radio signals that can be used by sensitive receivers to pinpoint the receiver's exact location on the face of the earth. This technology is called Global Positioning System (GPS). Initially, this sophisticated technology was limited to government and military use, but in the last decade the system has been open to anyone. The price and size of GPS receivers has dropped dramatically in recent years, making it affordable to all.

For many years I have roamed some of the earth's really wild places, including the Sierra Madre Occidental of North Central Mexico, the Eastern and Western Sahara Desert, and the Wadi Rum Region of the Arabian Peninsula, using only 1:250,000 air navigational charts. Throughout my travels I have relied on maps alone, and seldom felt the need for any sophisticated GPS navigational system.

Nevertheless, in deference to the younger generation brought up on high tech gadgetry, I am bowing to reader pressure, and am including selected GPS coordinates in this publication. In doing so, the GPS minded reader can be reassured that he, or she, is indeed at the right road intersection. In case you are interested, our GPS readings are based on the commonly used WGS 84 datum.

For those of you from the old school of "dead reckoning", please forgive me, and just let your eyes breeze right across those silly numbers in parentheses.

(Death Valley Museum photo)

The Mitchell Scale

Everything seems to have its standard of measurement. Earthquakes have their Richter Scale. Temperature has its degrees. Sound has its decibels. Thus it is that I have attempted to quantify the degree of difficulty to the various SUV trails we describe. This scale, which I modestly call *The Mitchell Scale,* was blatantly stolen from rock climbers and mountaineers, who have their own peculiar brand of madness. It goes from Class I – the easiest, to Class VI – the impossible.

CLASS I: This includes just about any kind of semi-improved, not normally maintained road over which you can safely maneuver a standard automobile. A Class I route should cause no one problems.

CLASS II: This road is a bit more rough than Class I, and may have a high center or deep potholes requiring vehicles with greater clearance. Four-wheel drive may not be absolutely necessary, but extreme care should be taken, if you don't have a vehicle with high clearance.

CLASS III: Here high clearance and four-wheel drive are a necessity, perhaps low range gears and limited slip differentials, too. But the route is not so difficult that your SUV should be damaged, if reasonable care is taken.

CLASS IV: The going gets rougher still. If you are not a skillful and experienced off-road driver, the body of your vehicle may suffer a little. You may wish to have a passenger outside the vehicle to act as a spotter, guiding you through the tight places. To avoid damage, drivers of SUVs should attempt these areas with extreme caution.

CLASS V: Most people will turn back before attempting a road of this severity. It is highly questionable whether the abuse your vehicle is taking is really worth the effort. Vehicle damage is always a possibility. Skid plates under everything are a must. Don't try this trail alone!

CLASS VI: This is for the foolhardy only. The route is so extreme that the use of a winch or two is often required. "Road building" and other creative feats of engineering are a likely necessity. You certainly don't want to try this trail without a second vehicle along, one equipped with a master mechanic, a welding torch, a complete set of spare parts, and a world-wide satellite communications system. (No Class VI routes are described in this book.)

Class I

Class II

Class III

Class IV

Class V

Class VI

16

Days Gone By at Furnace Creek Ranch

Cabins at Furnace Creek Ranch in the 1940s

Pacific Coast Borax Company's bunkhouse-kitchen located in Twenty Mule Team Cyn
before it was moved to Furnace Creek Ranch, where it is now the Borax Museum.

Furnace Creek Camp circa 1932
(Frasher photos from the author's collection)

Chapter I

Trails Out of Furnace Creek

The Furnace Creek Ranch area is the heart of Death Valley National Park. The name "Furnace Creek" was coined by Darwin French, who led an expedition through here in 1860 while searching for the ever-elusive "Lost Gunsight Mine". French had come upon a small ore-roasting furnace made by prospector Asabel Bennett earlier that same year at a spring near the mouth of a canyon. He named the tiny watercourse Furnace Creek. It would not be until 1874, however, that any thought was given to using the waters of Furnace Creek for agricultural purposes. In that year Andy Laswell cleared a few acres of land, and utilized the waters of Furnace Creek to irrigate alfalfa. The venture was a success, with the crop being sold at the booming mining camp of Panamint City. The Panamint market lasted only a year, however, and when the bloom fell off the mining boom in late 1875, Laswell abandoned his fields and moved on. In 1881 a Swiss emigrant by the name of Rudolph Neuschwander was appointed by William Tell Coleman to become superintendent of the newly opened Harmony Borax Mine located just 1½ miles north of present day Furnace Creek Ranch. Even before the first shipment of borax was made, Neuschwander had dug a mile-long irrigation ditch to bring Furnace Creek water down the alluvial fan to forty acres of land he had cleared. The energetic Swiss laid out his Greenland Ranch and planted not only alfalfa, but also fruit trees, melons, sweet potatoes and other garden vegetables. The Harmony workers who lived at the ranch ate far better than most of Death Valley's other borax miners. The Harmony Borax Works closed in 1888, but the Greenland Ranch survived. The extensive date-palm groves, mostly the Deglet Noor variety, were planted as an experiment by the Pacific Coast Borax Company in the 1920s, and still produce fruit to this day. When the luxurious Furnace Creek Inn opened in 1927, more rustic accommodations were offered at Greenland Ranch, and in 1933 the name was changed to Furnace Creek Ranch.

Today Furnace Creek Ranch remains an island of greenery amid a sea of brown. Not only are the park's administrative offices here, but there is also the Death Valley Visitor Center complete with museum, theater, and bookshop. Slide shows and films in the theater augment the visitor's introduction to Death Valley. In addition, ranger-guided tours add to the understanding and appreciation of this unique place. There is a second museum in the ranch complex, which highlights borax and hard-rock mining, as well as early transportation in the Death Valley area.

18

Facilities provided by concessionaires include a general store, a restaurant and bar, a gas station, an 18-hole golf course and a 3,000-foot paved airstrip (no AV gas). The elegant hospitality of the nearby Furnace Creek Inn has been well known for more than half a century. For the less affluent, there are three campgrounds here: Furnace Creek, Texas Spring, and Sunset (the latter for self-contained trailers and motor homes only).

The author took this photo of Texas Spring Campground in 1956.
Notice the absence of motor homes and camp trailers.

(Frasher photo from author's collection)

1

To Echo Pass via Echo Canyon

Primary Attraction:	Interesting scenery and geology, historic mines and mining camps, and a very challenging route across the Funeral Mountains into Nevada.
Time Required:	Plan to spend a half-day to Schwab and the Inyo Mines and return, or all day to cross Echo Pass into Nevada.
Miles Involved:	It is fourteen miles from Highway 190 to Echo Pass; add another 3.1 miles from Furnace Creek Ranch.
Maps:	1:100,000 Death Valley Junction and Beatty sheets; 1:24,000 Furnace Creek, Echo Canyon and Lees Camp Quadrangles.
Degree of Difficulty:	The road past Eye of the Needle and on to the Inyo Mines is generally Class II. It is mostly Class III for three miles beyond Saddle Cabin, until bedrock in the canyon narrows creates one hundred feet of a very challenging Class V ascent. Once you are over that obstacle, the last mile is all Class III to the summit of Echo Pass. (The eastern side of the pass is generally Class III and IV as the route enters Nevada).

Lower Echo Canyon is one of the easiest and most delightful jeep trails in Death Valley National Park. Because of its close proximity to the Furnace Creek Ranch and Texas Spring Campground, it can easily be visited in a half-day. This outing offers typical "canyon scenery" of the Funeral Mountains, as well as an old mine with its ghost town thrown in as a bonus. Upper Echo Canyon, on the other hand, is the third or fourth most difficult route described in this guide.

Our backroad adventure begins at the entrance to Furnace Creek Ranch. Take State Route 190 eastward up the alluvial fan, passing the Badwater Road on the right after one mile. On the left side of the highway is the entrance to Furnace Creek Inn. Continue up the Furnace Creek Wash on Hwy 190 another 2.1-miles (N36°26.254 W116°49.425), and look to the left for a small sign displaying the jeep symbol and reading *Echo Canyon*. Reset your trip odometer to zero, and turn left up the wash; there should be tracks to follow. The first ten miles of this excursion are generally Class II.

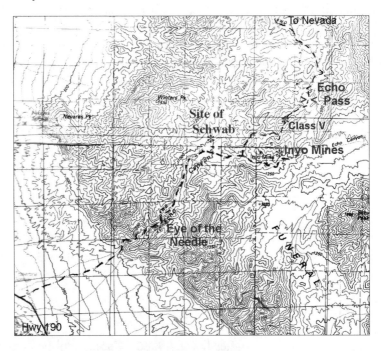

The dominant plant at first is creosote *Larrea tridentata* var. *glutinosa,* a hardy shrub well adapted to its desert environment. The creosote commonly has shallow roots that spread out many feet beyond the plant. Nature causes these bushes to be spaced well apart to reduce competition for moisture, and as the days grow longer, warmer, and drier, the creosotes drop many of their leaves to further reduce moisture loss. The veteran desert naturalist Edmund Jaeger once documented creosote bushes that went 32 months without a single drop of rain.

The flat-lying beds of rocks on either side of the wash are part of the Furnace Creek Formation, a fanglomerate deposited in the late Pliocene or early Pleistocene, a mere two or three million years ago. The appearance of those layers containing well-rounded rocks suggests that conditions then may have been very similar to those forming the alluvial fans in Death Valley today.

After ascending the gentle slope of Echo Wash for three miles, you will enter Lower Echo Canyon, where the geology changes and becomes very complex. Echo Canyon has eroded through old Cambrian marine sediments that are highly faulted. The Wood Canyon Formation, as it is known, has layers that range from sandstone to dolomite. These rocks were being deposited as silt at the bottom of a once great seabed more than 500 million years ago. The upper layers contain trilobite fossils, some of the very oldest and most primitive marine animals to be found in the fossil record. (Remember that collecting fossils within our National Parks is prohibited.) The older, lower layers of the Wood Canyon Formation are barren of fossils here, suggesting that they might have been deposited at the very dawn of sea life.

The road twists and turns as it winds its way up the canyon. Watch your odometer, because at a point 4.8-miles in from the pavement you will reach *"The Eye of The Needle"*, a natural window eroded out of the canyon wall to your right. If you take the time to climb to the window (easiest on the western side), you will find that the opening is more than ten feet from top to bottom.

Eye of the Needle

The canyon remains narrow for another half-mile, and then it opens into a small valley. At a point 7.8-miles from the highway, a faint set of tracks goes up a wash to the left (N36°29.794 W116°43.978). This was once the way to the site of Schwab. That road is now closed, but it is an easy walk of just 0.7-mile to the old townsite.

The book *Death Valley, A Guide*, published in 1939 as part of the WPA Federal Writers Project, describes Schwab as follows:

Schwab is an old mining camp with a few deserted and
tumbling houses and one or two that are still inhabited.

That may have been the case in the 1930s, but, alas, little is left today. You have to look close or you will walk right by the old townsite. It is the rusty tin cans strewn about that mark the site. Named for Charles M. Schwab, President of Bethlehem Steel and a noted financier of Rhyolite fame, Schwab was a typical Turn of the 20th Century gold camp. Like at its sister cities of Lee and Furnace, the veins of gold here proved to be as elusive as the hopes and dreams upon which they were built. The typical cycle of birth, boom and bust did not take long at Schwab.

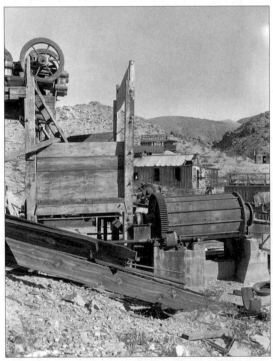

Jaw crusher and ball mill at Inyo Mines in 1968

To continue on, stay to the right following the clearly defined Class II tracks. A few prospect holes are passed, and at 9.1-miles the road forks. Here a slab foundation is all that remains of a structure once known as *Saddle Cabin*.

By taking the right fork for a half-mile, you will come to the camp and mill site of the Inyo Mine. This mine was discovered as part of the Greenwater Excitement in 1905, which caused prospectors to pour over every inch of the Funeral and Black Mountains. The actual mines are high on the hillside to the north; it is the camp and mill site that are in this canyon bottom.

If you take the left fork at Saddle Cabin, the road immediately crosses a low ridge and forks again. The National Park Service has closed the left fork that once went 0.8-mile down the wash to Schwab; stay to the right.

Soon the country closes down into a canyon once again, and the road deteriorates to Class III. In a little less than two miles from Saddle Cabin, you will see a cable stretching from the canyon bottom to the ridgetop high above. This was once a crude device used to drag machinery up to the Furnace Mine some four hundred feet above. Another cabin site is passed on a knoll to the right.

The canyon narrows to a series of three dry waterfalls 2.9 miles above Saddle Cabin. The first of these is Class IV; the second and third are an even more challenging Class V. The second obstacle is the worst, but fortunately there is a handy anchor rock above it for those who need to winch themselves up. **Caution: Stop and scout the route on foot before attempting to drive any farther. This Class V pitch should not be underestimated.** I would not recommend that the drivers of pickups or long wheelbase vehicles attempt these dry falls. When I last scouted this route, a Jeep CJ5 with large tires went up and down the obstacle with ease; however, a Land Rover got hung up on the rocks, and its driver had to winch himself up and over the last half of the ledge. A short bobtail rig can probably make it, if the driver first scouts the route and is a skillful and experienced off-roader. This is not a place you would wish to get stuck or have a breakdown.

Beyond the dry falls, it is a relatively easy Class III road to the old 1907 mining camp of Echo, atop 4400' Echo Pass on the crest of the Funeral Range. If you thought Schwab was short lived, Echo was a mere flash in the pan. There are two rusting tin cans at Schwab for every one remaining at Echo.

From the summit of Echo Pass, it is 5½ miles down to the site of Lee CA (sometimes called Lee's Camp), and another 7.4 miles to Valley View Road, the nearest paved road in the Amargosa Valley. For the route description coming up to the pass from the opposite side, see the trail description coming out of Beatty (see Excursion #19).

2

Hole in the Wall

Primary Attraction:	Rugged austere scenery of the Funeral Range, interesting geology, and Mother Nature's cactus garden.
Time Required:	Three to four hours out of Furnace Creek Ranch and return.
Miles Involved:	It is 3.7 miles from Highway 190 to Hole in the Wall, 2.4 miles more to the wilderness boundary near the old quarry.
Maps:	1:100,000 Death Valley Junction sheet; 1:24,000 Furnace Creek and Echo Canyon Quadrangles.
Degree of Difficulty:	Mostly Class II, but Class III conditions may exist in sandy spots.
Remarks:	The floods of 2004 badly washed out this trail. Nearly two years later, it was still not reopened, though it is expected to reopen eventually.

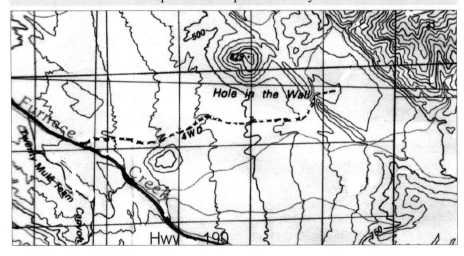

Hole in the Wall is an easy excursion out of Furnace Creek Ranch, generally no more difficult than Class II, unless the sand is soft. The route goes up an unnamed wash, through Hole in the Wall to end at an old rock quarry. Along the way you'll see some fascinating geology.

Our backroad adventure begins at the entrance to Furnace Creek Ranch. Take State Route 190 eastward up the alluvial fan, passing the Badwater Road on the right after one mile. On the left side of the highway is the entrance to Furnace Creek Inn.

While the first facility in Death Valley catering to tourists was the Stovepipe Wells Hotel opened by Herman Eichbaum in November of 1926, the Furnace Creek Inn was not far behind. As early as 1906, "Borax" Smith openly spoke of building a first class tourist hotel in Death Valley, but it was not until Eichbaum started his own resort project in November of 1925 that the Pacific Coast Borax Company, who had owned and operated Greenland Ranch (to later be renamed Furnace Creek Ranch) for many years, became sufficiently motivated to proceed with their own plans for a competing hotel. The project was to proceed under the direction of Frank Jenifer, manager of the Tonopah & Tidewater Railroad, a Pacific Coast Borax Company subsidiary. In March of 1926, a low ridge at the mouth of Furnace Creek Canyon was selected for the site of the new hotel. Water was piped in from nearby Texas Spring and, with it, the making of adobe bricks began in earnest. Furnace Creek Inn opened for business on February 1, 1927, with a dozen rooms, a dining room, and a kitchen. The hotel staff lived in tents and small cabins behind the hotel.

Furnace Creek Inn in the mid 1930s
(Frasher photo from the author's collection)

In those days, most promotions lured the public to Death Valley with the promise of easy and comfortable rail travel via the Union Pacific Railroad to Ludlow, then the Tonopah & Tidewater Railroad to Death Valley Junction, with the final 28 miles via tour buses. The public responded, and the inn's Terrace Wing was built by 1927-28, adding 20 more rooms, as well as the swimming pool. A nine-hole golf course and the airstrip were added in 1929 for the convenience and enjoyment of the public, and 20 more rooms were built the next year. By the early 1930s, Death Valley was well established as a tourist attraction, but the public turned to coming in its own automobiles, rather than by rail. Furnace Creek Inn has changed management several times in the past fifty years, but it continues to maintain a reputation for excellence. While not quite as old, the Furnace Creek Inn nevertheless carries on the elegant tradition of Yellowstone's *Old Faithful Inn*, Yosemite's *Ahwahnee Hotel*, and the Grand Canyon's *El Tovar*, all grand old hostelries in our National Park System.

Furnace Creek Inn circa 1950
(Frasher photo from the author's collection)

Passing the Inn, continue ascending State Route 190 as it makes it way up Furnace Creek Wash. At a point five miles up the wash and 0.7-miles above the entrance to Twenty-Mule Team Canyon, look for a sign with the jeep symbol on your left. Reset your trip odometer to zero and turn left here (N36°24.267 W116°46.904), starting up this side wash. There are usually tracks that have been left by previous vehicles, depending on how recent the last rain was. (Yes, Virginia, it does rain in Death Valley. The average precipitation at the Furnace Creek Ranch is 1.92 inches per year. That statistic is meaningless, however, as a single thunderstorm on August 15, 2004, caused a major washout on Hwy 190 that took some eight months to repair at a cost of $10 million. In the process, the jeep trail to Hole in the Wall was washed out. It has subsequently been restored.

Damage to Highway 190 in Furnace Creek Wash
after the August 15, 2004 flash flood
(National Park Service photo)

The road into Hole in The Wall is usually no more severe than Class II.

Make your way up the wash. The sand is soft in places, but that is why you have four-wheel drive.

At first the most noticeable desert plant is the creosote bush. This shrub spreads its roots out wide in search of moisture. After periods of rainfall, the creosote will quickly react, producing tiny yellow blossoms.

Notice, too, the very abundant growth of Desert holly *Atriplex hymenelytra* thriving in the wash. With its whitish or pale green spiny leaves, this hardy little shrub often grows quite well in soils that are much too salty for other plants. For this reason, it is common in the bottom of Death Valley, particularly on the eastern side.

As you proceed up the wash, also notice the gently dipping beds of light brown sandstone that are capped with a darker colored alluvium. The lower layers are part of the Furnace Creek Formation deposited during the Pliocene epoch, just before the massive glaciation of the Pleistocene that made lakes in many of these desert valleys. The Furnace Creek series of sediments is one of the more important geologic formations in Death Valley, because the borate mineral colemanite is found in these layers of compressed mud. The capping layer of desert alluvium was deposited in much later times.

This gash in the Funeral conglomerate is called Hole in the Wall.

At a point 3.7 miles from Highway 190, you will encounter a fascinating geologic phenomenon called *Hole in the Wall* (N36°24.852 W116°43.431). As the name implies, a small gap bisects a natural wall of rock some four hundred feet high. It is immediately apparent by the color, texture, and composition that this wall of rock is very much different than the other sediments back down the wash. This formation is the Funeral fanglomerate, and it is older than the Furnace Creek Formation. The band of sediments is composed of both smoothly rounded as well as angular rock fragments, all laid down together in an ancient alluvial fan during the Pliocene some one million years ago. The Furnace Creek Fault on the eastern side of "the wall" has caused these deposits to be pushed upwards, so that the once nearly horizontal layers are now standing on end.

After passing through the Hole in the Wall, turn sharply to the right and you will see the remnants of an old road. Driving farther up the wash, you can easily observe five of the thirteen species of cactus to be found in Death Valley. While cacti do not like the salty soils on the floor of Death Valley, they seem to thrive on the alluvial fans and in the washes. Perhaps the most conspicuous cactus here is the so-called cottontop or many headed barrel cactus *Echinocactus polycephalus,* which typically has six to ten barrels growing out of single root mass. The solitary barrel cactus *Echinocactus acanthodes* is much less common, but also present. Two species of cholla cactus can be seen here: the Strawtop cholla *Opuntia echinocarpa,* and the other spiny-fruited cholla *Opuntia erinacea.* Equally abundant are the beaver tail *Opuntia basilaris, while p*resent in smaller numbers is the mound cactus *Echinocereus mojavensis.* Cacti have done a remarkable job of adapting to arid climates. They have the ability to retain moisture when it does rain, and their waxy skins retard moisture loss when it is dry.

E. polycephalus   *E. acanthodes*

Follow the old roadway up the fan. After going 2.4 miles from Hole in the Wall, you will find an old rock quarry. Here slabs of nicely layered travertine were cut and split into convenient sizes for shipping. They were then transported by truck and rail to Los Angeles, where they were used in the construction of the Pacific Coast Borax Building on Shatto Place. The jeep trail now ends at the quarry.

3

Furnace, Kunze, and Greenwater

Primary Attraction:	Three Turn of the 20th Century mining camps in the Black Mountains.
Time Required:	This outing can be done in a half-day out and back from Furnace Creek, or it can be combined with a Gold Valley excursion for a full day of historical backroad wanderings.
Miles Involved:	It is no more than thirty miles out of Furnace Creek Ranch to the three camps.
Maps:	1:100,000 Death Valley Junction sheet; 1:24,000 Dantes View and Greenwater Canyon Quadrangles.
Degree of Difficulty:	The route is generally Class I and II, with only a little easy Class III between Kunze and Greenwater.

It has been said that the Yukon gold rush of 1898 was the last great gold rush in this nation's history. Don't tell that to Shorty Harris. His discovery at Bullfrog touched off a whole series of gold rushes. In his excellent book *Nevada's 20th Century Mining Boom,* Russell Elliott chronicles the major boomtown of Tonopah in 1900, followed by Goldfield in 1903, Bullfrog and Rhyolite in 1905, Silver Peak, Ramsey, Wonder and Fairview in 1906, and lastly Rawhide in 1908. In 1907 Goldfield was the largest city in the entire State of Nevada!

These mining booms created enormous transportation needs in an area where roads were primitive at best. Half a dozen railroads were built to fill this need. Not only could they bring in heavy mining and milling equipment, but they could also carry out the ore concentrates and bullion. The Tonopah and Goldfield Railroad made connections with the Carson & Colorado near Candelaria. In the other direction, the Las Vegas & Tonopah Railroad came up from the south, as did the Tonopah & Tidewater. The Bullfrog Goldfield Railroad laid some track, too. These railroads created their own prosperity in towns like Las Vegas and Reno, but also spawned new supply points like Beatty and Gold Center. Places like Shoshone and Tecopa were mere sidings, somehow managing to hang on and survive long after the rails were pulled up.

While all of this activity was going on, prospectors were pouring over
every mountain and canyon in western Nevada and Eastern California. A few
were lucky, finding mineral wealth overlooked in the previous half-century of
prospecting. These finds gave rise to new, smaller camps. In Nevada, towns
like Round Mountain, Manhattan, Silver Peak, Kawich, and Fairview suddenly
sprang up overnight. The same was true in eastern California. In the Death Valley
region places like Lee, Echo, and Schwab briefly sprang up out of nowhere and
had their day in the sun (See Excursion #1). In this easy outing, we will visit the
sites of three such camps: Furnace, Kunze, and Greenwater.

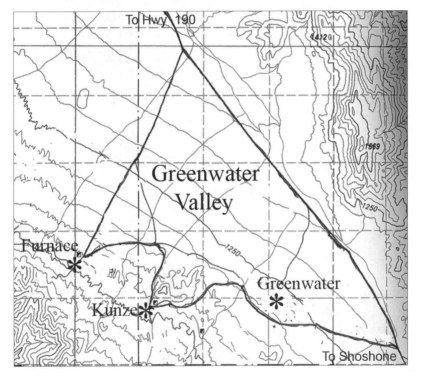

We start by taking Highway 190 southeast out of Furnace Creek Ranch,
ascending Furnace Creek Wash. At a point 10.8 miles above the Furnace Creek
Inn, the paved Furnace Creek Wash Road turns south towards Ryan and Dante's
View (N36°21.781 W116°42.542); turn right here. Soon the modern-looking works
of the Billie Mine are passed on the left. After 2.4 miles a paved road to the
left (N36°20.009 W116°41.344) goes to Ryan, an important borax producer between
the years of 1915 and 1927. It was the terminus of the seventeen-mile long
Death Valley Railroad, which connected with the Tonopah & Tidewater at Death
Valley Junction.

The author took this photo of Ryan in 1958.

Continue south on the road toward Dante's View. At a point 7.5 miles south of Highway 190, reset your trip odometer to zero and keep to the left on the graded Greenwater Valley Road, rather than following the pavement on to Dante's View (N36°16.131 W116°39.793). After 2.8 miles of the moderately washboard surface, you will be glad to turn off to the right onto a more comfortable Class I desert road (N36°14.117 W116°38.222), which makes its way to the southwest into the Black Mountains. Simply follow this road straight up the bajada, and after 3.5 miles you will be in what once was downtown Furnace.

The cycle of birth, boom, and bust all took place in Furnace in three years' time, 1905 to 1907. One is tempted to say that Furnace was a suburb of Greenwater, but that is not entirely true. Furnace had its own industry (copper mining) and its own surveyed townsite, complete with a downtown business district composed of the usual enterprises: a saloon, restaurant, boarding house, stable, and even a post office. The largest structure in Furnace was the Miner's Hospital with eight rooms. (A few months after it was built, the building was cut into thirds and moved to Zabriskie, where it was pieced together and used as a boarding house for the next eleven years. It was then dismantled again and moved to Shoshone, where it still stands to this day.) Furnace also had stage service to Amargosa, a stop on the Tonopah & Tidewater Railroad. Alas however, there was no bank in

Furnace. For such financial transactions, one had to go to Greenwater. The fact that most of the structures in Furnace consisted mainly of tents is irrelevant. The good citizens of Furnace took pride in their community, right up until the time that they shut the town down and moved to Greenwater!

Main street in Furnace in 1907

As you might expect from a tent camp, there are no Rhyolite-like ruins to mark the townsite, rather just a few stone walls and flat areas where tents were once pitched. High up on the ridge, several hundred feet above the townsite are most of the copper mines that briefly gave life to the community. The largest block of claims were the Furnace Creek Copper Company, financed by Seattle businessman, "Patsy" Clark, who had made a fortune in the Yukon Excitement. There are several Class II roads that go from one mine to the next. Specimens of copper ore minerals can be found on some of the mine dumps. The bright green mineral is malachite; the blue mineral is azurite. **(Note, however, that rock hounding and mineral collecting in Death Valley National Park is prohibited.)**

The Patsy Clark Mine
(Above photos from the author's collection)

To continue on to the old camps of Kunze and Greenwater, keep right on the road below Furnace, heading east. In about a mile, look for a Class I road going to the right up a canyon. In 1.2 miles a side road to the right turns south, climbs the fan, and within a mile you will come to stone ruins marking the lower residential district of Kunze, a camp even more obscure than Furnace. Continue driving up the wash another quarter-mile to reach the downtown district.

In his little book *Greenwater,* the noted desert writer, Harold O. Weight, retells the controversy as to who it was that first found copper in this part of the Funeral Range. By some accounts it was Arthur Kunze, right here in this little canyon early in 1904. Others say it was late in 1904 that Phil Creasor and Fred Birney, who had been grubstaked by "Patsy" Clark, found copper. That argument aside, there is no doubt that Arthur Kunze sold his claims to eastern steel magnate Charles Schwab in July of 1906, and it was this action that set off the stampede to the Greenwater Mining District.

Kunze was the smallest of the three camps, perhaps doomed by its close proximity to Greenwater just to the south. The founding fathers had drawn a plot map with streets laid out and lots subdivided, but the camp didn't have time to develop much more than a city of white canvas tents. Ironically however, the stone structures put up in Kunze have lasted far longer than the wooden buildings of Greenwater. Of this trio of camps, more history survives in Kunze, but admittedly, that is limited to mine dumps, a few stone walls, and a lot of broken glass.

The last surviving building in Kunze

From downtown Kunze, a Class II road goes east over a saddle in the hills, where it passes a mine tailings dump, and briefly deteriorates to Class III as it makes its way down the hillside. From the last mine in Kunze, it is only 1.5 miles on to the site of Greenwater (N36°10.765 W116°36.986). Alas, there is little left to mark the site today. Some rascal has created a monument of rusty metal to artistically mark the major intersection of downtown Greenwater.

Named after a small spring on the hillside two miles to the south, Greenwater was laid out on the bajada where it had room to grow. Situated at an elevation of nearly 4,300 feet, Greenwater had everything a town could want: fresh desert breezes, a great view, and of course, the promise of great mineral wealth that would rival and exceed the great copper deposits of Butte, Montana. Oh sure, Greenwater had its shortcomings, too. There was no water within miles, and the nearest railroad was nearly twenty miles away. But surely Greenwater sat upon the greatest copper deposit in the world, and all of those problems would be quickly resolved.

As word of Schwab's investment leaked out, the saloons and boarding houses of Goldfield and Tonopah emptied overnight. The population of Greenwater went from seventy to more than one thousand in late 1906 and early 1907. More than 2,500 claims were staked in the surrounding hills in a matter of weeks.

Staking claims was no easy task. This is Inyo County, and in order to record a claim, one had to go to the Inyo County Courthouse in Independence. This meant getting a seat on one of the automobiles that carried passengers north to the southern end of the Bullfrog Goldfield Railroad, which would take you north to Goldfield. From there one had to next get on the northbound train of the Tonopah & Goldfield Railroad, taking it to McSweeney Junction east of Tonopah. Here there was another train change that would take you west to Tonopah Junction, where a southbound train of the Carson & Colorado would take you to Kearsarge Station. From there a buckboard took passengers the last five miles into Independence. Altogether, the four hundred-mile trip from Greenwater to Independence was a journey of two days by rail. The only alternative was an arduous 180-mile trek across Death Valley and Panamint Valley to Keeler, where you could catch a train north to Kearsarge.

Nevertheless, Greenwater prospered for a year, even though not a single ounce of copper had been smelted. No less than fifty companies were formed, each burrowing in the ground and issuing stock fast and furiously. Stock in the Furnace Creek Copper Company went from an initial offering of $.25 a share to $5.50 in a matter of weeks. The Greenwater & Death Valley Copper Company did not do as well. It too went to $5.50 a share, but it had an initial offering price of $1.00. Altogether an estimated thirty million dollars was invested in Greenwater mining ventures in a three-month period.

Greenwater's Glory Days in 1906

Main Street in Greenwater
(Nevada Historical Society photo)

Greenwater Times and post office

Main Street
(Photos from the author's collection)

Greenwater started as a tent city, but by late 1906 more substantial buildings appeared, built with lumber carried by train from Tonopah to Death Valley Junction, and then by mule-drawn freight wagon over Deadman Pass. At its peak, Greenwater had the usual mining town amenities: several saloons and general stores, a drug store, livery stable, bank, many boarding houses, and of course, a red light district. The Tonopah & Tidewater Railroad even opened an office here in anticipation that a spur line would be brought in. The people were so keenly interested in the goings-on here, that Greenwater soon had two newspapers, "The Greenwater Miner" and the "Chuck-Walla". They sold as many copies in San Francisco, Tonopah, and Goldfield, as they did in Greenwater.

Alas, it all came crashing down in the summer of 1907. By then it had become clear that while Greenwater had copper, it simply was not in concentrations high enough to make it worth mining. With the mines closing down, there was no longer a reason for anyone to live here. The population left as rapidly as they had come. In January 1907, Greenwater had a population of seven hundred; by September it was down to one hundred. One of the last to leave was Deputy Sheriff Charles Brown, who departed in 1909. Desert freight-hauler, R.J. Fairbanks bought most of the abandoned houses for a song, had them dismantled and then rebuilt in Shoshone. Thus it has often been said, "If you want to see Greenwater, look in Shoshone!"

There is a good Class I road heading northeast from the Greenwater "monument" 1.8 miles down the fan to rejoin the graded Greenwater Valley Road (N36°12.086 W116°36.174), where a left turn takes you back to the paved road to Dante's View. Or you can choose the fork that heads southeast, and after nearly twenty miles come out onto State Highway 178 at a point six miles west of Shoshone. Still another alternative is to head for Shoshone as described above, but to turn to the left off the Greenwater Valley Road at a point 12.2 miles from Greenwater. This will take you over lonely Deadman Pass, and put you on State Highway 127 at a point 7.6 miles south of Death Valley Junction. Yet another possibility is to proceed southeast 2.4 miles down to the Greenwater Valley Road and then on another 9.3 miles where a right turn will head you into Gold Valley (as described in Excursion #20).

Greenwater "monument" of rusted cans

4

Trail Canyon

Primary Attraction:	Of all the well-watered canyons that you can drive into on the east side of the Panamints, Trail Canyon is the most northerly and easily accessible from Furnace Creek Ranch. The road has been in use by miners for nearly a century.
Time Required:	If you hurry, and who wants to do that, this outing can be done in a half-day out of Furnace Creek Ranch.
Miles Involved:	The one-way distance from Furnace Creek Ranch to the end of the road in Trail Canyon is 23 miles. All but seven of those miles are over dirt roads.
Maps:	1:100,000 Death Valley Junction and Darwin Hills sheets; 1:24,000 Devils Speedway and Wildrose Peak Quadrangles.
Degree of Difficulty:	Most of the roads are of graded dirt or are Class I. Once you get into the canyon proper, it is mostly Class II, with only a little easy Class III.

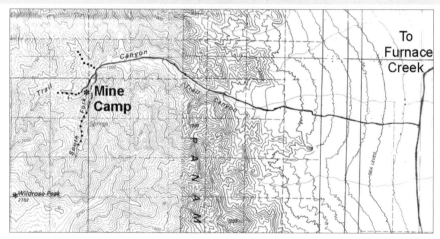

At one time, it was possible to drive up Trail Canyon all the way to Aguereberry Point and Harrisburg Flats. You were able go from 276 feet below sea level to 6,240 feet above sea level on Class II and III roads in that eleven-mile journey.

You can still drive into Trail Canyon, and you can still drive to Harrisburg Flats and Aguereberry Point, but the four miles of spectacular road between the two points have been too severely washed out to restore them. A trip into Trail Canyon is still interesting even with the heart cut out of this breathtaking route.

Trail Canyon is found by taking the Badwater Road for six miles south of the Furnace Creek Inn to where the West Side Road goes off on the right (N36°21.931 W116°50.675). Turn right here and follow this wide graded road south across the salt flats of the Devil's Golf Course for another five miles. Here (N36°18.162 W116°53.415) an NPS sign saying *Trail Canyon* points west to a road heading towards the still distant Panamint Mountains; reset your trip odometer to zero and turn right here. This easy Class II road begins its climb up the alluvial fan. No camping is permitted along the first two miles. At a point three miles up from the West Side Road, our route crosses the main wash and soon enters the canyon proper. The road deteriorates in the wash, and while four-wheel drive is not absolutely necessary, there are some easy Class III sections.

The road into Trail Canyon is mostly Class I and II.

In the springtime after a wet winter, the wild heliotrope *Phacelia* can put on an awesome display of colorful purple splendor here in Trail Canyon. A word of warning, however; the genus *Phacelia* is very large and some of its species, like *crenulata,* can cause a reaction on human skin similar to poison oak! Not only is it against NPS regulations to pick the wildflowers, but if you do so, your punishment may swiftly come from Mother Nature, if not from Smokey The Bear!

Another plant you do not want close contact with is known as cottontop, Mohave Redhead, or many-headed barrel cactus *Echinocactus polycephalus.*

Its spines are very sharp. Growing in clusters of from five to thirty barrels in a bunch, it is very abundant on the hillside to the left, a mile into the canyon. There are thirteen different species of cactus in the park, representing four different genera. The cottontop is one of the most common, and where you see one, you are likely to see many. Trail Canyon is no exception. To catch its fragrant flower you must see it in the heat of summer. The fruit produces seeds that were a staple in the diet of the Shoshone Indians.

Although not present in as many numbers, another common cactus in the canyons of the Panamints is the Engelmannn's hedgehog or calico cactus *Echinocereus engelmanni*. This species and its close cousin, *Echinocereus mojavensis,* can both be seen in Trail Canyon. Look for them on the left, two miles inside the canyon.

Engelmannn's hedgehog
Echinocereus engelmanni

Mound cactus
Echinocereus mojavensis

Notice the bedrock geology as you make your way up the canyon. These are largely marine sediments ranging from the late Precambrian Period, some 560 million years old, to the late Ordovician, 435 million years old. This is a time span of more than one hundred million years. Tilted at a steep angle Ordovician age rocks of the Ely Springs Dolomite are encountered as you enter the canyon. These are the youngest rocks in the sequence you will see. As you go up the canyon, the rocks will become older. The next formation is Eureka Quartzite, once a very white sand deposited at the bottom of an ancient sea during the middle of the Ordovician Period. In sharp contrast to the white Eureka Sandstone, the next sequence is the Pogonip Series of shale interspersed with dolomite. Its layers were deposited very early in the Ordovician times. The upper most layers of the Pogonip sometimes contain fossil gastropods and brachiopods, shellfish that lived on the sea bottom. The Cambrian layers begin in the time sequence below the Pogonip, and are encountered as you go farther into Trail Canyon. Representing the late Cambrian Period is the Nopah Formation, which was once limestone, and has now mostly metamorphosed into dolomite. The next oldest is the Bonanza King Formation consisting mainly of shale, limestone and dolomite. Older yet in Cambrian times come the various layers of silt, shale and limestone of the Carrara Formation. In places, this formation is rich in trilobite fossils, the very first hard-shelled animals to scurry about the sea bottom. Next comes its slightly older cousin, the Zabriskie Point Formation, a quartzite that never contains fossils. Finally, where Trail Canyon forks into three, we find the Wood Canyon Formation. These early Cambrian layers of shales and limestones contain the oldest fossils found in Death Valley National Park. They represent a time in the earth's history when marine animals made the transition from soft organisms, like worms and jellyfish, to hard-shelled bottom dwellers. Beyond the forks you come to the oldest layer yet, the Sterling Quartzite that goes back into the late Proterozoic Era, when life forms on earth were extremely primitive, leaving no fossil record.

So it was not until the early Paleozoic Era that sea life began to evolve to the point where traces of them can be easily found in the fossil record. Even then sea life consisted mostly of hard-shelled creatures such as trilobites, brachiopods and gastropods, and soft tissue organisms like sponges and worms. Can some of these marine fossils be found in the strata of Trail Canyon? Yes. Can you collect specimens? No. **Fossil collecting is prohibited in our National Parks.**

After you have ascended the canyon for five miles, the canyon divides into three branches. The right branch once had a mining road connecting up to the Aguereberry Point road, but it was washed out in the 1970s, and Mother Nature has reclaimed it. If you wish to walk up it for a half-mile or so, you will come to the Tarantula Mine.

Tungsten was in great demand for use as an alloy to harden steel during the Korean Conflict era of the early 1950s. California was a major producer of tungsten, with mines at Atolia near Randsburg, Coyote and Pine Creeks near Bishop, and several locations in the High Sierra above Bass and Shaver Lakes. The Tarantula Mine in Trail Canyon was Death Valley's contribution to meet the demand for tungsten. The mineral scheelite, the most common tungsten ore, was first found here during World War II in quartz veins in a metamorphosed zone between limestone and granite. At that time, the property was named The Victory Tungsten Mine. The mine shipped but one ton of ore because of its remote location and difficulty of access. That was in 1943. A decade later when the price of tungsten shot way up, the access road switch-backing down from Aguereberry Point was built, and the mine was reopened under the name of the Tarantula Mine. This time hundreds of tons of ore with assay values of from 2 to 12% tungsten were shipped. Production peaked in 1958, although continued exploration of the orebody is said to have gone on until as recently as 1971.

Scheelite gives off a unique sheen under ultra violet light. If you should have a battery powered UV light, you might look over the mine dump after dark. The scheelite will be obvious. You might also find the copper minerals of azurite (blue), malachite (green) and bornite (bronze looking), although they do not fluoresce under a UV light. Remember that with the passage of the Mining in the Parks Act of 1976, **rock hounding and mineral collecting are no longer permitted in Death Valley.**

If you are really ambitious, you can continue to hike the remaining 3.5 miles up to the graded road, then another 1.5 miles out to Aguereberry Point. Such a walk involves a vertical gain of 2,400 feet.

Leaving this one time fork in the road, today's road swings to the left and within fifty yards forks again (N36°19.211 W117°02.533). The left fork is in a wash, and can be easily missed. This fork soon deteriorates to Class IV, as it goes up the south fork of the canyon another mile to where there are some springs and, with them, the new Wilderness boundary. Further vehicle traffic is prohibited. You can walk up the old mine road a mile to the McBride Camp, called the Morning Glory Camp by some, where several buildings still remain. In this heavily mineralized area was the Old Dependable antimony mine, and high on the hillside, the Morning Glory Mine whose tramline brought down lead, silver, zinc and copper ores.

The main road keeps to the right at this second fork. The Tarantula Mine Camp is reached within a quarter-mile. This makes a good campsite, particularly for groups, as there are adequate flat places among the deteriorating buildings, and it is far enough from the nearest water so that camping is not prohibited.

The Tarantula Mine Camp

5

Hanaupah Canyon

Primary Attraction: Interesting geologic features and old mines.

Time Required: Hanaupah Canyon alone can be seen in a half-day out of Furnace Creek, but when combined with jaunts into Trail Canyon to the north, or Johnson Canyon to the south, a full day of backroad exploration is required.

Miles Involved: It is 17.8 miles from Furnace Creek Ranch to Shorty's Well. From there to the end of the road in Hanaupah Canyon is another eight miles.

Maps: 1:100,000 Death Valley Junction and Darwin Hills sheets; 1:24,000 Hanaupah Canyon and Telescope Peak Quadrangles.

Degree of Difficulty: Mostly Class II or better, except for the last 1½ miles, half of which are Class III.

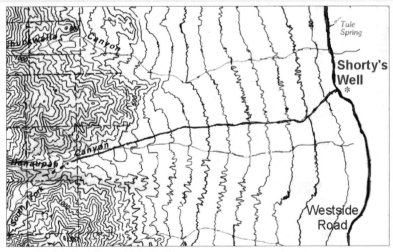

Hanaupah Canyon is one of a score of canyons in the east slope of the Panamint Range that contain reliable year around water. The presence of this life giving liquid has not only attracted wildlife, but also early Indians in Death Valley. In later years, it was sourdough prospectors who were scrambling over every inch of these mountains in search of that elusive rich vein.

Hanaupah Canyon is accessed off the West Side Road. Go south on the Badwater Road down the valley from the Furnace Creek Inn 6.1 miles to the West Side Road (N36°21.931 W116°50.675); the turnoff to the right is well marked. This graded road goes down the western side of Death Valley for some 35 miles to rejoin the paved Badwater road near the Ashford Mill ruins.

For Hanaupah Canyon, however, we are taking the West Side Road only 10.2 miles to Shorty's Well. The site of the well is a few hundred yards east of the West Side Road. The story is that Alexander "Shorty" Borden (not to be confused with his contemporary, Frank "Shorty" Harris of Bullfrog fame) dug this well by hand. Although it was a shallow well at the edge of the salt flats, the water was said to be fresh. I first sampled the water in 1956, and the notes I scribbled on my topo sheet were *hand-pump, brackish.* The well has all but disappeared since then.

While you are looking around, notice the mounds of pickleweed *Allenrolfea occidentalis,* a low sprawling shrub very common at the edge of the salt flats all along the West Side Road. This is the most salt tolerant of all the desert plants, even more so than the two exotic tamarisk species introduced into Death Valley by man around the Turn of the 20th Century.

A Class I road at Shorty's Well (N36°13.542 W116°52.864) heads westward up the alluvial fan. You reach sea level at a point 0.8 miles from the West Side Road, and a tenth of a mile beyond, cross a north/south trending earthquake fault. The escarpment can be clearly seen, but perhaps best when backlit in the late afternoon sun. The vertical displacement along this fault scarp measures between twenty and fifty feet.

Geomorphologists have closely studied the Hanaupah fan, because at least four surface depositional layers can be identified: one at 550-800 thousand years, one at 120-190 thousand years, one at 15-30 thousand years, and the most recent surface laid down a couple of thousands of years ago. The layer of patina on the rocks, so-called desert varnish, has dated the most recent layers. The older surfaces have been dated by a more complex carbon isotope method.

As you make your way up the alluvial fan, you might appreciate the road a little more to know that all nine miles of it were built solely by Shorty Borden, using only simple hand tools, with his two burros as his only companions. He had found a lode of silver in Hanaupah Canyon, and needed a road to properly work it, even though he himself owned no vehicle. He started the project in September of 1932, and completed it six months later in March of 1933.

When I scouted this road during the unusually wet spring of 1998, I was struck by the vast quantity of bright orange dodder that covered all of the native vegetation. Dodder is a parasite, because it contains no chlorophyll, and hence cannot manufacture its own food like most green plants do. Once established on

Dodder, genus *Cuscuta*

another plant, it relies on its host plant for nutrients, and eventually kills its host. Dodder seemed to be much more widespread than I ever recall seeing it before. Another visit to the Hanaupah fan in the spring of 2004, after a dry winter, revealed relatively few of these striking plants. The lesson learned: parasites respond to stress conditions just like their hosts do. Dodder is common even in dry years, however. There are five species, and five sub-species of dodder in the California desert.

Curiously, as you make your way up Hanaupah Canyon, cactus is noticeable by its absence. How can this happen, when Trail Canyon just to the north has lots of it, as does Johnson Canyon just to the south?

As you drive up the fan, you cannot help but notice Telescope Peak, the highest point in Death Valley National Park. The elevation at the summit is 11,049 feet. It typically carries a mantle of snow from November well into April. A few hardy souls attempt to climb the peak from the end of the road in Hanaupah Canyon. It is a grueling two-day siege involving a vertical ascent of 7,500 feet. I always preferred the conventional route, by trail from Mahogany Flat, which involves a still respectable climb of 3,000 feet.

At a point 4.8 miles from the West Side Road, Shorty's old road drops down into the wash. Before descending this short grade, stop a moment and look around. To the west, of course, Telescope Peak dominates the skyline. Behind you, to the east are good views of the salt flats 2,000 feet lower in the bottom of Death Valley. But looking to the south and west notice as well how the old alluvial fan surface coming out of Hanaupah Canyon has been deeply cut into by today's wash. This suggests that sometime after this older fan was deposited, the Panamint Mountains began a new cycle of uplift, causing more recent flash floods of the last ten thousand years to cut down through the older fan surface. The new floods have caused erosion, rather than deposition. Studies of the old levels of Ice Age Lake Panamint on the western side of the range confirm this recent uplift theory. Geologists say that the Panamint Mountains are 67 feet higher today than they were 15,000 years ago when Lake Panamint was full and overflowing down Wingate Wash.

The road drops into the wash, and at the bottom of this short but steep grade Chuckawalla Canyon comes in from the right. This is probably the best place in Hanaupah Canyon where camping is permitted, particularly if you have a group of several vehicles. At a point 6.8 miles in from the West Side Road, the canyon makes a turn to the south, and with it the road turns to Class III. The canyon swings west again in a mile, and soon you may see your first trickle of water upon the sand. At one time, the old road went all the way to Shorty's mine, but it has been overgrown and closed for several years. It is about a mile walk to the mine; be sure to camp away from the spring.

Archaeologists have excavated sites in Hanaupah Canyon that show Indian occupation well over 1,000 years ago. In the Death Valley context this may not be so remarkable, because stone tools from other sites go back 9,000 years or more. Nevertheless, Hanaupah Canyon suited the Indians well, providing not only water, but also game and natural plant foods ranging from wild grapes to piñon pine nuts.

If you are of a mind to climb Telescope Peak, avid Death Valley hiker Michael Digonnet recommends a trailless ascent of the ridge between the south and middle forks of the canyon to the 10,000-foot level, where you can pick up the trail from Mahogany Flat. Good luck!

Hanaupah Canyon Road

6

Johnson Canyon,
Where Hungry Bill Once Lived

Primary Attraction:	Johnson is my favorite of all the canyons on the eastern slope of the Panamints, because of its scenery and historical connection with Panamint City.
Time Required:	This is an all day outing from Furnace Creek, even if you don't leave your vehicle. The hike up to Hungry Bill's Ranch is highly recommended, however, and to do that, you had better plan on a two-day excursion and camping in the canyon.
Miles Involved:	From Furnace Creek Ranch to the start of the Johnson Canyon Road is 27.8 miles, plus another 10.4 miles to the end of the road.
Maps:	1:100,000 Death Valley Junction and Darwin Hills sheets; 1:24,000 Mormon Pint, Galena Canyon and Panamint Quadrangles.
Degree of Difficulty:	The first six miles are mostly Class I and Class II. The last four miles are both Class II and Class III.

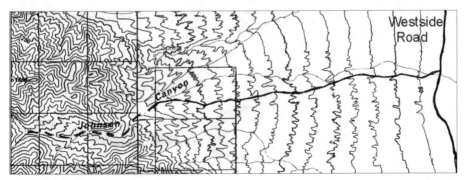

Those interested in history, hiking, nature, and wildlife photography will all find the trip into Johnson Canyon a worthwhile endeavor. Take the Badwater Road south of the Furnace Creek Inn. After going south 6.1 miles, take the graded West Side Road turning off to the right (N36°21.931 W116°50.675). Soon you will be crossing the barren salt flat known as "The Devil's Golf Course". This three to five foot thick layer of gleaming white crystals is almost pure sodium chloride (NaCl), better known as common table salt. It is an evaporite deposit left behind when a 30-foot deep lake dried up about 2,000 years ago. Below the rough surface lies more than a thousand more feet of similar deposits left behind during the past million years, when several other lakes filled and then dried up during the Pleistocene Ice Age. At the time, meltwater from glaciers along the eastern slope of the Sierra Nevada flowed down the then mighty Owens River into the China Lake and Searles Lake basins, overflowing into Panamint Valley and finally into Death Valley by way of Wingate Wash. At its peak, Death Valley's ancient Lake Manly covered some 618 square miles, was 100 miles long, and some 600 feet deep.

The road across the Devil's Golf Course in the early 1930s
(Death Valley Museum photo)

Five miles from the pavement, the Trail Canyon Road is passed, and after four more miles you will come to Tule Spring. This is could be the site of "Bennett's Long Camp", where in January of 1850 the exhausted and starving Bennett-Arcan Party of emigrants could go no farther. They sent two of their younger men, William Manly and John Rogers, ahead with meager rations and $60 in coin. "The Boys" were to scout the way to civilization, buy fresh horses and supplies, and return. They did just that, going to Rancho San Francisco (near today's Newhall) and back in only 26 days (see pages 263-264).

Continue south on the West Side Road heading towards Shorty's Well. Notice the prominent fault scarp on the Hanaupah alluvial fan about ¾-mile to your right. This twenty-foot embankment was caused when the eastern side of the fault dropped in relation to the western side. The escarpment is still fresh, exhibiting only minor erosion, suggesting the faulting took place relatively recently, perhaps even within the last thousand years.

Along the West Side Road 1½-miles south of Shorty's Well are the graves of two noted Death Valley sourdoughs, Jim Dayton and Shorty Harris. Dayton died here in the summer of 1898. Harris died three decades later in 1934, and at his own request, Shorty Harris was buried here beside his friend.

(Frasher photo from the author's collection)

A half-mile farther to the south are the ruins of the Eagle Borax Works, the very first borax mining operation in Death Valley. Unfortunately for its owner, it was also the first such operation to go broke. A sign and an unsold pile of borax, still awaiting shipment, mark the site.

Finally, after you have gone south on the West Side Road for 19.7 miles, a Park Service sign points the way to Johnson Canyon; reset your trip odometer and turn right here (N36°10.210 W116°52.431). As you start up the alluvial fan, a groan of protest from your engine advises you that the grade is steeper than it appears. The road surface hovers someplace between Class I and Class II. Notice how barren and devoid of life the bajada surface is. Only a few hardy creosotes manage to grow in the small gullies. In the loose and disturbed soil along the road, however, the curious Desert Trumpet *Eriogonum inflatum* has managed to find a foothold. Some people use the tender tips of the stems to add zest to salads, but, of course, picking native plants is not permitted in our National Parks. If you want to sample this morsel, plenty can be found outside of the park in Panamint and Searles Valleys.

At a point 6.4 miles up from the West Side Road, the Johnson Canyon Road drops down into the wash and deteriorates. Sometimes the route is Class II, sometimes an easy Class III. The canyon forks at a point 8.7 miles from the West Side Road. At one time, it was possible to drive up the left or south fork for a short distance. The NPS has now closed that road, so you must keep to the right in the north fork.

Ten miles off the West Side Road, you encounter the first flowing water. The canyon is alive with wildflowers if you venture into here in the springtime. The "P's" are well represented by phacelia, primrose, phlox, popcorn, paintbrush, and pentstamen. Other blossoms you are likely to see come from chia, fiddleneck, gilia, and mallow.

The road used to force it way upstream through a thicket of willows, but the park service requests that you utilize the parking area just before the water for camping or day hikes. It is a short walk to carry supplies to the old campsite under the cottonwood trees.

By walking a quarter-mile beyond the end of the road, you will see an old arrastra on the south side of the trail. Miners commonly used this crude device in the 1850-80s to crush and pulverize ore so that the gold could be extracted. A single horse or burro would walk around and around, pulling a horizontal beam that pivoted on a vertical shaft. The beam would drag a large boulder around within a circular rock-lined race. Ore and water were added occasionally and the pulverized ore, now the consistency of fine sand, was drawn off so that the gold could be panned out. While this simple method was not very efficient, the device was relatively easy to construct and cheap to operate.

A short distance up the trail are the rock outlines of a second arrastra, an aqueduct, and what appears to be a primitive reduction furnace. Beyond, the trail climbs the south wall of the canyon to avoid the willow-choked streambed. After hiking an hour or so, a little less than two miles, you will come to the massive stone walls that mark the site of Hungry Bill's Ranch.

Death Valley historian, Richard Lingenfelter, says that the site of Hungry Bill's Ranch was once the site of the Shoshone village of *Puaitungani* (said to mean "Mouse Cave"). During the boom days of Panamint City's heyday, a Kentuckian by the name of William Johnson moved in, cleared, terraced, and irrigated land, and grew a variety of vegetables that he sold for a good price to the hungry residents of Panamint City. He made so much in his first growing season that he terraced even more land and started orchards of apples, pears, peaches, apricots, and figs. Alas, the boom at Panamint City died before his fruit trees were mature. No longer having any customers for his crops, Johnson abandoned his works and moved on to the Kern River country. Upon Johnson's departure, Hungry Bill, a Shoshone chief of immense size and appetite, moved onto the land and filed a homestead claim. He lived there off and on until his death in 1919. Although Hungry Bill's Ranch has been abandoned for years, some of the orchards, vineyards, and terraced and fenced lands remain. When I first visited the site in the 1950s, the trail in was reasonably good. I recall gathering enough of the stunted and half worm-eaten apples to make a pie. There were a few figs, too. The last time I was in there, the trail had become overgrown and I didn't see any edible fruit. If you don't mind a little hike of a couple miles, the trip into Hungry Bill's Ranch is one of the more interesting walks in the park.

The really ambitious can continue on up the canyon to 8,070' Panamint Pass. Even forty years ago, this trail was badly washed out in places and sometimes hard to find. It has only deteriorated further in recent years. Nevertheless, if a car shuttle can be arranged, a two or three day traverse of the Panamints from Johnson Canyon to Chris Wicht's old camp in Surprise Canyon is a memorable experience.

As late as the 1930s, this wickiup stood at Hungry Bill's Ranch.
(Death Valley Museum photo)

7

Galena Canyon,
The Home of "White Gold"

Primary Attraction:	An opportunity to see, close-up, how talc was once mined.
Time Required:	Because of its semi-remote location and distance from the major areas of the park, Galena Canyon will be an all day excursion, but one that can be combined with the Queen of Sheba Mine (Excursion #8).
Miles Involved:	The Galena Canyon Road leaves the West Side Road at a point 32.6 miles south of Furnace Creek Ranch, or 41 miles west of Shoshone. The distance up the canyon is another 5.6 miles.
Maps:	1:100,000 Death Valley Junction sheet; 1:24,000 Mormon Point and Galena Canyon Quadrangles.
Degree of Difficulty:	The Galena Canyon Road is mostly Class I; however, Class III roads will be encountered in visiting some of the mines off this road.

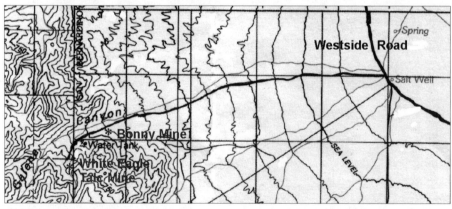

The mineral *galena* is the major ore mineral of lead. Presumably then, in a place called Galena Canyon one might understandably expect to find lead and lead mines. Right? Wrong. Galena Canyon in Death Valley is not noted for the heavy dark gray lead mineral, but a soft, lightweight, sparkling white mineral that is used to dust a baby's bottom - talc! You figure it out; I can offer no explanation.

The lack of lead notwithstanding, Galena Canyon makes an interesting destination for an outing in the southern end of Death Valley. The Galena Canyon Road leaves the West Side Road 10.2 miles north of the south intersection of the Badwater Road and the West Side Road (N36°1.919 W116°49.867). This is 25.5 miles south of the north intersection of those same two roads. Clear enough, huh?

Turning west off the West Side Road, the Galena Canyon Road gradually starts up the alluvial fan. At one time this road saw heavy traffic from fully loaded ore trucks. Since the mines closed, road maintenance has also ceased, and the roadway has deteriorated a bit to Class I.

Try to time your visit to Galena Canyon in late April or early May. Once you leave the salt flats of the valley floor, there is a mile or so along the north side of this road where the Beavertail Cactus *Opuntia basilaris* grow in great abundance. In the springtime, their deep rose color blossoms are quite beautiful. This is a good place to see and enjoy them.

Beavertail Cactus *Opuntia basilaris*

There were four major talc mines in Galena Canyon, all operated at one time or another by the Minerals, Pigments, and Metals Division of a major pharmaceutical firm, Pfizer, Inc. As you come to them, they are the Bonny Mine, Mongolian Mine, Mammoth Mine, and finally, White Eagle Mine.

At a point 4.4 miles in from the West Side Road, the first of these talc mines can be seen off to the left. It is here that the road to the Bonny Mine's giant open pit left the Galena Canyon Road. Although intentionally scarified by Pfizer, the Bonny Mine Road remains a passable Class III. The Bonny Mine was the largest producer of talc in Galena Canyon in the period 1970 to 1975, when it produced 29,645 short tons of talc worth $1,612,000. **Use extreme caution in wandering around these mines**.

You cannot help but notice two large rusting tanks standing upright on the hillside just a quarter-mile up the Galena Canyon Road. A steep, but otherwise good Class III road goes up to them. The route is a tenth of a mile beyond the tunnels of the Mammoth Mine. Unlike those of its neighbors, the Bonny and Mongolian Mines, the Mammoth orebody was worked from underground tunnels. **These tunnels, or adits, remain open today, but obviously, they should not be entered under any circumstances.** The talc came out of the underground works in small ore cars that were pushed onto a platform over the twin tanks, where the ore was stored for truck transport to market.

Rusting ore bunkers of the Mammoth Mine

What is talc and what is it used for, other than the obvious talcum powder? Pure talc is hydrous magnesium silicate, affectionately known as $Mg_3 (Si_4O_{12}) OH_2$ to the chemist. It is used by a number of industries including auto, paint, paper, ceramic, plastic, rubber, roofing, and petroleum manufacturers. Commercial talc is classified in four categories: "Soft platy talc", used in more products than any other type; "Steatite", the most pure and the most expensive for its excellent insulating properties; "Tremolite talc"; and "Mixed talc" (most commercial talc products are a mix of these four types).

All of the talc deposits in Galena Canyon and from adjoining Warm Springs Canyon (see Excursion # 9) come from the Crystal Spring Formation, which are among the oldest layers of the larger Pahrump Group. The talc was formed when diabase, an igneous rock, was intruded into limestone and dolomite beds in the middle of the formation. The heat and pressure created by the diabase altered the carbonate beds to talc.

The Crystal Spring Formation is Precambrian in age, and often 3,000 to 4,200 feet thick. I was once talking to a Johns-Mansville geologist in Warm Springs Canyon, who made the comment: *"You show me an outcrop of the Warms Springs Formation, and I will show you talc."* The Crystal Spring Formation is very widespread in the southern part of Death Valley. For years, Inyo County was a major producer of talc. Talc mining in the Death Valley area began in 1910, although the Galena Canyon Mines are not that old. The White Eagle is probably the oldest mine in Galena Canyon, and it was first opened in 1939.

From the turnoff up to the Mammoth Mine, the main access road passes two cabins of the Mammoth Mine camp. A Class II road turns off to the right, heading up Galena Canyon at a point 0.9 miles beyond the cabins. These tracks dead-end within a half-mile. The main road curves to the left and it, too, soon dead-ends at the enormous ore bunker of the White Eagle Mine. Again, **stay out of the underground workings**; they are no place for amateurs. Specimens of steatite grade talc can be found around the ore bunker. As strange as it may sound, prior to passage of the Mining in the Parks Act of 1976, talc miners could lawfully haul away thousands of tons of this material; however today, the collecting of even one small piece is illegal.

Ore bunker of the White Eagle Talc Mine

8

Carbonate and the Queen of Sheba Mine

Primary Attraction:	An obscure and short-lived Turn of the 20th Century mining camp.
Time Required:	This excursion can be done in a half-day out of Furnace Creek Ranch, but because of the distance it would be better to combine it with another west side outing for a full day's activity.
Miles Involved:	This site is 37 miles south of Furnace Creek Ranch via the West Side Road. It is 44 miles from Shoshone via State Route 178.
Maps:	1:100,000 Death Valley Junction and Owlshead Mountains sheets; 1:24,000 Mormon Point, Galena Canyon, and Anvil Spring Canyon East Quadrangles.
Degree of Difficulty:	The roads are all good, except for the last 3.9 miles that are Class II and III.

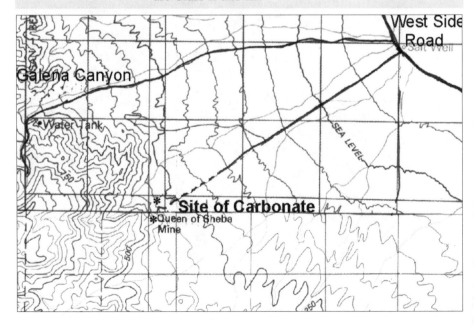

The site of Carbonate, the only mining camp on the eastern slope of the Panamint Range, is reached by taking the West Side Road south through Death Valley. At a point 32.6 miles south of Furnace Creek Ranch, the Galena Canyon Road goes off to the right. Continue south on the West Side Road another 0.1 miles. On the left are two rusting steel tanks. On the right a road heads south and west, straight up the bajada toward the distant hills (N36°1795 W116°49.773). This is the road to Carbonate.

This road was in much better condition when Goldfield Consolidated Mines was doing exploration work in the Queen of Sheba Mine back in 1952-53. The road has deteriorated since that time, and it has had several minor washouts. Today the road up from the valley floor is Class II for the first two miles, and then turns into a very easy Class III for the last two miles.

The Queen of Sheba Mine camp is reached at a point 3.9 miles up from the West Side Road. This mine was the last to be worked, and only a couple of its buildings and an ore bunker survive to this day. The old camp of Carbonate was situated down in the wash, just north of the Queen of Sheba Mine. Although the camp consisted mostly of white canvas tents, Carbonate was said to have had a saloon and a couple of stores. Practically nothing has survived. Up on the ridge above the camp was Chester Pray's Carbonate Mine.

In 1908 a drifter from Nevada named Chester Pray stumbled upon the mineral cerrusite (lead carbonate) on the mountainside just south of Galena Canyon. His find was in the Noonday Dolomite, 700 million-year-old marine sediments of the Precambrian Age. Pray dug several tunnels and otherwise explored his find for several years, but shipped no ore. In 1913 he approached Jack Salsberry, a big promoter from Tonopah. With Pray and one other partner, Salsberry formed the Carbonate Lead Mines. Pray had ore blocked out, but no means to ship it to a smelter. He began the arduous task of building a road for forty miles to the Tonopah & Tidewater Railroad station at Zabriskie. Sadly, Pray shot himself in the head before the road was completed.

Mining promoter Jack Salsberry completed the road late in 1913. Much of it is still there in the form of today's State Highway 178. The 3,315-foot high point still carries the name Salsberry Pass. Nevertheless after building all that road, Salsberry found the price of lead depressed. The value of the lead produced did not exceed the high cost of extraction, shipping, and smelting. Then a fortuitous event happened for Salsberry. World War I came along, and the price of lead doubled from 3½ cents a pound to seven cents. By the summer of 1915, Carbonate Lead Mines employed sixty men. There were just a handful actually working at the mine, because they could put the ore in the bunker faster than it could be hauled away. Most of those workers were engaged in transporting forty tons of ore per week. Mule drawn wagons were first used to haul the ore to Zabriskie siding on the Tonopah & Tidewater Railroad. From there it went by rail to Midvale, Utah for smelting. Later a fleet of sixteen trucks was utilized for the first leg of the journey. There was no water at the mine, so the otherwise empty ore trucks carried water on the return trip.

The price of lead continued to rise, reaching a peak of twelve cents by 1917. World War I ended with the armistice of November 11, 1918, and the bottom dropped out of the price of lead. However, in its first four years of production, the Carbonate Mine had produced 6,500 tons of ore worth about a third of a million dollars.

The story of the Carbonate Mine did not end there. Between 1923 and 1926 optimism was running rampant across the country. Salsberry worked a couple of stock deals with the mine that artificially inflated the value of the stock, and then, of course, he sold out, leaving others holding the bag. Many people lost their jobs after the stock market crash of 1929, and the wages for what work was available were low. Under these circumstances, Salsberry was able to reopen the Carbonate Mine and the adjoining Queen of Sheba Mine in 1930, and another

Queen of Sheba Mine

4,000 tons of ore were shipped between 1930 and 1935.

The Carbonate Mine was reluctant to close for good. It was leased out and worked again in 1948-49, when a new mill was built, and again in 1952-53. The neighboring Queen of Sheba Mine was worked as recently as 1972. Much of the machinery left on the sites dates from this later period. Historian Richard Lingenfelter says the Carbonate and Queen of Sheba Mines were the second most productive and profitable lead mines in the Death Valley country. State records indicate that, in their sixty year lives, the Carbonate and Queen of Sheba Mines produced five million pounds of lead, 146,000 pounds of copper, 100,000 ounces of silver, and 1500 ounces of gold.

Warning: The underground workings are not safe, and the visitor would be well advised not to attempt to enter them.

9

Mengel Pass via Warm Springs Canyon
and Butte Valley

Primary Attraction:	Talc mines, interesting geology, unusual scenery, and a little history all come together to make this outing one of the most interesting in the park. Smart backroad explorers make the traverse of the Panamint Range, going up Warm Springs Canyon and down Goler Wash, which is somewhat easier on your nerves and your vehicle than going in the opposite direction.
Time Required:	It is an all day trip to Mengel Pass and back, or on over the top and down into Panamint Valley. Three days could be spent exploring the various side roads.
Miles Involved:	It is forty miles from Furnace Creek Ranch to the beginning of the Warm Springs Canyon Road, and then another 24 miles to the summit of Mengel Pass. If you choose to go on, add another 25 miles down Goler Wash to Ballarat.
Maps:	1:100,000 Owlshead Mountains and Ridgecrest sheets; 1:24,000 Anvil Spring Canyon East, Anvil Spring Canyon West, and Manly Peak Quadrangles.
Degree of Difficulty:	The route through much of Warm Springs Canyon is Class I. Beyond the road deteriorates to an easy Class II as far as Greater View Spring. The last mile to the summit of Mengel Pass is Class III. **For those planning on going over the pass, be aware that the Goler Wash Road on the west may be just as bad, or even worse than the road on the east side of the Mengel Pass (see Excursion #35). Do not attempt this road in any vehicle not having four-wheel drive.**
Remarks:	**It is well over 100 miles from the gas pump at Furnace Creek Ranch to the next refueling point in Trona or Panamint Springs. Be sure your fuel tank is topped off before leaving Furnace Creek Ranch on this excursion.**

Prior to 1994, there were three jeep trails one could take across the southern portion of the Panamint Range between Death Valley and Panamint Valley. At the north end of this section, there was a steep road that switchbacked up and out of the north fork of Trail Canyon, to join the graded Aguereberry Point Road, where one could go on to Panamint Valley via Emigrant Pass and Wildrose Station. In the far south, there were two alternative ways to drive over Panamint Range. First, if you had arranged in advance for a one-day

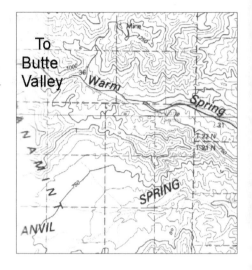

Recreation Pass from the China Lake Naval Ordnance Test Station, you could have followed the twenty mule team borax route up Wingate Wash, crossing one corner of the naval base, and descending into Panamint Valley via Goler Wash. Or, you might have driven up Warm Springs Canyon into Butte Valley and over Mengel Pass, descending into Panamint Valley by way of Goler Wash. Alas, the Trail Canyon switchbacks have subsequently been washed out, and any eventual restoration of the road seems highly unlikely (Historic Wildrose Station has also been torn down.) Then with passage of the *California Desert Protection Act* in 1994, Wingate Wash was classified as *Wilderness*, thus forever closing that route to vehicles. So only one of these three trans-Panamint routes remains open to motor vehicles today, the Warm Springs Canyon-Goler Wash road. It represents a scenic and historically interesting way to explore the southern portions of Death Valley and Panamint Valley, while leaving Death Valley by a route that most park visitors never see.

To find the Warm Springs Canyon Road, take the Badwater Road for 6.1 miles south of the Furnace Creek Inn, then turn right and continue south on the graded West Side Road another 33 miles. Watch for a sign pointing to the west that reads *Butte Valley*; reset your trip odometer, and turn right on this graded road (N35°57.223 W116°44.780). For years, heavily laden ore trucks used this road; back then it was a high standard road. Since the last talc mine in Warm Springs Canyon closed in the 1980s, the road has deteriorated some, but it still generally meets the Class I criteria of *The Mitchell Scale*.

Shortly after turning off the West Side Road, a side road to the left once went over to Wingate Wash, where a four-wheel drive route followed the path of the twenty mule team borax wagons up the wash on the long road to the railhead at

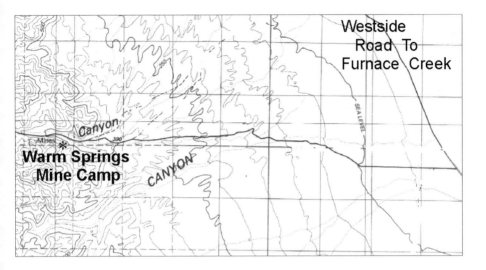

Mojave. The National Park Service closed this road in the early 1980s, because the United States Navy was having trouble with trespassers on NOTS Range "B". Wingate Wash is still open to hikers and backpackers willing to carry sufficient water.

Anvil Spring Canyon appears off to the left seven miles from the West Side Road. Fifty years ago there was a road through here going all the way up to Butte Valley. It was not Congress or some faceless government bureaucrat that closed this route. It was closed by one of Mother Nature's gully-washers in the 1940s.

Our road enters Warm Springs Canyon in a little more than seven miles. As you start up the wash, notice the rocks on the south side of the canyon. These old pre-Precambrian rocks are part of the Crystal Spring Formation. Millions of years ago these already formed limestone and dolomite layers were profoundly altered by heat and pressure, when a dike of molten igneous rock was intruded into the sediments. As a result of this metamorphism, a band of talc two miles long and up to 25 feet thick was formed next to the dike. You can get a close look at the mineral in numerous abandoned workings on the south side of the road. **Warning: Stay out of the underground workings; they are unsafe!**

The first mine encountered is the Big Talc Mine. The access road to it is 9.1 miles in from the West Side Road. The next mine is the Number 5 Mine, also on the left. The Number 5 and Big Talc had underground workings that connected and were all part of what was known as the Grantham Mine.

Of the one hundred or so women who have trod Death Valley's barren hillsides in search of mineral wealth, Louise Grantham was by far the most successful. In 1931, she and Ernest "Siberian Red" Huhn recognized the potential of the talc deposits and started staking claims up and down the canyon. These were the depression years, however, and the demand for talc was not great; nevertheless, talc mining began in 1933. With the advent of World War II, talc became an important commodity, and by 1943 it was crucial to the war effort. The mine's output was continuous in the post war years.

Johns-Manville Products purchased the property in 1972, and they operated the mine for another fifteen years. In those later years both mines had extensive underground workings on sixteen different levels. Many of the tunnels were big enough to accommodate the use of rubber-tired diesel haulers and front-end loaders. The ceilings of the tunnels and stopes were supported in one of three ways. At times extensive heavy timbers were utilized. In other areas, roof bolts were driven into the "hanging wall" (the ceiling). In yet other areas, room-and-pillar mining was employed, where large columns of ore were left in place to support the ceiling. As these levels were worked out, the last areas to be mined were the pillars themselves, leaving a very dangerous unsupported void. **None of these underground workings are now safe to enter!**

The third mine encountered off to the left is the Warm Spring Mine. It had an enormous open pit eight hundred feet long by four hundred feet wide by eighty feet deep. The access road to this mine is 9.6 miles in from the West Side Road.

At a point 10.8 miles in, a side road left goes to the Warm Springs Mine Camp, a worthy stop and a good overnight campsite. The Paiutes had camped at Warm Springs long before the first prospectors came this way. The Shoshone village of *Pabuna* was here when the Bennett-Arcan party made their long camp near Mesquite Well, just a few miles to the north. The remnants of this village are said to have been destroyed by a flash flood in 1897. Only the fig trees planted by Panamint Tom in 1890 remain.

Warm Springs has served as a comfortable base camp for the many talc miners who have come and gone since the 1930s. In her book *A Mine of Her Own: Women Prospectors in the American West, 1850-1950,* Dr. Sally Zanjani of the University of Nevada Reno postulates that it was the "woman's touch" brought by Louise Grantham that brought these amenities to Warm Springs Canyon. I recall that, when I was in here during the early 1970s, the place looked more like a mobile home park than a mining camp. While the last mobile home was pulled out over twenty years ago, many of the camp buildings remain in good condition, thanks in part to the Mojave River Valley Museum of Barstow, which has sort of adopted the place. They have placed a sign telling a little about the camp, and have a register for visitors to sign. The imported giant salt cedar trees still provide cool shade on a warm summer's day, and the spring of lukewarm water still feeds the swimming pool. Camping is permitted here, and there are even a couple of picnic tables. Campfires are not permitted.

Talc was not the only mineral commodity handled at Warm Springs. In 1939 gold miners erected a mill here to process gold ore from the Gold Hill Mine. The mill has suffered relatively little vandalism in recent years and looks very much like a reconstructed museum piece designed to display various types of ore dressing. Through a series of belts and gears, a single, horizontal-cylinder gasoline engine drives three different kinds of ore crushers. There is an arrastra, one of the most primitive ways of crushing ore, a small jaw mill, and a more efficient ball mill. Once it was reduced to sand-size particles, the ore and water combination flowed across shaker tables. Here the free gold was concentrated at one corner of the vibrating table, with the lighter waste material flowing off at another corner.

Gold Hill Mill

The road deteriorates to Class II beyond Warm Springs, but it poses no problem for vehicles with high ground clearance. At a point 15.5 miles from the West Side Road, Warm Springs Canyon is left and Butte Valley is entered. It will be a couple of miles yet before the Striped Butte, from which the valley gets its name, is visible. The road gradually turns to the south, and the scenery becomes dominated by Striped Butte, rising some nine hundred feet above the valley floor. The colorful layers of sediments in this butte make it geologically unique, for the surrounding country is made up of largely granitic rocks. When prospector Hugh McCormack passed through here in the 1860s, he named it "Curious Butte". Through the years, however, the name has changed to "Striped Butte".

At a point 20.7 miles in from the West Side Road, the main road goes straight; however, a Class II side road turns off to the right (N35°55.399 W117°4.950). By following it to the west 1.8 miles, the crest of the Panamint Range can be crossed at an elevation of 4,626 feet. On the other side, a deeply rutted Class III and Class IV road descends into Redlands Canyon all the way down to Redlands Spring nearly 2,000 feet below. Historian and tireless researcher Leroy Johnson thinks Redlands Canyon is the route used by Manly and Rogers in February of 1850, when they rescued the ill-fated Bennett-Arcan Party that was stranded in Death Valley.

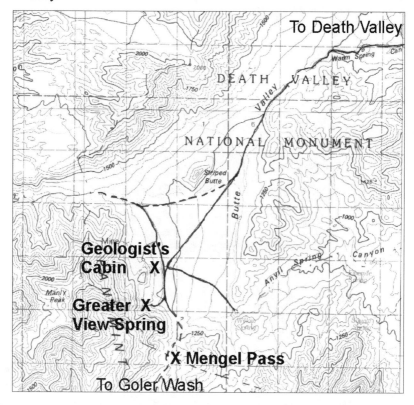

A side road to the left off the Redlands Canyon trail takes you into an old miner's camp in Wood Canyon. It is in this general area that Panamint Russ claimed he found, and then lost, a fabulous vein during a prospecting trip in 1925.

Continuing ahead on the main road for 1.8 miles, a lone cottonwood tree marks the site of Anvil Spring. The stone cabin above it is sometimes known as the *Geologist's Cabin,* after one of its original occupants. Supposedly Anvil Spring got its name from Lieutenant Charles Bendire, whose United States Army scouting party found an anvil here in 1867. Historian Richard Lingenfelter says that Charles Alvord's prospecting party had thrown it into the spring in disgust seven years earlier, after Alvord was unable to locate a rich vein of gold that he had found only five months previously.

The stone Geologist's Cabin is weather tight, stocked with food and water by passersby, and kept unlocked and available for public use. It is one of several such emergency shelters in the high Panamints. Use it if you wish, but please keep the place clean, and restock any food you might use. There is a register for visitors to sign. On occasion the backcountry ranger stays here, as do NPS volunteers. If the flag is flying, the ranger is in residence.

The "Geologist's Cabin" at Anvil Spring, with Striped Butte in the background

Less than a mile south of Anvil Spring is Greater View Spring, once the home of veteran prospector Carl Mengel, a buddy of Frank "Shorty" Harris and Pete Aguereberry. He also had a close relationship with Bill and Barbara Myers, who lived on a little ranch just over the pass in Goler Wash. Mengel, who lost a leg in a mining accident in Nevada, settled at the spring here in 1912, rebuilding an old preexisting cabin left by Mormon prospectors in 1869. In 1912 he also bought the Oro Fino Mine in Goler Wash. While trying to find a better route for his mules to haul ore out, he discovered a lode of high-grade ore that is said to have assayed as high as $35,000 per ton! Unfortunately, the deposit was small. Except for his financial interest in the nearby Lotus Mine, Carl died penniless of tuberculosis in 1944. His cremated ashes lie within his monument at the summit of what is today called Mengel Pass.

Mengel's cabin, too, is left unlocked and stocked with water and some food. It may be weather tight, but it is not rodent-tight like the Geologist's Cabin. Camp here if you wish, but remember: **mice and other small rodents sometimes get** into these cabins. Their feces, urine, and saliva can be the source of the **Hantavirus**, which can infect humans with a nasty often-fatal illness called **Hantavirus Pulmonary Syndrome.** Avoid all contact with rodent droppings, and do not stir up any dust where there is evidence of mice and rats. Inhalation of the virus is a common way of transmission to humans.

Oh yes, one convenience that Mengel's cabin has, which the Geologist's Cabin does not, is an outhouse!

Carl Mengel's cabin in the 1930s
(Death Valley Museum Photo)

Carl Mengel's cabin Today
Beyond Mengel's cabin, the first 0.3 miles is Class II, but soon that turns to

Class III, as the last 1.3 miles of climb to 4,800 foot Mengel Pass is made. If you have difficulty getting up this last mile, go no further. **Although downhill all the way, the descent through the Goler Wash side of Mengel Pass can be much worse than the Warm Springs side.**

Carl Mengel in the 1930s
(Searles Valley Historical Society photo)

Carl's ashes rest in this monument at the summit of Mengel Pass.

The Early Days at Stovepipe Wells

The Eichbaum Toll Road led to Stovepipe Wells.

Bungalette City at Stovepipe Wells circa 1932

(The above photos by Burton Frasher from the author's collection)

Chapter II

Trails Out of Stovepipe Wells

Today's Stovepipe Wells Resort dates back to the earliest days of tourism in Death Valley. In 1925, Herman William Eichbaum, an electrical engineer who had helped build Rhyolite's first electrical plant in 1907 and had started a successful sightseeing business on Catalina Island, returned to the Death Valley region with the idea of building a grand resort at Hell's Gate (on today's Daylight Pass Road to Beatty). First, however, he had to build a good road to the site, so that tourists might drive there in their own automobiles. In October of 1925 the Inyo County Board of Supervisors granted Eichbaum a franchise to build a toll road from Darwin Falls, over the Panamint Range and down to Stovepipe Wells, just east of the sand dunes. Within weeks he had a caterpillar tractor and a half-dozen men grading the new road. They had crossed Towne Pass by Christmas, and had extended the road to the sand dunes a month later. The 38-mile long Eichbaum Toll Road officially opened for traffic on May 4, 1926, even though the portion through the sand dunes remained a problem, and construction of the resort had not yet started. That summer, trucks delivering the first building materials became mired down in the sand dunes, still some twelve miles short of their destination at Hell's Gate. By this time, Eichbaum's capital from the sale of his business on Catalina Island was exhausted, and the entire project was in jeopardy. He made the decision to abandon the Hell's Gate site and build his resort on the valley floor on the west side of the dunes, where his trucks were mired down to their axles in soft sand. Never mind that the true Stovepipe Wells was still five miles to the northeast, his new resort would be known as the Stovepipe Wells Hotel.

The newly created Stovepipe Wells Resort opened its doors on November 1, 1926. Death Valley's first tourist facilities would consist of twenty open-air bungalows with screened windows, having a total of fifty rooms to rent. A restaurant, general store, and gasoline pump were also provided. Electricity to pump water from the well and provide lighting came from a diesel-powered electrical generator. Eichbaum even installed a large searchlight, pointed skyward to guide in guests arriving after dark. Some irreverently called the complex "Bungalette" or "Bungalow City".

In order to compete with the Pacific Coast Borax Company's Furnace Creek Inn, a few years later the Stovepipe Wells Hotel would add a swimming pool, tennis court, an improvised golf course, and an airstrip. Thus, Death Valley was already being heavily promoted as a tourist attraction when President Herbert Hoover created Death Valley National Monument in 1933. In 1934, the state purchased Eichbaum's road and stopped charging tolls. The Civilian Conservation Corps crews, which had been building new roads in the monument for a year, realigned the old Eichbaum toll road over Towne Pass, and tourism flourished in spite of the economic hard times of the Great Depression years.

Today, Stovepipe Wells remains a tourist center within Death Valley National Park. There is a Ranger Station here, where the latest road and visitor information can be obtained. Concessionaire services include a hotel, restaurant and bar, gift shop, general store, service station, and an RV park with full hookups. There is also a campground operated by the NPS, and even a paved airstrip (no AV gas).

LOBBY STOVEPIPE WELLS HOTEL
DEATH VALLEY, CALIFORNIA

The lobby of the Stovepipe Wells Hotel in the 1940s

(Frasher photos from the author's collection)

10

The Tucki Mine

Primary Attraction:	This outing goes to an old mine with interesting geology and canyon scenery along the way.
Time Required:	Budget at least a half day for this excursion out of Stovepipe Wells.
Miles Involved:	It is 21 miles, one way, from Stovepipe Wells Resort to the Tucki Mine.
Maps:	1:100,000 Darwin Hills sheet; 1:24,000 Emigrant Canyon and Tucki Wash Quadrangles.
Degree of Difficulty:	Much of the route is Class II, with only a few sections of easy Class III.

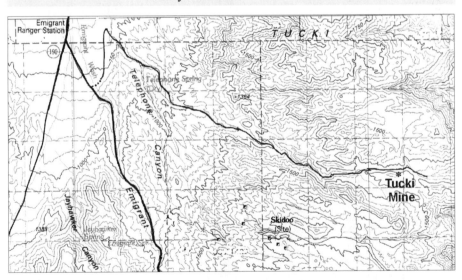

The rough road excursion into the Tucki Mine is interesting geologically, historically, and perhaps even politically. Along the way, the scenery isn't bad either. As this book is being published, the National Park Service has not placed a sign at the beginning of this jeep trail. Follow these instructions and watch carefully, or you might miss it. From the Stovepipe Wells Resort, drive south on State Route 190 some 9.2 miles to Emigrant Junction (N36°29.629 W117°13.611).

Turn left here on the Wildrose Road, and proceed 1.5 miles to the entrance to Emigrant Canyon. Just before entering the confining walls of the canyon, watch carefully for wheel tracks going to the left across the wash. If the sand is dry, you may need four-wheel drive to get across the wash; reset your odometer. If recent flooding has washed the tracks away, the route can be seen climbing up onto the bajada across the wash. Get there the best way possible. The way is clear from there on.

The jeep trail heads across the flat desert surface, with good views of the northern portion of Death Valley. At a point 1.3 miles from the pavement, the trail makes a sharp turn to the left, and in another 0.4 miles enters Telephone Canyon. This drainage has its headwaters below the site of Skidoo, a former mining camp that boasted of having 500 residents in the 1907-1909 era. A telephone line came through here in 1907 to connect Skidoo with the outside world at Rhyolite, then a booming metropolis connected with the world by two railroads. The telephone line is long gone, but the name has stuck.

You cannot help but notice the horizontal beds of reddish brown conglomerate rock on either side as you proceed up the canyon. This is part of the Nova Formation, a fanglomerate of the late Tertiary era formed about ten million years ago under similar circumstances as those under which the Emigrant Wash fan is being deposited today. The Nova Formation is so undercut at one point that you can drive your vehicle under it.

The Nova Formation overhangs the road in the lower Telephone Canyon.

The canyon forks at a point 0.7 miles above the mouth, with Telephone Canyon continuing to the right into what old timers call "Sheep Canyon". When I first published *Death Valley Jeep Trails* in 1969, it was possible to drive up Telephone Canyon another mile and a half, where it left the wash to rejoin the Wildrose Road. The California Desert Protection Act of 1994 designated the area as wilderness, but if you don't mind a short hike of less than a mile round trip, you can walk up the right fork to a natural arch and the now-dry Telephone Spring just beyond. The spring was the site of an old miner's cabin and an arrastra, a crude device to crush ore into sand-size particles so the fine gold could be extracted.

Natural arch in Telephone Canyon

From this fork in the canyon, the jeep trail keeps to the left gradually making its way eastward, as it climbs ever higher into Sheep Canyon and the northern Panamint Mountains. The younger Nova beds are left behind as you climb, and you enter the metamorphic core of the range. Here are steeply dipping slate and schist that, in the Proterozoic Era some 750 million years ago, were laid down as sea-bottom sediments.

The walls of Sheep Canyon dissipate at a point 8½ miles from the paved highway, and the road improves as the country opens up. In a half-mile, the crest of the Panamints is crossed at the 4,900' elevation. Since leaving the pavement, the jeep trail has gradually climbed some 2,500 feet. From the pass, it is an easy 0.6 miles down the Tucki Wash drainage to the Tucki Mine.

Small amounts of gold were discovered in this canyon in 1909, and first claimed by a Henry Britt as part of the Skidoo-Harrisburg frenzy. In 1927, Roy

Journigan grubstaked an informal partnership of three prospectors, Charlie Walker, John Millett and Sam Ball. It was this trio who found some interesting looking float in Tucki Canyon, at apparently the same location as Britt's discovery some eighteen years previously. They staked four mining claims on their find, and began to dig into the mountainside in search of a quartz vein; no vein was found. The gold just seemed to be disseminated throughout the bedrock that was quartzite. Fire assays had to be taken regularly to determine in which direction the richest gold ran. Initially, there was no road into the mine, so the ore had to be hand sorted and carried out by mules to the previously mentioned arrastre in Telephone Canyon. In 1929, Roy Journigan bought controlling interest in the mine from the original locators, and he began the first serious efforts to mine the orebody. The lack of water was always a problem at the Tucki Mine. By 1934, the inefficiency of the arrastre in Telephone Canyon prompted Journigan to construct a new amalgamation plant at the old Gold Bottom Mill, where there was ample water from a spring. The finely crushed ore was now mixed with water, and made to flow over copper plates coated with mercury. From time to time, the mercury was scraped off the plates and heated in a retort. The liquid mercury was evaporated off, and passed through a condenser to recover it. (The foundations of this mill can still be seen today.) With the advent of World War II, considered "nonessential to the war effort", gold mines were closed by an Executive Order signed by President Roosevelt.

When I first visited the Tucki Mine in the 1960s, there was less to see than there is now. In 1973, Roy's son Russ Journigan reopened the mine and, in order to rework the old tailing dumps, built a cyanide and carbon filtration mill at the mine site. However, the times and political climate in the 1970s were very different from those in the 1930s. Mining in Death Valley was no longer encouraged. The National Park Service could not prevent Journigan from mining and milling his ore, but they could prohibit him from using any water from within Death Valley National Monument in his new mill. Russ was forced to buy water from Panamint Springs for one cent per gallon, and transport it twice a week over Towne's Pass by tank truck. Nevertheless, in spite of the adversities, by 1974 Russ Journigan was smelting ingots of 99.8% to 99.9% pure gold, which he sold to a metals dealer in Las Vegas.

About this same time, Senator Alan Cranston introduced a bill that would prohibit mining in Death Valley National Monument. The legislation was passed by the full Congress in 1976, and signed into law by President Gerald Ford. The National Park Service told Journigan that he had to cease operations, close his mine, and clean the site up within 90 days. He spent the next five years seeking relief in Federal Court but, in the end, his money ran out before the government's did.

At the Sixth Death Valley Conference on History and Prehistory, 76 year old Russ Journigan presented a paper in which he outlined his family's 55-year history at the Tucki Mine, and how he lost it all with no compensation from the U.S. Government.

Two older structures and one from the latest period of operation remain. Charlie Walker built the building in the middle, shortly after the road was constructed in 1930. The cabin is unlocked, and available for use by backcountry explorers. Visitors often leave food and water so that the structure can be used as an emergency shelter. Stay there if you wish, but please, leave the cabin cleaner than you found it, and be sure the door is securely closed when you leave. **Warning: mice and other small rodents sometimes get into these cabins. Their feces, urine, and saliva can be the source of the Hantavirus, which can infect humans with a nasty often-fatal illness called Hantavirus Pulmonary Syndrome. Avoid all contact with rodent droppings, and do not stir up any dust where there is evidence of mice and rats. Inhalation of the virus is a common way of transmission to humans.**

The jeep trail ends just a short way beyond the mine A walk down the canyon might interest the geologist, for here can be seen a reddish brown dolomite of the Cambrian Age. From the end of the trail one gets only a glimpse of the floor of Death Valley, some ten miles and nearly 5,000 feet below.

Warning: the old tunnels and inclined shafts may look inviting to explore, but are in dangerous condition, and should not be entered under any circumstance.

The Tucki Mine

11

Cottonwood and Marble Canyons

Primary Attraction:	In recent years, these two interesting canyons have become a very popular destination for visitors having four-wheel drive and looking for a more secluded campsite.
Time Required:	Budget the entire day for this excursion, particularly if you decide to take a little walk up Marble or Cottonwood Canyon.
Miles Involved:	It is 19 miles from the Stovepipe Wells Resort to the end of the trail in Cottonwood Canyon. Add another five miles for the round trip drive into Marble Canyon.
Maps:	1:100,000 Saline Valley sheet; 1:24,000 Stovepipe Wells, Cottonwood Canyon, and Panamint Butte Quadrangles.
Degree of Difficulty:	The first 8.5 miles of dirt road out of Stovepipe Wells Resort are graded (but with a washboard surface). Once in the canyon however, the road is rated as mostly Class II, with a little Class III as you ascend the sandy boulder-strewn wash.
Remarks:	Camping is not permitted along the road for the first eight miles out of Stovepipe Wells, or once inside the canyon, within a quarter-mile of any surface water.

As everyone knows, Death Valley is as hot and dry and desolate as a place can be. Yet here is a paradox, for amid the sun-bleached sands flow streams of sparkling water supporting a wide variety of plant and animal life. One such spot lies hidden deep within Cottonwood Canyon near the floor of Death Valley, only a few miles west of Stovepipe Wells Resort. Here a rare desert stream is forced to the surface by layers of bedrock. In its brief length of only a few miles, the life-giving stream supports a small forest of cottonwood trees and an untold variety of native wildlife. Exploration of this isolated region is not for everyone. Soft sand and boulders make it difficult to get close in a standard automobile. Four-wheel drive vehicles, particularly those with high clearance, should have little trouble.

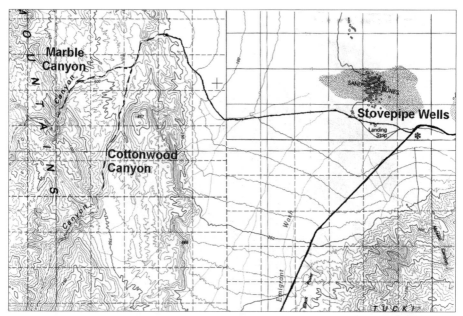

The route begins on the western side of Highway 190 just south of the Stovepipe Wells General Store. Take the road past the entrance to the campground and the north end of the airstrip (N36°36.406 W117°09.309). Here there is the customary jeep symbol with a sign reading *Cottonwood Canyon,* and a graded desert road heads west across the valley floor. It is difficult to understand why the NPS made the decision to grade this jeep trail, an act that created a washboard surface making the road far worse than it was originally. The washboard surface finally ends in 6.5 miles, and the road turns into a more comfortable Class I.

After 8.5 miles you will begin to enter a gorge cut from beds of dolomite comprising the massive front wall of the mountain's face. This is the gateway to Cottonwood Canyon and its secrets.

Upon entering the gorge, the road deteriorates further from Class I to Class II, perhaps even a few short areas of Class III. Indeed, the "road" may actually cease to exist at all, depending on conditions at the moment. Nevertheless, start up the canyon carefully picking your way through the maze of half-buried boulders. Cottonwood Canyon has become a popular off-road destination in recent years; it is very likely that a number of vehicles have left tracks for you to follow. It was also a popular place with the ancient Indians who occupied the Death Valley area for the last two thousand years. They left their marks pecked into the rocks of the canyon walls.

On one occasion, my wife Loris and I were camped on a sandy bench at the entrance narrows in Cottonwood Canyon. Just after sunset when it was still light, the air became alive with motion as hundreds of bats emerged from the pockmarked rock walls above us. Within fifteen minutes, they had all disappeared up the canyon.

A Sierra Club outing explores Cottonwood Canyon. The
National Park Service requires large groups to obtain a permit.

As soon as you become accustomed to the confining walls of the gorge, the canyon opens into a large flat, and forks. When I was first here in the 1960s an old metal Automobile Club of Southern California sign was still standing, without a single bullet hole in it! (The Auto Club placed hundreds of these signs in the California desert in the 1930s.) The sign is no longer there. I hope it found a good home.

As soon as the canyon opens up, there is the temptation to turn to the right in order to go to Marble Canyon; resist the temptation. You must go up Cottonwood Canyon nearly a mile after the first narrows before a sign points right to the Marble Canyon Route (N36°37.909 W117°17.732). This turnoff is 10.8 miles from Highway 190.

Marble Canyon has a much different ambiance than Cottonwood Canyon. There is no water along the road and no cottonwood trees. The canyon narrows with towering walls of solid rock on either side. At least part of the route is Class III. The canyon narrows to a seven-foot width 2.6 miles above the turnoff from Cottonwood Canyon. Here the NPS stops further vehicle traffic, although the road once continued on another 1.1 miles to a point where a house size boulder rolled off the hillside to make an impassable obstacle.

The reason for this cessation of the jeep trail is that the NPS wants to keep some space between visitors and the Indian petrogylphs found further up the wash. They are reluctant to reveal the exact whereabouts of these sites, because of past incidences of theft and senseless vandalism. You need look no farther than the mouth of Cottonwood Canyon for that. Indeed, the one time jeep trail through Greenwater Canyon was closed entirely, because people were destroying irreplaceable archaeological sites.

Rock art buff Geron Marcom says there are at least 158 prehistoric rock art sites in Death Valley National Park, with about a third here in the Northern Panamints. With the new lands added to the park in 1994, I am sure those figures are very low. Donald Martin, who catalogued and studied the Death Valley rock art sites for 25 years, thinks they had magical or religious significance associated with hunting. Many, but by no means all, were near water or game trails. Rock art takes on three forms: petrogylphs, designs pecked into the rock surface; pictographs, designs painted on rocks with primitive pigments; and geoglyphs, stone alignments on the desert floor. Petrogylphs are the most common, and are likely to be the best preserved. Some were made long enough ago that the *desert varnish*, a natural patina that develops with time, covers even the etched surfaces within the rock. Such petrogylphs could have been made as long ago as 3,000 years. Only seventeen of the 158 known rock art sites contain pictographs. These sites are particularly sensitive to the weather and the elements and, in spite of man's best efforts, are slowly being weathered away. Other very sensitive sites are those locations in Panamint Valley and elsewhere where archaic man has aligned stones on the desert floor in mysterious patterns called geoglyphs. While none of those in the Death Valley area can compare to those on the Colorado River near Blythe, California, they nevertheless remain an archaeological mystery just as much as the famous ones at Nazca, Peru.

The Marble Canyon narrows

If you leave your vehicle at the end of the road and walk up Marble Canyon a ways, you might be rewarded by one of these rock art sites. Keep your eyes open! They are easy to miss. For those who can arrange a car shuttle, Goldbelt Spring (see Excursion # 28) is a vigorous hike of twelve miles up the Marble Canyon.

Once you leave Marble Canyon and return to Cottonwood Canyon proper, you will want to turn right. Cottonwood Canyon generally heads south now. Soon the vertical walls of the highly metamorphosed limestone will once again enclose the main wash. At a point four miles above the fork, look for a large cave hollowed out of thick layers of fanglomerate. Carved out by floodwaters coming down the canyon, it is difficult to estimate the age of this cave; the most popular place in the canyon to camp today. It seems reasonable to assume that it has in its past provided shelter for the ancient and more modern Indians who lived and farmed in this canyon.

This cave is a popular place to camp.

A short distance up the wash from the cave, the canyon walls suddenly turn from fanglomerate of Tertiary age to limestone of Mississippian age. You can climb up and put your hand on the contact point of the two vastly different rock types. When doing so, your hand will cover a missing gap of 340 million years in the earth's history.

Almost immediately, the road passes a second set of narrows cut through the marine sediments of the Perdido Formation. In wet years, the first surface water from Cottonwood Creek may be encountered 17.4 miles from Highway 190. A mile beyond is the first cluster of cottonwood trees from which the canyon gets its name. The road deteriorates to Class III and a little Class IV in its last 0.8 miles.

By all means hike up the stream a ways from the end of the road. Watch the moist soil along the creek for various animal tracks. When I would come in here thirty and forty years ago, feral burros were everywhere. Thanks to the National Park Service's relocation program, they are rarely seen today.

Cottonwood Canyon teems with wildlife. Less conspicuous dwellers of the canyon are various kinds of small rodents, rabbits, foxes and, of course, the ubiquitous coyote. Keep your eye on the high ridges, too. Desert bighorn sheep *Ovis canadensis nelsonii* have been seen here. Birdwatchers will also find Cottonwood Canyon fascinating. At almost any time of the year, the huge spreading cottonwood trees are alive with the flutter and chatter of various birds. Here the normally hushed desert is so noisy that nature seems unbalanced somehow.

Cottonwood trees line a small stream in Cottonwood Canyon.

12

Jean LeMoigne's Retreat

Primary Attraction:	This rough road excursion goes to a hiker's trailhead leading to the former camp and mine of one of Death Valley's *old timers*.
Time Required:	It is an hour to the present end of the jeep trail near the mouth of LeMoigne Canyon. Add another four to five hours to hike up to LeMoigne's mine camp and return.
Miles Involved:	It is about 11 miles from the Stovepipe Wells Resort to the present-day road's end at the mouth of LeMoigne Canyon.
Maps:	1:100,000 Saline Valley sheet; 1:24,000 Stovepipe Wells and Cottonwood Canyon Quadrangles. (Those hiking up into LeMoigne Canyon may wish to have the Panamint Butte Quadrangle as well.)
Degree of Difficulty:	The route is rated at Class III most of the way, and should not be attempted in any vehicle not having high clearance.

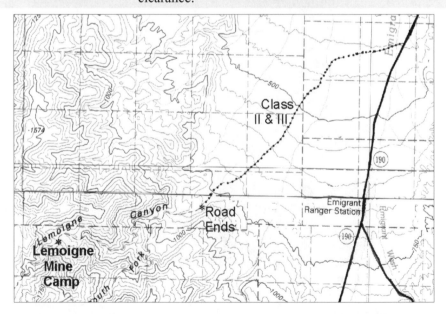

If you thought Cottonwood Canyon was off the beaten path, you should visit LeMoigne Canyon just to the south. This largely forgotten spot was once the home of a spunky little Frenchman named Jean LeMoigne. Prior to passage of the California Desert Protection Act of 1994, it was possible to drive right up to LeMoigne's mine and home site, but, with that legislation, both have been classified as *Wilderness*. Nevertheless, it is still possible to take a Class III route a short distance into LeMoigne Canyon, and walk the last several miles to see his retreat.

From the Stovepipe Wells Resort take Highway 190 south starting up Emigrant Wash. At a point 6.1 miles from the hotel, (coming the other way, go 2.7 miles beyond the Emigrant Ranger Station) you will have to watch carefully to see some wheel tracks leading off to the right (N36°32.319 W117°12.812); this is where you leave the pavement. Engage your four-wheel drive here, for you will need it the rest of the way.

The roadway cuts across the grain of the drainage pattern coming down Emigrant Wash for the first 1½ miles. This is an endless series of ups and downs. Eventually high ground is reached, and the road swings to the south to climb the bajada. Here among patches of reddish brown basalt boulders are textbook examples of *desert pavement*, the tightly packed surface of largely soil-free rocks, which seems to have been laid out and compacted by a steamroller.

The road gradually climbs the alluvial fan, and 4.3 miles from the pavement there is a good flat campsite high above the wash. The road drops from here down into the wash and continues on another 0.4 miles, before coming to an abrupt end. This is today's *Wilderness* boundary; further vehicle travel is prohibited.

For those who want to continue on, Jean's camp is a walk of nearly four miles, in which the elevation gain is some 1800 feet.

Jean LeMoigne's life seems to be a series of contradicting stories. The tale told most often is that in 1883, Isadore Daunet wrote to his friend and fellow Frenchman Jean LeMoigne, enticing him to come from Paris to America. LeMoigne was a chemist and engineer, and Daunet needed help operating his Eagle Borax Works. LeMoigne accepted his friend's offer, but, by the time he got to Death Valley in 1884, the bottom had fallen out of the price of borax, Daunet had gone broke, his wife had left him, and pal Isadore had committed suicide. There was no job for Jean LeMoigne. Some Death Valley historians doubt that version, because LeMoigne's name is mentioned as part owner of a mine near Panamint in 1880, three years before Daunet ever started mining borax. Whatever the story, Jean, or Cap as he was known to his many friends, liked the desert and spent the next forty years prospecting in the Death Valley country.

The legend persists that Cap had a silver mine that supported his modest needs, and on occasion even grubstaked his friends. Here again however, stories differ as to where this mine was located. Some think Cap found the "Lost Gunsight Lode", which had been found by a group of Georgians in 1849. Was it this lode that kept Cap in beans and bacon? *Death Valley in 49* author John Southworth contended that Cap's mine was right here in what is known today as LeMoigne Canyon. However, friend and fellow prospector Frank Crampton claims that LeMoigne's silver mine was just north of Skidoo and his lead mine was in LeMoigne Canyon. Again, the stories differ.

Jean LeMoigne and his friends in 1915
(National Park Service photo)

We do know that Cap built a small stone cabin and was mining lead in LeMoigne Canyon in 1918; however, his mine was a long way from markets and transportation was difficult. With the World War I armistice on November 11, 1918, the price suddenly dropped, and Cap stopped mining lead.

In August of 1919, 71-year-old Jean LeMoigne decided to make a fateful trip to the outside world. Cap was camped near Salt Creek between Stovepipe Wells and Furnace Creek, when he went down. He crawled under a mesquite bush and died, leaving his two faithful burros tied nearby. Death Valley Scotty claimed that he discovered Jean's body, together with those of his two animals. Scotty said that he buried Cap there on the spot. Another account is that Shorty Harris and Frank Crampton found Jean's body. Harry Gower also claims that he and Tom Wilson buried Jean in one grave and his two burros in their separate graves. Thus, the list of people who claimed to have buried Cap is endless. A pile of rocks and a bleached wooden cross marking Cap's grave can still be seen to this date, if you know where to look.

Cap's grave down near Salt Creek

After Cap's death a couple of local boys, Bill Corcoran and Bev Hunter, quietly went into LeMoigne Canyon and relocated all eight of Cap's claims. Twice they tried to sell the property, only to have the buyers die before the deals could be consummated. They finally did sell the property in 1924. The new owner shipped 200 tons of lead ore between 1925 and 1927. Further exploration has been sporadic since then, with activity as recently as 1975, but little ore has been shipped.

Early Days at Scotty's Castle

Walter Edward Scott, aka Death Valley Scotty

Death Valley Scotty and his benefactors Albert and Bessie Johnson
(Photos above by Burton Frasher from the author's collection)

Scotty's Castle circa 1931
(Nevada Historical Society photo)

Chapter III

Trails Out of Scotty's Castle

Scotty's Castle is the principle attraction in the northernmost part of Death Valley National Park. It is sort of a Hearst Castle in the desert. As a young boy, Walter Scott ran away from his home in Kentucky to join his brother on a ranch in Nevada. He bounced around doing odd jobs, including a twelve-year stint in Buffalo Bill's Wild West show. He apparently honed his con man skills there, for he started telling potential investors that he had a rich gold mine in Death Valley. He must have been a smooth talker, because they put up the money and he spent it. Scotty lived a lifestyle far beyond his own limited means. This lifestyle included the building of a Mediterranean-style villa in the sheltered oasis in Grapevine canyon. Construction on Scotty's Castle started in 1925, seemingly with money provided by Scotty's friend and benefactor, Albert Johnson, an insurance magnate from Chicago who enjoyed Scotty's humor and wild stories so much, that he did not mind bankrolling Scotty just so that he would stick around. For his part, Scotty far preferred living in his "hideaway", a small bungalow located a few miles away at Grapevine Spring. The castle project never really was completed, but what you see today was finished in 1931. When Albert Johnson died in 1948, Scotty was not mentioned in Johnson's will and his estate went to the Gospel Foundation of California. The castle remained a tourist attraction, and Scotty was permitted to stay on as one of its attractions. Scotty died of a gastric hemorrhage on January 5, 1954, while on his way to a hospital in Las Vegas, and is buried on a hill overlooking the castle. The Gospel Foundation continued to operate the castle until 1970, when the National Park Service bought it for $850,000.

The National Park Service conducts living history tours during the peak winter season (sign up as soon as you arrive) and they will tell you the whole story. Visitor services at Scotty's Castle are limited to a snack bar, gift and book shops, and gas pump, all of which are only open from 9:00 a.m. to 5:30 p.m. There are no overnight accommodations. The nearest campground is at Mesquite Spring 4.8 miles to the south. In between Scotty's Castle and Mesquite Spring is the Grapevine Ranger Station, where park and road information can be obtained.

13

Skating Stones of Bonnie Claire Playa

Primary Attraction:	Would you like to see first hand, tracks gouged in mud by small rocks that have seemingly moved by themselves? This phenomenon has been most often observed and reported at the park's Racetrack Playa. A visit to the Racetrack involves a half-day journey out of Scotty's Castle, with a round trip distance of 54 miles over semi-maintained dirt roads. If you don't wish to subject the family automobile to that sort of punishment, or if you don't have the half-day to spare, then the same natural phenomenon can be observed here at Bonnie Claire Playa, about a 25-minute drive east of Scotty's Castle. The rocks at both playas move in just the same way.
Time Required:	This is outing can be done in a couple of hours out of Scotty's Castle.
Miles Involved:	The one-way distance from Scotty's Castle to the skating stones on Bonnie Claire Playa is about 16 miles, of which all but the last mile or two are on a paved highway.
Maps:	1:100,000 Last Chance Range sheet, 1:24,000 Bonnie Claire NW Quadrangle.
Degree of Difficulty:	If the playa surface is dry, which it must be in order to drive on it, the most difficult portion of the excursion is the first few hundred feet between the highway and the flat playa surface. Once on the dry lakebed anywhere you choose to drive is likely to be Class I.
Remarks:	**Get out of your vehicle, and inspect the playa surface carefully before driving on it. A seemingly dry crust may only be an inch thick, hiding a quagmire of bottomless mud beneath it!**

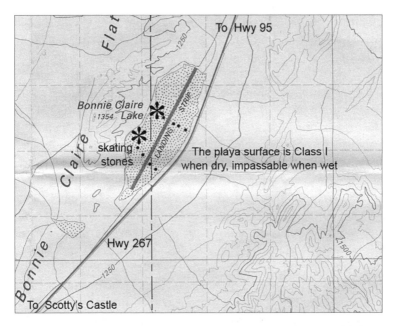

To see the phenomena called "skating stones", turn left on the highway upon leaving the front entrance at the Scotty's Castle parking lot. Reset your trip odometer to zero as you make that left turn onto Grapevine Canyon Road. During the construction of Scotty's Castle, the only road here was a rough 20-mile bone-jarring dusty dirt track from the railroad depot at Bonnie Claire, Nevada. The Civilian Conservation Corps improved the road when, in the words of the NPS, "crowds of people began braving the dangers of the desert for a glimpse of Death Valley Scotty and 'his' fabulous home."

For the next mile, you can't help but notice the green vegetation in this part of Grapevine Canyon. The source of the water that supports this vegetation is a year-around spring above Scotty's Castle about a mile up the canyon.

Wild grape is abundant in Grapevine Canyon

Water means life in this very arid land. Within a three-mile radius of the mouth of Grapevine Canyon there are no less than four permanent springs that were relied upon by paleo-Indians long before the Shoshone moved into this area 800 to 1,000 years ago. A clear picture of the prehistoric occupancy still awaits discovery through careful and systematic archaeological excavation. We do know, in historic times, about 1849 when the Jayhawker party entered Death Valley, that a band of Shoshone Indians, consisting of four extended families totaling about 30 in number, lived here in Grapevine Canyon in the vicinity of what is today Scotty's Castle. The clan spent about six months of each year here, from autumn well into the spring. They called their winter home *Mahunu* and they lived relatively well eating the wild grapes that grew here in abundance, as well as seeds, berries and piñon nuts they had collected the previous fall. Each family had several acres under cultivation where they would grow corn, beans, squash and pumpkins. In the fall and winter months, the tribe's hunters made regular trips to Grapevine Springs, just three miles to the west, where they created artificial ponds to attract migratory ducks that they would shoot with obsidian-tipped arrows from brush covered hunting blinds. In the late spring, many in the tribe temporarily move to Mesquite Spring, a place they called *Panuga*. Here they would collect the seedpods of the mesquite, an item that stored well for consumption later. The summer months found the band living high in the mountains around springs such as those in the vicinity of Phinney Canyon. It was much cooler there and, if their hunters were lucky, venison was a periodic part of their diet. About September, the tribe migrated down to Sarcobatus Flat where they would join other nearby clans in large rabbit drives that would last several weeks. Once the rabbit meat and pelts were gathered, it was time to return to the Grapevine Mountains for a few weeks to harvest the annual crop of piñon nuts. The last event of the post-harvest season was the annual gathering of the clans at Ohyu at the northeast edge of the sand dunes (shown as Surveyor's Well on the 1913 Ballarat topographic sheet). Here families from Cottonwood Canyon, Gold Belt Spring, Panamint Valley, Saline Valley, and other places, would gather to rekindle old acquaintances, and possibly the young men could return to their winter homes with a wife. Life was not idyllic at Mahunu in the 1850s, but these peoples probably had conditions a little easier than the Shoshone living elsewhere. It might be noted that several generations later, some of the descendants of the same Shoshone band returned to Grapevine Canyon to help build Scotty's Castle. Because of the isolated location of the jobsite and the warm temperatures, the contractor had a difficult time in keeping workers. The Shoshone construction workers never complained and proved themselves to be reliable.

At 4.3 miles the highway crosses the State line, where it leaves Death Valley National Park to enter Nevada and becomes State Route 267. In another nine miles, the west end of the Bonnie Claire Playa will begin to appear on the left. The first place to leave the highway and enter the dry lakebed is at 14.1 miles. If you miss this turnoff, don't worry; there is another at 14.8 miles, and yet another at 15.1 miles.

Once you are on the playa surface, there is no need to follow any particular roadway. If the surface is dry, vehicles can usually be driven just about everywhere. **Remember: Before driving out onto the playa, get out of your vehicle, and check the condition of the lakebed surface carefully. This is particularly important in the springtime or after winter storms.**

In recent years, the best place to see the "skating stones" has been on the north side of the playa. Simply drive around and look for them. As you drive across the surface of the dry lake, do not expect to see the fifty to two hundred pound rocks for which Death Valley's Racetrack is noted. The Racetrack playa has steep slopes on its south and east sides, which allow boulders to roll down off the hillsides onto the dry lakebed. There are no such steep slopes here. The rocks on the Bonnie Claire Playa are usually no larger than a baseball. Nevertheless, under the right conditions, they move about just like their much larger cousins at the Racetrack. They leave the classic tracks, and clusters of small stones often seem to have moved together *en-echelon.*

A skating stone on the Racetrack Playa

Skating stones on the Bonnie Claire Playa

Although nobody has ever been present to fully document on film the movement of these rocks, in theory three elements must be present: first, winter storms must leave water standing on the playa surface; next, it must be cold enough that the water around these stones freezes, capturing them within a large sheet of ice; and finally a strong wind must be blowing with sufficient velocity to move the ice sheet. The bottoms of the rocks leave grooves in the mud below the ice, which still remain once the ice melts and the playa dries up. At first blush, this explanation seems quite reasonable. The theory quickly breaks down, however, when we see the parallel grooves left by two rocks moving together only a few feet apart. Then suddenly, the tracks left by one rock turn to the left, while the tracks left by the second rock go to the right! It seems unlikely that the winds would be so fickle as to blow in one direction, while blowing in another direction just a few feet away. One might suspect a prankster perpetrating a hoax; yet, there are no telltale signs left in the soft mud. So how do you explain that? I don't. (I don't explain crop circles either!)

While your eyes are looking down at the skating stones, be watchful for those that look a little peculiar, with their sharp edges seemingly smoothed and rounded by heat. In 1998, a fellow by the name of Nicholas Gessler says he found two olivine-rich stony meteorites here just a few feet apart. These visitors from outer space may have had companions!

Bonnie Claire Playa was also known to NASA and US Air Force test pilots at Edwards Air Force Base in California, as it was one of several designated emergency landing strips for the X-15 rocket plane and other experimental projects taking place in the 1960s and 70s.

14

A Four Camp Tour Through Yesteryear
Gold Mountain, Oriental, Tokop & Gold Point

Primary Attraction:	This tour visits four historic, picturesque mining camps.
Time Required:	This is an all day journey back through time.
Miles Involved:	The entire loop from the Grapevine Ranger Station to Gold Point and return is 88 miles. Be sure to top off your gas tank at Scotty's Castle before starting off.
Maps:	1:100,000 Last Chance Range sheet; 1:24,000 Ubehebe Crater, Sand Spring, Gold Point SW, and Gold Point Quadrangles.
Degree of Difficulty:	When I re-scouted and updated all of these roads, I found them to be generally Class I, with a little Class II between Old Camp and Tokop. However, for much of its one hundred-year history, the route up Oriental Wash has been Class III, because of soft sand. One good flash flood, and it could easily be Class III again. Check current conditions with the Rangers at Scotty's Castle.

There seem to be two different types of historic mining camps in the Death Valley Region; those like Greenwater, Rhyolite, and Goldfield about which millions of words have been written, and those communities whose very existence is little known, even to historians. In this outing we will visit four of those old camps in the last category.

We begin our nostalgic journey through the places of yesteryear at the road junction three miles south of Scotty's Castle, north of the Grapevine Ranger Station. Take the paved Racetrack Valley Road north towards Ubehebe Crater (N36°59.928 W117°22.005). It goes off to the left after 2.5 miles (N36° 00.485 W117°23.579) (see Excursion #15); you will want to stay right on the graded dirt road. This is the start of 13.4 miles of the most awful washboard road in the entire park. It is bone jarring at any speed! My only suggestion to make it more pleasurable would be to take this road in May, when the cottontop and prickly pear cacti are in bloom.

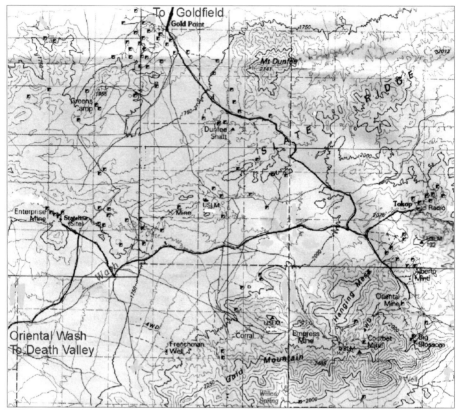

Just before reaching Little Sand Spring, at 15.9 miles, look for an unsigned graded road going off to the right (N37°10.004 W117°32.137). Reset your trip odometer, and turn right on the Class I road. Death Valley National Park is left behind, and you enter Nevada in 4.3 miles (N37°13.004 W117°30.390). This is now federal land administered by the Bureau of Land Management's Tonopah Field Office. Rock hounding, camping, and campfires are permitted here, but please do not burn wood from historic sites. A side road goes right a quarter-mile beyond the state line; stay to the left on the main road (37°13.606 W117°30.292). A remote weather station is passed a mile from the state line and, one tenth-mile beyond, the road from Tule Canyon comes in from the rear. Stay right, going up Oriental Wash. In a couple of miles, as you gain elevation, yuccas and their close cousins, the Joshua trees, will begin to appear.

The next key intersection is at 12.6 miles. The left fork at this desert crossroads goes 0.8 miles to the remains of the old mining camp of Gold Mountain, later called Stateline after the principal mine of the area.

The armies of blue and gray had just laid down their arms when Leander Morton first found gold-bearing rock on what would become known as Gold

Mountain. Morton did not feel the lode was rich enough, so he sought his fortune elsewhere. He robbed a train in 1870, was caught and sent to prison; he escaped, was caught again, and then hung by a posse at what is now Convict Lake. So much for Morton's judgment!

A fellow named Tom Shaw came along in 1868 and discovered a quartz outcrop twelve feet thick and nearly a half-mile long. He and his partners staked four claims along the ledge. They pecked away for several years, but had no way to mill the ore. In 1871 Shaw built a mule-powered arrastra at a spring some five miles away, and with that he was able to eke out $9.00 per day, about twice the wage of a working miner. Historian Richard Lingenfelter says Shaw's Stateline Mine was the first profitable mine in Death Valley. The Stateline Mine passed through several hands, and then a con man by the name of George D. Roberts bought the mine in September of 1880. He broke it up into quarters, one for each claim, formed four companies and set out to sell stock in each one. He enlisted the aid of various experts, who promptly called it "the greatest gold mine on this continent". All the activity at Stateline attracted a lot of attention. Investors in the east were lining up to buy Roberts' stock, the price of which he was carefully manipulating. Out west people began pouring into Stateline, hoping for a piece of the action. By November of that year, Roberts had laid out a townsite, called it "Gold Mountain", and was selling lots for $50 to $500 each.

By March of 1881, a small mining camp had sprung up, complete with the usual assortment of saloons, stores, livery stables, bawdy houses, boarding houses, blacksmith shops, a bakery, butcher shop, post office and other essential services needed at the time. He set about building an impressive forty-stamp mill. At the same time he bought some 65,000 feet of six-inch spiral wrapped pipe, and began to lay a twelve-mile long pipeline in from upper Tule Canyon.

The stock in Robert's venture soared, even though not a single ton of ore had been crushed. When the stock reached a peak of around $25 a share, Roberts began to quietly sell off his substantial holdings. By August, with the pipeline still miles away and the mill not yet complete, Roberts slipped away. He knew full well that the ore in the Stateline Mine was worth only about $10 per ton, not the exaggerated $100 per ton the experts had proclaimed a year before. By December of 1881, the Roberts' stock transactions were recognized for what they were - a swindle of gigantic proportions!

Some mining continued around Gold Mountain, but by 1891 the post office had closed. The Goldfield Excitement of 1905 brought renewed interest, and the mines of Slate Ridge briefly reopened. They have closed and reopened several times since then, once even with the construction of a new mill. As you enter Gold Mountain, you pass the stone ruins of many miners' cabins. The lonely headframe of the Stateline Mine is halfway up the hillside. Just below it are the foundations of the Enterprise Mill. You will find several dugouts and several wooden structures in various stages of decay if you look around. The camp's sole resident occupies the best house in Gold Mountain. **For your own safety, stay out of the tunnels and shafts!**

The State Line mill in 1915
(Nevada State Historical Society photo)

By turning right at this desert crossroads, it is just four miles to Gold Mountain's sister city, Oriental, later called "Old Camp". Tom Shaw, the same guy who first found gold veins at Gold Mountain, also found gold here in 1864. Once again Shaw was unable to take advantage of his findings, and it was not until 1871 that the Oriental Mine was developed on one of the more promising veins. The Oriental Mine produced some very rich *specimen ore*, several pieces of which were put on display at the 1876 Centennial Exposition in Philadelphia. Oriental, too, had a post office that lasted until 1900.

With the Oriental Mine, a small camp of the same name sprang up two miles to the west on the northern slope of Gold Mountain at the 7,000' elevation. Unlike the town of Gold Mountain, Oriental had a small well nearby to service the residents' needs, but it was insufficient to run an ore mill. At least one could get a drink of water here, and the piñon forest just above town provided firewood for heating and cooking. Somewhere along the line, the name of the community changed its name from Oriental to Old Camp, the name used on the 1911 1:250,000 topographic map, and the current Automobile Club of Southern California *Death Valley National Park* map. Today the site consists of the ruins of eleven stonewalled structures, plus several wood cabins and an old boiler.

Oriental today

The miners of the 1870s were by no means the first humans to call this country home. With its dark basalt lava, Hanging Mesa was frequented by the Indians, who left petroglyphs and obsidian chips on its summit and around its perimeter.

The camp of Tokop lies a few miles to the northeast, and it is also at 7,000 feet. Mineral exploration did not begin here until the 1890s, but it took the Greenwater Excitement of 1904 before serious attempts at mining were made. Gold was indeed found, but the ore bodies were of too low grade to turn into anything great. Today only one wooden building marks the site of Tokop. There is a good graded road from Tokop past the Senator Mine, over Slate Ridge and into Gold Point, the fourth camp on our journey. This is the only camp to survive into modern times.

Tokop was a busy place in 1926.
(Nevada State Historical Society photo)

Gold Point started as Lime Point in 1868, when a short-lived lime quarry was established here. It became re-established and re-inhabited in 1880 under the name of Hornsilver, when a silver mine opened. That operation lasted only two years, primarily due to its then remote location and the long ten-mile haul to Lida for milling and ore dressing. The Goldfield-Greenwater Excitement of 1903-05 rekindled mining interests in the area with the opening of the Great Western Mine in 1905. Silver mining was now less expensive with the railroad now only fourteen miles away at Cuprite. New silver discoveries created yet another stampede in 1908, and overnight Hornsilver gained its place on the map of Nevada. In May and June, Hornsilver grew from a small collection of tents to a townsite complete with mapped streets, the usual saloons, sporting establishments, restaurants, general stores, boarding houses, livery stables, a gasoline pump, and even a post office. The newly established *Hornsilver Herald* proclaimed the community would be the brightest star in Nevada's crown.

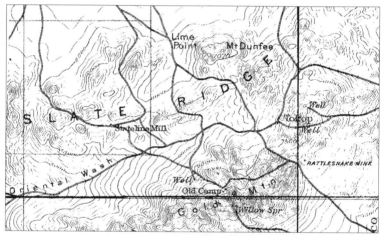

On the 1913 topographic sheet, Gold Point is shown as
"Lime Point" and Oriental is shown as "Old Camp".

The largest mine, the Great Western, had legal as well as ore milling problems that caused on and off operations for several decades. As the mines went deeper, gold began to become more important than the silver. By the 1930s the community had changed its name to Gold Point, seeming more appropriate under the changing circumstances. The Great Western Mine was closed in 1942 by President Roosevelt's proclamation that all gold mines were to be closed so that the workers could be better utilized in the war effort. Gold Point was abandoned at that point, leaving its fifty-some wooden buildings to bleach in the sun.

Fortunately for history buffs like myself, Gold Point has not changed much in the last fifty years. However, I am sure that with the passage of each year the wooden buildings will weather and deteriorate a little bit more, and it will only be a matter of time before the site returns to the sand. Gold Point is not a *ghost town*. In 1998 there were still 22 mailboxes in use on a rail in the center of town. When asked why they choose to live here, many of the local residents said they wanted to stay away from the hustle and bustle of Goldfield, the seat of county government for Esmeralda County. Here in Gold Point, life proceeds at a more leisurely pace.

The first bakery in Hornsilver
(Central Nevada Museum photo)

Gold Point today

From Gold Point it is only seven miles via paved highway to State Route 266 where roads lead in three directions. A turn to the left will take you over Westgard Pass and on into Big Pine. Those 79 miles will take about a two-hour drive. A right turn onto Highway 266 will soon put you onto U.S. Highway 95, where another right turn will have you in Beatty in less than an hour. If you choose to go north, a left turn onto Highway 95 will have you in Goldfield in fifteen minutes or in Tonopah in less than an hour.

15

White Top Mountain

Primary Attraction:	Recent volcanic craters, some interesting sedimentary geology, old mines, and some very remote country with nice views down into Death Valley make this an outstanding backcountry drive.
Time Required:	This is an all day outing from Scotty's Castle, or anyplace else.
Miles involved:	From the parking lot at Scotty's Castle to the end of the road at the Silver Crown Mines is 45 miles.
Maps:	1:100,000 Saline Valley sheet; 1:24,000 Tin Mountain, Teakettle Junction, Sand Flat, and White Top Mtn. Quadrangles
Degree of Difficulty:	The 21 miles from Ubehebe Crater to Lost Burro Gap are generally Class I. The remaining 14.5 miles are generally Class II, but may contain a few short sections of Class III.
Remarks:	**Be sure you leave Scotty's Castle with a nearly full fuel tank.**

Looking for a place to get away from the crowds in Death Valley? I can promise more solitude on White Top Mountain than just about any other destination within the park.

To begin this back road odyssey, take the paved road from Scotty's Castle down the canyon three miles to the road junction just north of the Grapevine Ranger Station; turn right (N36°59.928 W117°22.005). As you drive north up the valley, notice the line of mesquite trees at the base of the hills to the right. A geologic fault runs along here and, in that zone of weakness and sheared rocks, ground water seeps to the surface. It was at one of these springs that Walter Scott, Death Valley Scotty, had a small bungalow that he far preferred over the "castle". A side road right goes to Scotty's bungalow, at a point 1.5 miles north of the Grapevine Ranger Station. The site is closed to visitors.

A road junction is reached at a point nearly three miles north of the Grapevine Entrance Station (N36°00.485 W117°23.579). To the right, a graded dirt road with a

washboard surface goes north up the valley, ultimately reaching Big Pine. Stay
left on the pavement for another 2.5 miles to the side road to Ubehebe Crater
(N37°00.844 W177°27.236).

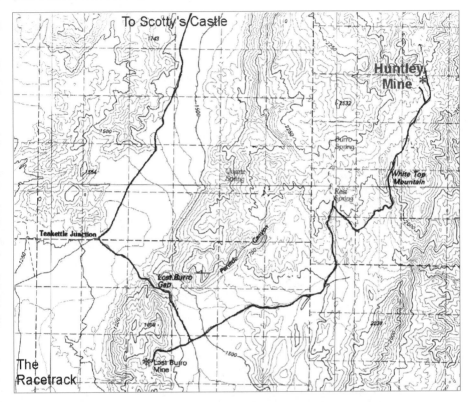

There are more than a dozen distinctly separate volcanic craters at the site
generally known as Ubehebe Crater. All seem to be explosive events, with little
or no lava emitted away from the craters. Explosive events like these typically
occur when magma deep within the earth rises and comes in contact with
groundwater. The water flashes to steam and, in the expansion process, the force
of the explosion is directed upwards. In all likelihood, the entire eruption cycle
from beginning to end takes only a few minutes. In the case of Ubehebe Crater,
the resulting hole is 750 feet deep and 2,000 feet across. Cinders and ash were
thrown out from two to five miles in every direction. As noted geologist Tom
Clements pointed out, the emitted cinders lie on top of, rather than within the
sediments formed in the bottom of Pleistocene Lake Rogers. This would suggest
that the first eruption occurred after the lake dried up some 10,000 years ago.
The lack of erosion around the crater suggests that the event occurred a few
hundred, or perhaps only a few thousand, years ago, although ash found with

archaeological artifacts suggests an age of 6,000 years. If you have the time, take the 1.5-mile foot trail that circles the rim of Ubehebe Crater, or walk at least the half-mile trail over to Little Hebe Crater.

Ubehebe Crater

Beyond Ubehebe Crater, a graded dirt road heads south up Racetrack Valley. The first two miles of road cross a thick mantle of volcanic ash that was thrown out by the volcanic explosions. Soon the countryside returns to sandy alluvium, as you begin the ascent up the valley. In the twenty miles from Ubehebe Crater to Teakettle Junction, the road very gradually climbs from 2,600 feet to 4,100 feet.

To the left is an impressive high ridge of mostly limestone and dolomite layers, which culminates in 8,953' Tin Mountain. As you allow your eyes to climb up the mountainside from the bottom, you look through sediments of the Cambrian, Ordovician, Silurian, Devonian, and Mississippian Ages. The time span represented in these layers is some 250 million years. The rock layer on the summit is appropriately named the Tin Mountain Limestone. It was deposited in the sea bottom about 325 million years ago. The summit of Tin Mountain is garnished with a scattering of piñon and juniper trees. A light sprinkling of snow can often be seen here after winter storms. I have never climbed this summit, but I know people who have done so. From the road, the four-mile walk with a vertical gain of 4,100 feet took four hours one way.

Teakettle Junction is reached at a point 19.8 miles south of Ubehebe Crater (N36°45.606 W117°32.536). This road junction gets its curious name from the variety of teakettles that people have placed on the road sign over the years. Turn left here; the right fork goes to the Racetrack Playa (see Excursion #28).

Teakettle Junction

The road remains Class I for the next mile, and then deteriorates a little as it passes through a little canyon known as Lost Burro Gap. While this canyon is only a mile long, the steeply dipping limestone rocks here represent one hundred million years of the earth's history. The first and youngest rock stratum encountered is the Tin Mountain Limestone of Mississippian age. The Lost Burro Formation of Devonian age is reached after 0.2 miles. Once out of the canyon, off on the right, a small exposure of the Hidden Valley Dolomite of Silurian age can be seen. All three of these formations contain fossils of the primitive animals that lived in the sea at that time, although this is not the best place to look for them.

Lost Burro Junction is reached 3.2 miles beyond Teakettle Junction (N36°43.812 W117°30.348). A Class II road to the right goes 1.2 miles to the Lost Burro Mine. The quick side-trip visit is recommended if you have the time. A gold bearing vein was found here at the contact point where the Cretaceous granitic rocks forced their way up through the Tin Mountain Limestone. The main vein averaged about two feet in width and contained *free gold*. The first claims were staked in 1907 and, between then and 1912, the mine is said to have produced $85,000 in gold. Some estimate the mine's production from 1935 to 1942 to have been in excess of $100,000. The mill built in 1917 has been salvaged for use elsewhere; however, the timber frame remains. There is a weather-tight cabin at the mine that can be used as an emergency shelter in a storm, if you don't mind sharing your quarters with the mice and packrats. **Remember, these rodents can carry the Hantavirus, and should be considered potentially hazardous.**

For the White Top Mountain area, turn left at Lost Burro Junction and note your odometer reading or reset it. The Class II road heads east up the bajada. After 1½ miles, the gently dipping limestone beds of the Andy Hills are on the right. They are more of the Lost Burro Formation that you saw a few miles back. At a point 3.3 miles in from Lost Burro Junction, faint tracks go to the right; stay left as the road swings to the north (N36°44.771 W117°27.182).

Soon you will be entering Rest Spring Gulch. At first the Tin Mountain Limestone of early Mississippian age will be off the road to the left and right. But as the gulch narrows, the road enters the next strata up, the Perdido Formation of late Mississippian age. This dark rock stratum contains a variety of fossils including the *Cravenocerus* genus of ammonite, a rounded nautilus-type shell. Also present are crinoid stems, the only hard part of a plant-like animal that lived on the sea bottom. While these 320 million-year-old marine critters are interesting to look at, keep in mind that **fossil collecting in the park is strictly prohibited**.

At a point 4.9 miles in from Lost Burro Junction, the road goes up and over a few feet of bedrock in the canyon bottom. This dry waterfall or cascade should cause no real problem, although caution should be exercised, and the use of four-wheel drive might be prudent, but not usually necessary. Once over that obstacle, the Perdido Formation is topped and the road enters the Rest Spring Shale strata. These soft and easily eroded layers of shale are thought to be of early Pennsylvanian age. The road forks a tenth of a mile above the bedrock cascade; you must stay right on the main road for White Top Mountain (N36°46.263 W117°27.017).

The Class III road to the left here goes up the narrow gulch a half-mile to Rest Spring. Here a short tunnel dug into the soft shale has produced a seep of brackish water. As uninviting as this water may appear, wildlife in the surrounding hills depends on it. When I approached the spring on foot in December of 1998, I startled a huge covey of fifty or more chukar partridges. They took to the air in one mass, flapping their wings and making quite a racket. They landed again a few hundred feet down the wash and quickly seemed to loose interest in me, although a few curious birds did watch me walk back to my car.

Some 52,000 chukars were imported from India by the California Department of Fish and Game back in 1932. Those placed in the high deserts adapted readily to their new habitat and flourished. Like the burro, the NPS considers them to be an exotic species, and thus to have no place in Death Valley National Park. Unlike the burro, however, there are no current plans to eradicate the chukar; there are simply too many of them. They are found everywhere in the park where there is year around water.

Chukar partridge *Alectoris chukar*

You can walk up the draw from Rest Spring to Burro Spring, about a mile to the north. Please do not camp within a quarter-mile of Rest Spring.

From the turnoff to Rest Spring, the main road turns east, crossing a rolling ridgetop. From here the first views down into Death Valley can be seen. To the north is 7,607' White Top Mountain. This is a bit of a misnomer. The light-colored dolomite and quartzite rocks near the summit are not actually white, but they look so much lighter than the dark summits of surrounding mountains that the name was chosen.

The road winds around through the soft shale, drops down into a wash, and once again heads north up a canyon. This canyon was eroded out of the broken and crushed rocks along a north-south trending fault, where one side has slipped in relation to the other side. As you enter the canyon, and for nearly the next mile, the rocks on the east side of the narrow canyon are different from those on the west. At first the stratum on the right is the Ely Springs Dolomite, followed by the Hidden Valley Dolomite. At the same time, the rocks on the left are the Perdido Formation, followed by the Tin Mountain Limestone, and then the Lost Burro Formation.

Strangely eroded pinnacles appear in the Ely Springs Dolomite high on the ridge to your right eight miles in from Lost Burro Junction. Here, too, the first piñon and juniper begin to appear. No matter what time of year you visit, the air should be getting cooler here at 6,600 feet.

The road forks at a point 8.5 miles in from Lost Burro Junction. The left fork went to some mining claims in existence prior to the creation of the national park; stay right (N36°48.148 W117°24.828). A side road right in another 0.4 miles winds its way up the hillside. This was one of several roads put in to access the Huntley claims. The remains of the camp set up by Huntley Industrial Minerals are another 0.6 miles up the main road. The site consists of a wooden cabin and several metal tanks.

The carbonate rocks in this area have been intruded by a younger granite-like, igneous rock called syenite. Where these two rock units come in contact, the carbonate sequence, particularly the Ely Springs Dolomite, have developed lenses containing the amphibole suite of minerals. One of these minerals is tremolite, an ore of asbestos that was the commodity that the miners had been seeking since the deposit was first worked in 1900. Prospect pits are everywhere. A few hundred tons were shipped, but in general the impurities were too great, and the asbestos fibers too short, to warrant the long haul to the mill and market. Being careful not to raise any dust, the author did find a single specimen of long fiber chrysotile asbestos in one of the test pits years ago before Death Valley National Park was created. Today **mineral collecting is prohibited.**

Huntley Mine Camp

Beyond the Huntley Mine Camp, the road forks after another 0.3 miles; some call this Syenite Junction. The left fork is a Class III route, which after a couple of miles ends at the Silver Crown claims in O'Brien Canyon. Veins containing copper and fluorite minerals were discovered in 1912 in the Tin Mountain and Perdido Formations. Although one 75-foot tunnel was dug and several shafts sunk, no real production has ever taken place here. **Warning: Do not enter any underground workings. They are not safe!**

From Syenite Junction, the right fork proceeds up the draw another half-mile to where there are many spur roads to prospect pits. The syenite rocks of this area are somewhat unique in that they contain the mineral nepheline. While rocks of this type are common in Ontario, Canada, this is the only such locality ever reported in California.

There are some waterless, but otherwise fine campsites here among the piñon pines. The elevation here is 6,800 feet. On the ridge to the right are nice views down into Death Valley. If you want to escape the crowds in other parts of the park, this is the place to do it. To get back to reality, you will have to return the way you came.

Bygone Beatty

Beatty in 1905 before any permanent structures had been built
(Nevada Historical Society photo)

The Montgomery Hotel had its grand opening in 1907.
(California State Library photo)

Remick's Garage was a busy place in the 1930s.
(Central Nevada Historical Society photo)

Chapter IV

Trails Out of Beatty

Prior to 1904, there was nothing in this remote part of Nevada, except a few scattered ranches, one of which was owned by Montillus Murray Beatty, who planted some trees near a spring and cultivated a variety of crops. Then in the summer and fall of 1904, that all changed, when the mining excitement from Tonopah and Goldfield moved south. Rich discoveries were made in what would soon become the boomtowns of Rhyolite and Bullfrog. Beatty was born of necessity, to be the regional center where freight was brought for redistribution to the nearby mines and camps. By 1905 streets had been laid out in an orderly manner. It didn't matter that most people here were still living and doing business in tents. The post office opened in January 1905, with "Old Man" Beatty as its first postmaster, even though he could neither read nor write, except for his name. Beatty had its own newspaper by April of 1905, and by fall, the town's founder, Bob Montgomery, had built a fine two-story hotel that quickly became the center of social life. For the next few years, Beatty had a population of one thousand people, and was served by three railroads, the Bullfrog Goldfield Railroad, (1906-1928), the Las Vegas & Tonopah, (1906-1918) and the Tonopah & Tidewater (1907-1940).

Of all the Turn of the 20th Century mining camps in the Bullfrog Mining District, Beatty is the only one to survive to modern times, in part because of the availability of water. The town was given a rebirth after World War II, when it became home to thousands of workers involved in the Nuclear Weapons Test Programs conducted just to the east at Frenchman Flat, Yucca Flats and, later, Yucca Mountain. As those programs have wound down, Beatty continues to hang on, relying on servicing the needs of highway travelers going between Reno and Las Vegas, and tourists going to Death Valley from Nevada locations. Until the Bullfrog Mine closed late in 1998, mining had still been important to Beatty's prosperity. The Department of Energy has spent billions of dollars in recent years developing a nuclear waste storage facility under nearby Yucca Mountain. The project is controversial, however, and whether the project will gain its final approval is still uncertain. Either way, Beatty's economy will be unchanged.

The Beatty of today has a population of about 1800. For the traveler, the town is pretty much open 24 hours a day, offering motels, restaurants, towing service, auto parts and, of course, a casino or two for Nevada style entertainment. The Phoenix Inn and the Rio Rancho RV Park offer laundry facilities. Nobody should leave Beatty without a visit to the local museum, a couple of blocks west of downtown on State Route 374. The volunteer docents are friendly and knowledgeable and admission is by donation.

16

Forgotten Phinney Canyon

Primary Attraction:	Take a peek at a remote and seldom visited portion of the Grapevine Mountains.
Time Required:	This is pretty much a full day's outing.
Miles Involved:	From downtown Beatty, it is 11.8 miles up Highway 95 to the dirt access road, and then another 21 miles to the summit of the Grapevine Mountains.
Maps:	1:100,000 Pahute Mesa and Last Chance Range sheets; 1:24,000 Bullfrog Mountain and Wahguyhe Peak Quadrangles.
Degree of Difficulty:	The dirt roads are mostly Class I and II, with a little Class III as you near the crest of the range.

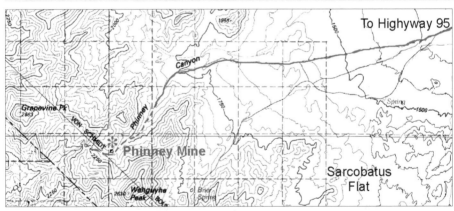

If you are one who comes to the desert to find peace and quiet, free from the hustle and bustle of the megalopolis, then a visit to Phinney Canyon should be your goal. There certainly are no crowds here. Indeed, this particular corner of Death Valley has never really been discovered, much less visited. You will probably have to share the solitude with only an occasional piñon jay. Much of its undiscovered nature lies in the fact that it is off the beaten tourist path, coupled with the fact that it is really not near anything else.

From downtown Beatty, take U.S. Highway 95 going in the direction of Goldfield and Tonopah. After 9.5 miles you will pass the small settlement of

Springdale. There are several natural springs here, which are today's source of that tiny trickle of water known as the Amargosa River. From Springdale, the river flows south through the Oasis Valley, past Beatty, through the narrows, and into the sands of the Amargosa Valley. It reemerges again near Tecopa, where it flows through a gorge, before turning west at the Dumont Dunes to eventually flow north into the Death Valley sink.

An unmarked Class I dirt road 1.6 miles beyond Springdale goes left, heading west off the highway (N37°02.951 W116°46.305). This is 0.3 miles north of highway milepost 71. Reset your trip odometer and turn off here, closing the gate as you pass through. This is rolling rangeland where cattle pretty much roam at will. Good at first, the road gradually deteriorates to Class I, as it makes its way across the vast expanse of Sarcobatus Flat. This tongue-twisting geographic name comes from the plant species *Sarcobatus vermiculatus,* common greasewood that grows in great abundance here. The term greasewood is sometimes used synonymously for creosote, but that is not correct. They are two distinctly different plants. While both plants are common in the deserts of California and Nevada, and both are shrubs growing up to six feet or more, each comes from a completely different plant family, and each occupies its own ecological niche. Greasewood grows up to 7,000' elevations, and tolerates very salty soils. It is common around the alkaline sinks in the Great Basin. Creosote *Larrea tridentata* is even more widespread, but prefers a habitat below the 3,000' elevation. It can easily be recognized by its small yellow flowers and the short sticky leaves that emit a resinous odor when crushed between your fingers.

There are four side roads going off to the left in the first 6.5 miles; always go straight ahead on the main road. However, the road forks at 6.6 miles (N37°01.085 W116°53.067); this time go left. Soon you will enter Death Valley National Park (N37°01.014 W116°53.207). A crossroads is reached at 10.7 miles (N36°59.779 W116°56.896). The fork to the left goes 2.4 miles south to Currie Well, a watering place and stage stop on the road from Bullfrog to Goldfield. In 1907 Currie Well was also the site of a construction camp for the Las Vegas & Tonopah Railroad that was being built just a few hundred yards up the hillside. Today none of the structures from the stage stop or railroad days remain. Continue heading west.

One fine spring day, my wife Loris and I were at the south end of Sarcobatus Flat, within the boundaries of Death Valley National Park, heading north towards the Phinney Canyon Road. I had apparently forgotten and left the radar detector on my dash turned on since leaving Highway 95 in Beatty earlier. All of a sudden the little box started emitting all sorts of sounds we had never heard before. I was about to reach up and whack it with my hand when a shadow flashed over our car accompanied by a very loud roar. My immediate reaction was to look at the instrument panel, because I thought my engine must have exploded. Loris was pointing out the front windshield to a jet aircraft rapidly receding into the flat horizon, but not before the pilot wiggled his (or her) wings at us. Once we had regained our composure and forced our hearts back down into our chests, we realized we had just had an encounter with a U.S. Air Force A-10 Warthog, probably flying out of Nellis AFB in Las Vegas. I surmised that the pilot had spotted us creeping across the desert below, and decided to liven up our morning by swiftly coming in behind us, fast and low, locking the aircraft's weapons radar system on our little 4Runner. It was a perfect training scenario for air to ground combat in the desert!

Our view of the A-10 Warthog as it buzzed us about 100 feet overhead.
(U.S. Air Force photo)

This could happen to you, too, and it would be entirely lawful. The Department of Defense has designated a large area from the Sierra Nevada to nearly the California-Nevada state line as Airspace Complex R-2508. Here military aircraft can fly very low and very fast for training purposes. In 1977 the military voluntarily agreed not to fly below 2,000 feet over Sequoia and Kings Canyon National Parks and Death Valley National Monument, but this 2,000' restriction does not apply to the new lands added when Death Valley became a national park in 1994. While it does not happen very often, do not be surprised if you should see military aircraft flying very low in the Panamint, Saline, or Eureka Valleys.

At a point 12.2 miles from the highway (N36°59.633 W116°57.444) you will cross the grade of the old Las Vegas & Tonopah Railroad, whose tracks were pushed across Sarcobatus Flats in 1907. However, it is still another four miles before the road enters Phinney Canyon. Before long the brush-covered hillsides turn into a forest of piñon pine and juniper.

The scattered junipers give a distinctly *high desert* atmosphere to the countryside. Junipers are well adapted to arid lands. Two species of juniper grow within the park. The species most common in California is the *Juniperous californica*. Those growing here are their eastern cousins *Juniperous osteosperma,* which grow throughout the Basin and Range province. During lean times, the Native Americans sometimes dried the berries to be later ground and roasted, often making them into mush or cakes. Tea and other beverages were also made, as were medicines used for colds and fever.

Another plant in this part of the Grapevine Mountains that was utilized by the Indians is the hardy ephedra, often called Squaw tea or Mormon tea. When boiled in water, its tender young shoots produce an astringent tea said to cure intestinal ailments. I use to brew some from time to time, but always found it more palatable with some sugar or honey to offset the bitter tannic acid it contains. In recent years however, the FDA has issued a heath warning about this plant. Ephedra contains the drug epinephrine, a cardiac stimulant. **Do not drink tea made from ephedra, if you have any kind of cardiac problem. Prolonged use may also cause personality changes and other psychiatric disorders!**

The Phinney Mine in 1968

A closed side road branches off to the right at a point 19.5 miles from Highway 95, where a short hike up the canyon will bring you to the Phinney Mine. Two brothers from Beatty, Charles E. and F.C. Phinney, located this mine in 1930. The two men toiled away for several years, with a net production of some fifty tons of ore worth about $17.00 per ton. The tattered remains of their tent cabin still cling to the top of the tailings dump.

Continue up the main canyon; the road by now is Class II. In a half-mile there will be another old mine shaft on the right side of the road. From here on it is mostly Class III.

You will discover that you are on the crest of the Grapevine Mountains after another 0.7 miles. Below to the west is the floor of Death Valley. Beyond, peaks of the High Sierra are clearly outlined on the skyline, even though they are seventy miles away. Prior to the California Desert Protection Act of 1994, you could drive down the other side to a spring. The area is now designated as *Wilderness,* and vehicles are prohibited. If you wish to get out and stretch your legs, look for Doe Spring, a small seep on the north side of the canyon. This is one of the few places in Death Valley National Park where mule deer can be found. Remember that our national parks are game preserves, where hunting is prohibited.

For really ambitious hikers, 8,738' Grapevine Peak is a modest climb of 1,200 feet, about two hours and two false summits to the north. At the highest point in the Grapevine Mountains, the view is superb. On your way up, keep an eye open for a tree that has needles in bundles of fives and looks very much different from the piñon pines all around you. This new tree is the Limber pine *Pinus flexilius,* whose habitat is limited to only the highest peaks in the Basin and Range Province. Very old sheltered packrat middens reveal that the Limber pine was very widespread during the Pleistocene Ice Age. But as the southwest became warmer and drier, its habitat retreated uphill, so that today these trees are only found near the tops of the highest peaks.

Limber pine *Pinus flexilius*

And speaking of unusual plants, Phinney Canyon has another interesting story to tell. In 1890, the U.S. Department of Agriculture sponsored a *Death Valley Expedition,* in which nine scientists from various areas of natural science spent months looking for new species and surveying the geographical distribution of plants and animals. The expedition was a success in one respect. It identified two dozen new genera and 150 new species, but it failed to reveal much in the way of potential new farmland.

One expedition member, botanist Frederick Funston, came into Phinney Canyon on June 9, 1891. At the time it was called Wood Canyon. Funston found a new species of wild pea, although he failed to recognize it as such. He incorrectly identified the plant as *Lathyrus paluster,* a pea that is common along the California coast. Nevertheless, a specimen was sent to the National Herbarium in Washington DC, to be forgotten for the next eighty years. (Funston later fought in the Spanish American War as a brigadier-general, and died of a heart attack in 1917 while chasing Pancho Villa on the Mexican border with Blackjack Pershing.) Then in 1970, modern day botanist James Reveal found in the Bullfrog Hills a wild pea that he could not identify. He suspected that he might have discovered a new species, the dream of every field biologist. After months of research, it was discovered that Reveal's 1970 specimen matched Funston's 1891 specimen in the National Herbarium. However, in the process it became recognized that Funston's find was not *Lathyrus paluster* after all. Funston had discovered a new species, and had not known it. The new species was named *Lathyrus hitchcockianus* in honor of Dr. Leo Hitchcock, who pioneered study of the genus *Lathyrus*

In the early 1980s, the Strategic Air Command was looking at the Bullfrog Hills as a potential MX missile site. Being sensitive to rare and endangered species, the U.S. Air Force, through the U.S. Fish & Wildlife Service, asked noted Inyo County botanist Mary DeDecker to determine if the wild pea was still growing and, if so, to what extent. Mary and her husband Paul searched Phinney Canyon from top to bottom. All of the plants that Funston had found eighty years earlier were still there, all that is, except for this elusive little pea. She then moved on to Sawtooth Mountain near where Reveal had made his discovery. Sure enough, a healthy population of *Lathyrus hitchockianus* was found growing on the volcanic soils. The 1980 edition of *Inventory of Rare and Endangered Vascular Plants of California,* which listed this little pea as *presumed extinct,* was wrong on two counts. The pea was certainly not extinct, and while it may have once grown in California's Phinney Canyon, today's population was now entirely in Nevada.

17

Down Titus Canyon

Primary Attraction: Titus Canyon has a little something for everyone: interesting geology, the site of a short-lived mining camp, and some very colorful desert scenery. Do not go into Titus Canyon seeking solitude. It is one of the most popular dirt road destinations in the park.

Time Required: You will want to allow at least a half-day for this outing.

Miles Involved: The distance is about 33 miles from Beatty down to the floor of Death Valley. The dirt road portion is 26.4 miles in length.

Maps: 1:100,000 Beatty and Saline Valley sheets; 1:24,000 Daylight Pass, Thimble Peak, and Fall Canyon Quadrangles.

Degree of Difficulty: The first nine miles of dirt road have a washboard surface, but the entire Titus Canyon road is generally Class I, with perhaps only a few Class II spots. Drivers should be watchful for large rocks in the roadway.

Remarks: Check with a park ranger before attempting Titus Canyon. Because of the flash flooding hazard in the narrows, the NPS tends to close the road during the summer months, and at the slightest hint of rain. During the winter, snow on White and Red Pass summits can close the road. **This is a one-way road only. You must start at the Nevada end, going downhill into Death Valley.**

I had great reservations about including the canyon in this book about jeep trails and backroads. The National Park Service has posted the road with a jeep symbol, recommending the route for high clearance vehicles with four-wheel drive. In reality, however, this is usually a very good road by backcountry standards. You will be disappointed if you seek a "challenge" in your route selection. By all other standards, Titus Canyon is an outstanding excursion worthy of your time. Incidentally, for those who wonder about such things, Titus Canyon takes its name from Morris Titus, a tenderfoot-mining engineer who perished here in the summer of 1906, while prospecting with two companions.

From Beatty, take Nevada State Route 374 southwest toward the park. About 3½ miles from town, the highway passes the few remaining modern day buildings of Bullfrog Mine. This mine closed in 1998 after producing some $910 million in gold during the previous decade. At a point four miles from Beatty, a paved side road right goes to the ghost towns of Bullfrog and Rhyolite. A visit to these historic camps is highly recommended.

Unfortunately only a few structures of Rhyolite's 1907 heyday remain, and there is even less left of Bullfrog. Of these Turn of the 20th Century boom towns only Beatty has survived. It was in August of 1904 that Shorty Harris and Ed Cross, a couple of prospectors from Ballarat, made a big find here, gold ore that had assay values up to $10,000 per ton. As soon as they staked their claims, the word got out. The saloons of Tonopah and Goldfield emptied as thousands rushed down to the Bullfrog Hills. The first camp to spring up was called Orion; it was soon renamed Amargosa City. Meanwhile the tent camp of Bonanza also sprang up three miles to the east. Both camps were at the base of steep hills where future growth was limited. Thus it was that both camps merged and relocated on the flat, where proper streets and utilities could be laid out in an orderly manner. The new town was then named Bullfrog. Bullfrog had a population in excess of 1,000 by early 1906, with permanent buildings and connections with the outside world by telephone and automobile. The Las Vegas & Tonopah Railroad bypassed Bullfrog a half-mile to the north, and had its station in the competing town of Rhyolite.

Only a few of Bullfrog's original buildings remain.

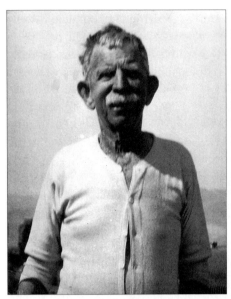

Shorty Harris
(Searles Valley Historical Society photo)

And what ever happened to Ed Cross and Shorty Harris, whose discovery touched off this mining boom? To celebrate his good fortune, Shorty Harris bought a few drinks for himself and his friends. He reportedly woke up six days later to find he had sold half of his interest for a paltry $1,000. Shorty went on to make more mineral discoveries, but frittered them away as well. He died broke in 1934 at the age of 77, and is buried next to a prospecting buddy in Death Valley near the site of the old Eagle Borax Works (see page 49). A young and sober newlywed, Ed Cross eventually sold his share for a respectable $125,000, and used the money to buy a large ranch near Escondido, California.

At a point 2.1 miles beyond the road into Rhyolite, watch for a graded dirt road turning right, heading west (N36°51.562 W116°50.751). Turn right here on the Titus Canyon Road, and reset your trip odometer. Within two miles you will enter Death Valley National Park. A park service sign announces that camping is not permitted anywhere along the Titus Canyon Road.

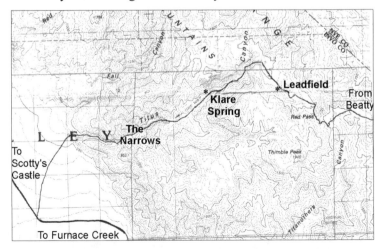

In its first six miles, the graded road gradually climbs 800 vertical feet up the alluvial fan, before entering the Grapevine Mountains. The country becomes more interesting once the wash is entered. The surrounding mountains are Tertiary volcanic rocks, representing several phases of volcanism occurring over a span of five to eleven million years ago. Many of the peaks are actually volcanic plugs, the hardened material in the throat of a volcano left exposed after the cone has weathered away.

A very common plant along the roadside here is ephedra, sometimes called Squaw Tea or Mormon Tea. There are seven species of ephedra in California, five of which are found within the park. Three of those five species are found here on White Pass: the very common *Ephedra viridis,* the less common, but still abundant *E. nevadensis,* and *E. funerea,* which is on the California Native Plant Society's list of rare and endangered plants. Originally it was thought to grow only in the Funeral Mountains near Ryan, but in recent years it has been found here in the Grapevine Mountains and in San Bernardino County as well. Note however, ephedra contains the drug epinephrine, a cardiac stimulant, about which the FDA has issued a health warning. **Do not drink tea made from ephedra if you have any kind of cardiac problem. Prolonged consumption may also cause personality changes and other psychiatric disorders!**

The summit of White Pass is reached 12.8 miles from the pavement. The elevation here is slightly over 5,100 feet. Winter snows can sometimes cause this road to be closed for a few days.

In the next two miles, the road descends some 500' through layers of green, red, and black sediments. This is the upper basin of Titanothere Canyon, so named for a large rhinoceros-like animal that roamed this area during Oligocene times. The 32-million-year-old fossilized remains of this critter were excavated from the red sandstone member of the Titus Canyon Formation near Leadfield in 1933. The Oligocene landscape was much different than what you see today. In those prehistoric times, this was a savanna-like terrain, with lakes and slow sluggish streams around which the plant-eating animals browsed and the carnivores hunted for prey. Other fossil animals uncovered in these beds were camel-like creatures, deer, tapirs, dogs and various rodents.

The road now switchbacks from the low point back up through layers of red sediments to the colorful summit of 5,250' Red Pass. This is the high point of the road, an ideal place to stop and enjoy the expansive views. Once you get down into Titus Canyon, that feeling of wide-open space will be lost.

The road descends Red Pass for the next three miles, passing a number of prospect holes, to come to the site of Leadfield 15.4 miles in from Highway 374. The Bullfrog excitement brought prospectors through here in 1905. Specimens of lead and copper minerals were found, and claims were filed, but the remoteness of the area and the low-grade ore combined to discourage mining. All was quiet until 1924, when there was renewed interest in the lead deposits. Jack Salsberry raised some capital and formed a company known as Western Lead Mines. He bought twelve claims in 1925 and staked forty more. Salsberry had one crew digging prospect holes in the upper part of Titus Canyon, while another crew was building a road in from Beatty.

In 1926, at the peak of the Roaring Twenties, an oilman from Los Angeles by the name of Charles Julian wrestled away control of Western Lead Mines, and set out to promote his new company's stock. Like some modern day real estate promotions, he induced potential investors to come out to Titus Canyon for a free meal and a tour of the mine. By this time, the road started by Salsberry had been completed. For those investors who did not choose the rigors of driving to Death Valley, Julian chartered a fifteen car special train using a Southern Pacific locomotive as far as Ludlow, from where a Tonopah & Tidewater engine brought the train into Beatty. A fleet of autos brought the potential investors from Beatty on into Leadfield. Waiting for them was a band and a grand lunch at which well over a thousand people were served. The scheme worked. A week or two after this promotion, some 330,000 shares of stock in Western Lead Mines had been sold. In late January 1926 that stock had been selling at $1.57 a share. At the end of March, Julian's scheme had boosted the price to $3.30. It did not seem to matter that the nearest water was some 2½ miles down the canyon at Klare Spring. Leadfield was on the map. In April the townsite of Leadfield was laid out with 1,749 lots in 93 blocks. Businesses opened and they advertised in the newly formed newspaper, the *Leadfield Chronicle*. The post office opened on June 25th, and Leadfield's prosperity seemed assured.

There were a few problems, however. By this time Julian was under investigation for securities irregularities. And then there was the matter of the lead ore. There wasn't any! The speculative bubble burst, and by December 31, 1926, the post office closed its doors in Leadfield for the last time. So 1926 was the best of times and the worst of times for Leadfield. It was born, matured, and died all in the course of twelve months. In spite of its short life, Leadfield was added to the National Register of Historic Places in 1975.

Legendary Leadfield

Leadfield in 1926
(Death Valley Museum photos)

Thanks to National Park Service protection, little has changed
in Leadfield since the author took this photo in 1956.

The geology suddenly makes a dramatic change a half-mile below Leadfield. The 30 million-year-old Titus Canyon Formation disappears to be replaced by a sequence of 550 million-year-old sedimentary rocks laid down during the Cambrian period. The park service used to have an interpretive sign "Where Rocks Bend", but it was removed because it is in fact an optical illusion. Titus Canyon now truly begins as the walls of these rocks begin too close in on both sides.

Where rocks bend

Klare Spring is reached 2½ miles below Leadfield. This is the only water in the canyon. Prehistoric Indians knew the site well; they left their petroglyphs etched in a rock outcrop just up the canyon from the spring. When these primitive rock carvings portray things like bighorn sheep, the object, if not the message, can be easily recognized. Many of the drawings are abstract geometric designs, and the meaning of these has been lost in antiquity. Even present-day Native Americans are not sure of their interpretation. Archaeologists have many theories as to what these doodles mean but, in fact, nobody knows for sure.

At a point 1.9 miles below Klare Spring, look to the left where the flat surface of the bedding plane in the marble is exposed. On top of the gray limestone rock is a thin layer of hardened brown mud containing fossil ripple marks. These ripples were made in the bottom of a shallow Cambrian sea some 500 million years ago.

Four miles below Klare Spring begin the narrows that so delight tourists. For the next 1.7 miles the canyon walls soar hundreds of feet up, but are barely twenty feet apart in some places. Six miles below Klare Spring, 23.8 miles from Highway 374, the magic of the canyon suddenly ends. The roadway abruptly leaves the canyon and you find yourself overlooking the vast expanse of Death Valley. It is only 2.5 miles down the alluvial fan to the paved road that leads to Scotty's Castle.

The Titus Canyon Narrows

18

Chloride City

Primary Attraction:	An historic mining camp of the 1870s, with great views of Death Valley all the way to Mt. Whitney and the Sierra crest.
Time Required:	This is pretty much an easy all day trip out of either Beatty or Stovepipe Wells, particularly if you hike down to the Monarch Mine.
Miles Involved:	It is sixteen miles of highway from Beatty to the turnoff, and then another seven miles into Chloride City.
Maps:	1:100,000 Beatty sheet; 1:24,000 Daylight Pass and Chloride City Quadrangles.
Degree of Difficulty:	Of the dirt road portion, about half is Class II, and about half an easy Class III.

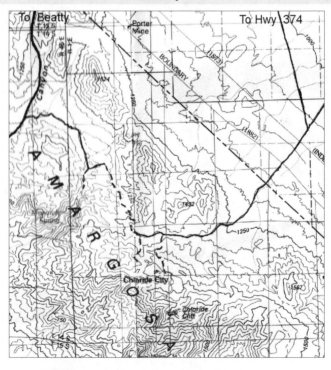

Chloride City arose out of silver discoveries in Chloride Cliff in 1873, the earliest of all the Death Valley mines. The mines of this small community struggled for a few years, but by 1880 none were working and everyone had moved on. The Rhyolite excitement of 1904 brought in new capital. The Chloride Cliff Mine was bought by investors in nearby Rhyolite and reopened in 1908. Sufficient ore was produced in the following years to warrant the construction of a cyanide mill in 1916. It is questionable whether that investment paid off, because by 1918 the camp was deserted again.

From downtown Beatty take State Highway 374, the Daylight Pass road, southwest towards Death Valley. Before leaving town the highway passes the local Death Valley information office where the latest road information can be obtained. At a point 3½ miles outside Beatty, the highway passes the huge Bullfrog Mine operated by the Barrick Corporation in the 1990s. During the good times in 1997, Barrick had 289 employees at the Bullfrog Mine. They produced 206,571 ounces of gold and 351,348 ounces of silver. By 1999, the number of workers had dropped to 52 employees turning out a mere 76,159 ounces of gold and 90,967 ounces of silver. The year 2000 found both the mine and processing plant closed.

Just beyond the mine, a side road goes right up the hill to the site of Rhyolite, just a couple of miles to the west. Rhyolite certainly warrants a visit. (For a more interesting route into Rhyolite, see *Great Basin SUV Trails, Volume II – Southwestern Nevada*, where we follow the old roadbed of the Tonopah & Tidewater Railroad into the ghost town.)

Rhyolite's origin goes back to February of 1905 when promoters left out of the Bullfrog boom selected a site a mile away, drew up a plat map, named streets, and subdivided the land into lots. To attract business and settlement, free parcels were offered to merchants; the ploy worked. Within three months the basin contained a sea of white tents, and within a year Rhyolite had eclipsed its slightly older neighbor, Bullfrog, just a mile to the southwest. In 1906 the Las Vegas & Tonopah Railroad extended its tracks to Rhyolite. By 1907 the town of only two years had a population of 6,000. By this time Rhyolite had substantial buildings made of wood and stone, and at least one made of empty bottles (it still stands as a museum). However late in 1907, a financial panic spread across the nation and, with the loss of financial support, the mines of Rhyolite closed, many to never open again. With this bursting of the bubble of optimism, the citizens of Rhyolite drifted away. By the 1910 census, Rhyolite only had a population of 700; by the 1920 census, nobody was left.

The John S. Cook Bank Building

Going strong .....

Going away.....

Gone forever
(all photos from the author's collection)

Nevada Highway 374 crosses the flat expanse of the Amargosa Valley, and begins a steady climb into the mountains to the southwest. The state line is crossed at a point 12.7 miles from downtown Beatty; the sign is so tiny that most people miss it. A 4,317' low point in the mountains, Daylight Pass is thirteen miles out of Beatty.

The newly built Daylight Pass Road
(Death Valley Museum photo)

Daylight Pass makes a convenient geographical boundary between the Grapevine Mountains to the north and the Funeral Mountains to the south. Note your odometer reading at the pass. Just 2.7 miles beyond the summit look for a desert road going off to the left. The NPS has marked it with the customary jeep symbol; this is the turnoff to Chloride City (N36°45.127 W116°56.168). (If you are coming from the Death Valley side, the turnoff is 3.4 miles above Hell's Gate.) Reset you odometer and turn onto the Chloride Cliff road.

The well-defined Class II road heads south and east. After two miles look for an abandoned closed road offering an easy hike of less than a mile to Keane Spring. As small as it is, this spring has been a reliable source of water. During the 1906 Rhyolite excitement when miners came flocking into these mountains by the thousands, a small village developed around this waterhole. Although short-lived, Keane Spring once had a boarding house, livery stable, and of course, a saloon. Even the Porter Brothers, who had a large general store in nearby Rhyolite, opened a branch here. When the Bank Panic of 1907 dried up venture capital, Keane Spring did not dry up, but the town did. A flash flood came down the wash a few years later and dispersed what little remained.

The road now begins a gradual descent and within a quarter-mile you will be in the Monarch Canyon wash. The road goes to the left, but there is an interesting

side trip right down into the confining walls of Monarch Canyon. At one time this
road went down to the Monarch Mine, discovered in 1905 and worked off and
on until World War II. Today you can take a vehicle down the canyon only 0.7
miles, where you will encounter the mother of all road washouts. Nevertheless,
this wash makes a fine campsite (in good weather) suitable for a 4x4 club outing.
From the present day road's end, you can hike down the canyon, past the spring
a mile or so, to the well preserved mine.

Back on the main Chloride Cliff road, a spring and a water tank are passed
on the left within a quarter-mile. The road now deteriorates to Class III as it
cuts across the grain of the landscape. On the hillsides to the right, mines and
prospect holes begin to appear. It returns to Class II after two miles. At a point
2.6 miles beyond the water tank, a major road intersection is reached; this is
Chloride Junction (N36°43.060 W116°53.137). The Class I road to the left heads
north to Highway 95 and Beatty; you will want to turn to the right for Chloride
City. The route has once again deteriorated to Class III.

A ridgetop with good views northeast into the Amargosa Valley of Nevada
is reached within 0.7 miles. To the west are some of Chloride City's outlying
mines, and beyond on the distant skyline, the crest of the Sierra Nevada Range.
At a point 1.1 miles from Chloride Junction (N36°42.426 W116°53.113), the road
forks at a viewpoint overlooking the site of Chloride City. Keep to the left for
another quarter-mile and you will be in what was once "downtown".

Chloride City has had a checkered past of boom and bust. It all started in the
early 1870s when A.J. Franklin discovered silver ore on what was to become
Chloride Cliff.

The author took this photo in 1958.

In his book *Mines of Death Valley,* Death Valley historian Burr Belden tells about the miners having to go 250 miles to the nearest grocery store in Barstow, California. Ten years later the road blazed in those days was adopted in part by mule trains from both the Eagle Borax Works, as well as the Harmony Borax Works. There were also several skirmishes between the miners and Paiute Indians in this part of the Funeral Range. The Franklin Mine could not be operated profitably because of its remote location, and it eventually closed in the late 1870s.

Not much happened here for the next 25 years, even though the silver mines of Panamint City, Lookout, Darwin and Cerro Gordo were going strong. The Rhyolite excitement of 1905 spurred new interest in the district, although the San Francisco earthquake dried up venture capital, and the mines of Chloride City closed. The Bank Panic of 1907 depressed the price of silver, keeping the mines idle. A few small mines reopened by 1908, and in 1916 Chloride City had its first cyanide mill. That operation was closed by 1918, but its foundations still remain. Since then, there have been several renewed efforts to wrestle the mineral wealth from these barren hills.

These are highly metamorphosed rocks - schist, gneiss and quartzite - some of the oldest rocks in Death Valley going back 500 million years to the pre-Precambrian. They have been cut by diorite dikes and with those intrusions came quartz veins, sometimes up to thirty feet thick, containing gold, silver, lead, and even cinnabar, a mercury mineral. Most of the gold and silver ores were low grade, containing one-half ounce or less per ton; nevertheless, it was sometimes economically feasible to mine it because the veins were so large. The major mines of the district were the Big Bell, Frisco, Gold Dollar, Chloride Cliff and the Keane Wonder Mines. The latter had production in excess of a million dollars. Because of their dangerous condition, the NPS has installed sturdy fencing over the entrance to many of these mines. Only the most foolhardy would try to enter.

Today Chloride City consists of a few wooden shacks of questionable ancestry, mines and tailings piles aplenty, and of course scattered dumps of rusting tin cans. The camp's only grave marks the final resting-place of one James McKay.

After wandering around Chloride City proper, be sure to drive ¾-mile to the ridgetop beyond the town; the view is grand and glorious. Not only can you look down upon much of Death Valley, including the sand dunes and that great slash in the Panamints caused by Cottonwood Canyon, but if the day is clear, you can clearly see the 14,495' summit of Mount Whitney, eighty miles away on the western skyline.

There are sufficient backroads and old mines in the Chloride City area to keep you engaged the whole day. It should prove to be an enjoyable one.

Chloride City

A "Cousin Jack" house in Chloride City circa 1906
(Death Valley Museum photo)

A similar house in 1998

Downtown in the early 1950s
(Death Valley Museum photo)

19

Echo Pass via Lee's Camp

Primary Attraction: Two Turn of the 20th Century mining camps, interesting geology and some challenging roads.

Time Required: This is an all day outing from Beatty to Echo Pass and return.

Miles Involved: It is 32 miles of highway or good graded road to the start of the Lee's Camp Road, then nearly three miles to the site of Lee, plus another three miles to Echo Pass. From Echo Pass to Furnace Creek Ranch is another fourteen miles.

Maps: 1:100,000 Beatty and Death Valley Junction Sheets; 1:24,000 Leeland and Lee's Camp Quadrangles.

Degree of Difficulty: It is Class II to the two sites of Lee, and Class III with a little IV from there on to the summit of Echo Pass. (The worst part of the road is on the western side of the pass, where it is Class V for a short distance.) **The road beyond Lee's Camp is not recommended for the timid and inexperienced off-road driver.**

The road over Echo Pass, in either direction, is one of the more challenging routes in the Death Valley country. Do not let this deter you, because Class II roads lead to the sites of interesting and little known old mining camps on either side of the pass before the difficult portions are encountered. The route up the west side of the pass is described in Excursion #1. I describe the road up the east side in this excursion.

Note your odometer reading in downtown Beatty, and take U.S. Highway 95 to the south. After going about 20 miles, look for a sign reading *Amargosa Farms* pointing to a paved road to the right; turn here onto Valley View Road (N36°40.837 W116°32.559). Going south, you can see Big Dune off on the distant right.

Big Dune is about 300 feet high, certainly higher than the sand dunes near Stovepipe Well and those in the Saline and Panamint Valleys, but not nearly as high as the 450' high Dumont Dunes at the southern end of Death Valley, or the 680' high Eureka Valley Dunes. Big Dune does have one unique feature not found in many other dune areas - the ability to generate sound. When conditions are just right, both Big Dune and the Eureka Valley dunes can produce an audible sound, variously described as a "barking" or sometimes "booming" noise. This strange process happens when small avalanches of sand roll down the slope of the dune. The internal shearing of the sand grains seems to produce the sound. Three factors must be in place before this phenomenon can occur: (1) the humidity must be exceedingly low; (2) the sand grains of the dune slope must be well sorted; (3) the sand grains must be medium in size. To be camped at the base of one of these dunes, quietly enjoying an evening campfire, when the dune begins to "sing" can be an unnerving experience for those who do not know what is happening.

Big Dune as seen from Valley View Road.

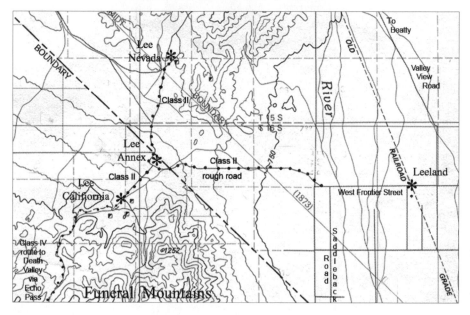

After driving south on Valley View for 6.6 miles, turn to the right onto West Frontier Street, a wide well graded road (N36°35.008 W116°32.547). After going west for about 2½ miles, look to the right for the barely discernable old roadbed of the Tonopah & Tidewater Railroad that passed through here during the years of 1906-1940. Where the railroad grade once crossed present day Frontier Street was the site of Leeland, a whistle stop on the railroad.

"Borax" Smith started building his Tonopah & Tidewater Railroad in 1905, largely for the purpose of hauling borax from his Lila C Mine, at the eastern edge of Death Valley, to Ludlow, California, from where the Atchison Topeka & Santa Fe could take it on to markets in the Los Angeles area. The T&T had its northern terminus in Gold Center, Nevada, just outside of Beatty. The line ran 169 miles south to connect with the AT&SF at Ludlow. Leeland was the first station south of Gold Center, and the last station in Nevada. Because of the abundant water available in the lower Amargosa Valley, there was a relatively large three-room station, and a water tank was established here to provide services to the nearby boom camps.

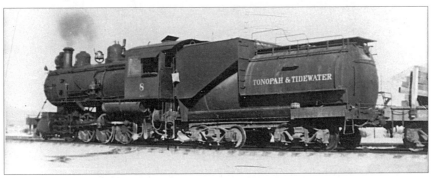

Tonopah & Tidewater locomotive No. 8 at Leeland
(Central Nevada Historical Society photo)

At a point 3.9 miles west of Valley View Road, you will see a Class II desert road going off to the right at an angle (N36°34.985 W116°34.976). This is the start of your rough road adventure all the way to the summit of Echo Pass. Reset your trip odometer to zero, and turn right.

The dirt road begins as Class I, but after a half-mile deteriorates to Class II as it turns to the west. A Class II side road goes off to the right 2.3 miles from Frontier Street (N36°35.267 W116°39.100). This is the first of several roads going north to the site of Lee, Nevada. Continue heading west. You will soon reach the state line (N36°35.214 W116°39.398) although no boundary sign marks its presence. Nearly three miles from Frontier Street, on the right there is a 100' by 100' rock enclosure evidently used as a corral. Together with some scattered rusting tin

cans, these rocks mark the site of the Lee Annex, a small community started by
L.P. McGarry in 1907 as a spin off of Lee, California, the more successful camp
just a mile to the southwest. The road going north from here goes to yet another
Lee, this one in Nevada. Gambling occurred in Lee, Nevada, but any resulting
disputes were settled on the California side of the boundary, where there was no
law enforcement!

Rusting cans mark the site of Lee, Nevada.

The road forks at Lee Annex. The road to Lee, California, and Echo Pass goes
to the left (N36°35.259 W116°39.698); keep to the left. Still Class II, the road actually
seems to become a little smoother, as it heads for a cove in the nearby Funeral
Mountains. Within 1¼ miles from Lee Annex, a fork to the left heads for a long
abandoned tunnel at the base of the nearby mountain (N36°34.797 W116°40.219).
Keep right, and in a few hundred yards you will be driving down Nevada Street
in downtown Lee, California. You will know you are there when again you see
piles of rusting tin cans strewn about. Among them are the low stonewalls that
were once the foundations of wooden structures.

Legend has it that two Shoshone Indian brothers, Dick and Gus Lee, together
with Henry Finley (who was well into his 70s), discovered a gold-bearing quartz
vein on the western slope of the Funeral Range as part of the Bullfrog excitement
of 1904. They staked their claims, set up camp near the outcrop, and started a
tunnel to tap the vein. Thus, the Hayseed and Stateline Mines were born. At first,
their small settlement became known as Lee's Camp (that name still appears on
USGS topographic maps). The Lee boys sold their claims to a trio of Tonopah

investors in February of 1906. The fact that they already sold those same claims to someone else didn't apparently bother them, for in late March they sold the same claims a third time, always a cash transaction. The Lee brothers then left for parts unknown, leaving the buyers to sue each other for custody. As it turned out, a fourth consortium of owners bought out the interests of the litigants, and mining began in January of 1907. At a depth of only 25 feet, the Hayseed Mine tapped into an 18" vein of gold that had assay values of $8,600 to $123,000 per ton! Unfortunately the vein soon pinched out, but there was the promise of more to come.

Lee, California in at its peak 1907
(Nevada Historical Society photo)

At the same time, promoters laid out the townsite of Lee, California, to compete with the townsite of Lee, Nevada, situated three miles to the northeast and laid out a few days before. Lee, California, boasted of having a rooming house, restaurant, general store, and of course, a saloon in its first 30 days, and by March it had added a bakery, another restaurant, rooming house and two more saloons. The town added a stage station, barbershop, meat market, icehouse, two lumberyards, two more restaurants, three general stores, three feed yards and two more saloons in April. It was obvious that Lee, California, had beaten Lee, Nevada, in the race for metropolis of the Funeral Range. By the late summer and early fall of 1907, the population peaked at somewhere between five and six hundred, including twenty women. There was a full range of goods and services available, including a post office and the *Lee Herald* newspaper. A telephone line connecting Lee with the outside world was strung to Leeland, and the railroad people even talked of running a spur line into Lee.

The Bank Panic of 1907 began to take its toll, as investment funds dried up and mines began to close. Within a year, most of Lee's population and businesses had moved on. The post office closed its doors in 1912, as did Lillard's General Store, and soon the entire town was deserted. Scavengers took the abandoned wooden buildings apart, using the materials elsewhere. As one looks around today, it seems incredible to think that this was once a thriving community of hundreds of people.

Today only low stone walls mark the site Lee, California.

The road continues above Lee, entering a small canyon and deteriorating to Class III in places. Watch for a wash on the left 1.6 miles beyond Lee. Although it may not look like it, this is actually a fork in the trail. The obvious route to the right dead-ends in a half-mile at a tunnel. You will want to turn left up this wash.

A canyon is entered within a mile, and soon the road becomes Class III, as it makes its way up the canyon's rocky floor. **Depending on conditions of the moment, there could be some Class IV sections in this canyon.**

The country opens up again a couple of miles after turning up the sandy wash. There are side roads going off to the right and left, leading to numerous prospect holes. Finally at a point five miles from Lee's Camp, the rounded summit over the Funeral Mountains is reached. Compared to the rocky canyon below, Echo Pass is anti-climactic.

Once on top you can turn around and return the way you came, or you can proceed on down Echo Wash into Death Valley (see Excursion #1). **If you elect** to go on into Death Valley, be aware that there is a dry waterfall about 1½ miles ahead. I rate the descent as Class IV for westbound traffic, but Class V for eastbound vehicles making the ascent of Echo Wash. My wife says, "Nonsense, it is Class V going in either direction!"

The dry waterfall on the west side of Echo Pass is rated as Class IV for westbound vehicles and Class V for eastbound vehicles.

Old Shoshone Still Lives On Today

Shoshone in 1940. The building on the left was originally built in Greenwater 1906. After it was moved to Shoshone, it became Charles Brown's gas station and general store, with a post office housed in one corner.
(Photo from the author's collection)

That same building houses the Shoshone Museum today.

Just beyond the Shoshone Cemetery are the "caves" of Dublin Gulch, hollowed out of soft ash and used as homes by local residents for well over 100 years.

Chapter V

Trails Out of Shoshone

Borax Smith's Tonopah & Tidewater Railroad started laying its rails northward from Ludlow in 1905. The construction crews finally broke through the formidable barrier presented by the Amargosa Gorge in the spring of 1907. A station was established in Tecopa in early May, and soon thereafter a siding was placed at what is now Shoshone. However, it would not be until three years later that Ralph J. 'Dad' Fairbanks partially dismantled many of the wooden structures (wood was hard to come by in the desert) in the abandoned town of Greenwater and transported them here by wagon. Thus, it has been said, "If you wish to see downtown Greenwater, come to Shoshone". Metbury Spring near the siding provided sufficient water to support a large grove of mesquite trees, as well as the needs of a small community. Soon Dad and his wife Celesta established a boarding house that catered to passengers on the railroad and local miners alike, as well as a store of general merchandise. On October 29, 1910, Ma and Pa Fairbank's daughter Stella married Charles Brown, starting a family legacy that persists in this remote corner of Inyo County to this day. Charles Brown was elected to the Inyo County Board of Supervisors in 1924, and in 1938 went on to serve in the California State Legislature for another 24 years. The T&T ceased its operations on June of 1940, and in 1942-43 its steel rails were torn out and salvaged for the war effort. The citizenry of lesser places might have packed up and moved on, but the good folks of Shoshone managed to hang on and survive.

With a population of only about one hundred, Shoshone makes a handy base of operations for exploration of the southern end of the Death Valley country. It offers a motel, general store, restaurant, gas station, and private camping and RV facilities. During your visit to Shoshone, I would highly recommend taking a few minutes to walk through its small museum. Displays include the fossilized remains of a 500,000 to 600,000-year old mammoth. Thought to be a teenage male, it is 28' long and weighs 15,000 lbs. The Shoshone Mammoth was dug up from the old lakebeds just southeast of Shoshone after being discovered by geology students from Sonoma State University in 1983.

In nearby Tecopa, Inyo County operates a hot spring spa, where weary muscles can be rejuvenated after a hard day of bouncing on the area's jeep trails.

20

Gold Valley Solitude

Primary Attraction:	Visit an isolated valley, once the site of three competing mining camps. If you are very lucky, bighorn sheep sightings are also possible.
Time Required:	This is an all day trip out of either Shoshone or Furnace Creek.
Miles Involved:	It is 29 miles one-way from downtown Shoshone to downtown Gold Valley. From Furnace Creek Ranch, the one-way distance to Gold Valley is 47 miles.
Maps:	1:100,000 Death Valley Junction sheet; 1:24,000 Funeral Peak and Gold Valley Quadrangles.
Degree of Difficulty:	The route is mostly Class II, with a few Class III sections near the end.

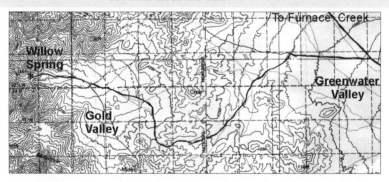

In the first decade of the 20th century, gold fever once again ran rampant throughout the west, and there was a frantic rush to anywhere one's fortune might be made. The excitement in the Black Mountains in 1906 emptied the saloons and boarding houses of Rhyolite, Goldfield, and Tonopah, as thousands headed south to the boomtowns of Furnace and Greenwater. The population of Greenwater swelled from 70 to 1000 in just one month. By 1907, more than 2,500 claims had been filed at the Inyo County Courthouse in distant Independence. Some of these claims extended south of Funeral Peak into a basin optimistically named Gold Valley. Like Greenwater, Gold Valley proved to be more sizzle than substance, and by 1910 there was nobody left.

I found this sign intact in 1958.

During the 1930s, the Automobile Club of Southern California placed a series of baked enamel road signs on the back roads throughout the California desert. They announced the distances to waterholes and other landmarks. When I visited Gold Valley for the first time in 1958, one of those old signs was still in place. In fact, the area was so isolated that not only was the sign still there, but it had not been shot full of bullet holes or otherwise vandalized! That sign was still there in the late 1990s, and still undamaged. Let's keep it that way!

To see Gold Valley as it was in 1910, take State Route 127 north out of Shoshone, immediately turning west on State Route 178 (N35°55.768 W116°15.414). At a point 5.8 miles west of Highway 127, reset your trip odometer, and turn right on the graded Greenwater Valley Road (N35°55.768 W116°21.828). Proceed up this road to the 16.4-milepoint, and there on the left you will find a Class II road heading into the Black Mountains (N36°03.339 W116°30.448); reset your odometer once again, and turn left. This road goes due west up the bajada for the first 2.5 miles, and then comes to a crossroads (N36°03.473 W116°33.067). The middle and right forks are now closed by *Wilderness* designation, so you will have to turn left, soon entering the Black Mountains. The crest of this range is crossed seven miles in from the Greenwater Valley Road, and Gold Valley is below you to the west. The road forks after a half-mile (N36°01.289 W116°37.358); take either branch, as they both descend into the valley. (The left fork passes some prospect holes, and is a half-mile longer than the right fork.)

The stampede to Greenwater in the summer of 1906 brought so many prospectors into the Black Mountains that there wasn't room for everyone. The overflow fanned out in every direction, and some wandered into an isolated valley just south of Smith Mountain. Here they discovered Willow Spring, an oddity in the otherwise dry and barren Black Mountains. Not only was there a spring here, but it had sufficient water to feed a year-around stream. Even before the first pound of ore was mined, the Willow Creek Mining District was organized. Chet Leavitt, a strict Mormon recently arrived from the Echo Pass area, proclaimed the area around Willow Spring to be the town of Copper Basin.

Not to be outdone, another newcomer Ernest Mattinson started a second competing town nearby that he called Willow Creek. Mattinson lacked the religious convictions of Leavitt, and had a saloon in his town. Within months, everybody in Copper Basin had succumbed to the lure of the demon rum, and moved to Willow Creek.

For the next ten months there was a lot of looking, but little mining. Traces of copper were everywhere, but none in sufficient quantities to mine. In May of 1907, Joe Witherell, a newcomer to the district, found not copper but gold, and the timing could not have been better. By this time the bloom was off the copper craze, and the prospectors were only too happy to go for the gold. Hundreds of them started pouring in from all the camps along the western side of the Amargosa River. Two enterprising brothers, appropriately named Goldsworthy, drew up a plot map, laying out 96 blocks in the City of Gold Valley. Everything was in place, awaiting the day that the first big mines started shipping ore.

At its peak in 1908, Gold Valley had the basic services to provide the needs of several hundred people. Unfortunately, there were no mines to support the community. By 1910, Gold Valley had been abandoned, and was but a distant dream. Gold Valley lasted no longer than Greenwater, its chief rival to the east.

Both forks of our road rejoin (N36°02.748 W116°39.506) and from here it is another 1½ miles to Willow Spring, where the road ends. Only the last half-mile becomes Class III. At the road's end, a half-mile hike down the canyon is a must. Here bedrock in the narrow gorge forces all the subsurface water in the Gold Valley drainage to the surface. Even in the heat of summer, there is usually enough water to trickle from one pool to the next. This water supports dozens of species of animals, including Bighorn sheep. Indeed, this is probably the best place in the park to see the Desert Bighorn during the warmer months. Obviously, the National Park Service discourages camping here at this very environmentally sensitive water hole.

The Desert Bighorn *Ovis canadensis nelsoni* appears to be a living remnant of the Pleistocene Ice Age that has been able to successfully adapt and hang on, as the land turned drier and warmer. There are an estimated four hundred to six hundred animals within the park, and naturalists are optimistic that their numbers are slowly growing. Bighorn like solitude, and are generally deep in the mountains far from the places that tourists frequent, although they have been sighted in the rocks a safe distance above Badwater, seemingly watching the crowds below.

There is an ongoing controversy concerning habitat competition between feral burros and the Bighorn sheep. Some say the wild burros foul waterholes and eat forage the sheep would otherwise eat. The conclusion is then made that Bighorn sheep populations have declined because of the feral burros, and as the numbers of burros increase, the sheep decrease. In their comprehensive study of the Bighorn sheep made in the late 1950s, Ralph and Florence Welles found no conclusive evidence to support this conclusion. I don't know who is correct, but it is interesting to note that during the late 1980s and early 1990s, some 6,000 wild burros were rounded up and removed from the park. Since that time, the Bighorn sheep population seems to be slowly increasing. Is it a coincidence?

The desert bighorn prefer solitude.

You must leave Gold Valley by the same route you came in from off the Greenwater Valley Road (N36°03.339 W116°30.448). Once at the intersection of the graded Greenwater Valley Road and the Gold Valley Road, you have at least three options depending on your next destination. If you wish to return to Shoshone, turn right and continue to retrace your route. It is about 18 miles back to Shoshone. If you are heading north towards Furnace Creek Ranch, turn left and you should find the roads good for the next 25 miles, at which point you will join State Route 190. From there, another left turn will put you at Furnace Creek Ranch in 12 miles. There is still a third option if you are heading for Death Valley Junction or Shoshone. Turn right, but go only a half-mile; then turn left onto the Class II Deadman Pass Road (N36°03.309 W116°30.003). From here, it is 13.6 miles over the very gentle rise called Deadman Pass (elevation 3,264') and down to Highway 127 at a point 7½ miles south of Death Valley Junction. According to a 1939 guidebook to Death Valley that was published as a WPA project, Deadman Pass was so named during the Greenwater boom when the body of an unknown man was found along the road.

21

The Ashford Mine

Primary Attraction: This route provides easy hiking access to a Turn of the 20th Century mine.

Time Required: From Shoshone (or Furnace Creek Ranch) to the mouth of Ashford Canyon is only an hour. Add another hour to walk up to the mine.

Miles Involved: It is nearly 33 miles from Shoshone to the Ashford Mill (45 miles from Furnace Creek Ranch) and then another three miles to the end of the trail.

Maps: 1:100,000 Owlshead Mountains sheet; 1:24,000 Shore Line Butte Quadrangle.

Degree of Difficulty: It is Class II from the Ashford Mill to the end of the road.

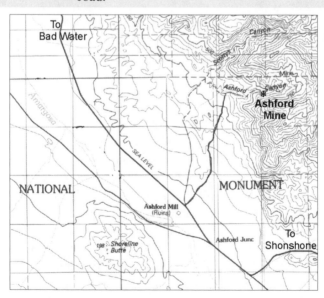

Every day thousands of folks drive on the Eastside Road between Badwater and Shoshone, passing the crumbling ruins of the old Ashford Mill near Shore Line Butte. The NPS has the spot marked by a sign, short access road, and parking area. During the course of a busy spring day, a few hundred may actually stop for a closer look at the ruins. As you might guess, the mill site itself is just part of the larger picture of what once went on here. This rough road excursion tells the rest of the story.

From Shoshone, take State Route 127 north 1.7 miles (N35°55.768 W116°15.414). Turn left on State Route 178 proceeding westward over Salsberry Pass and Jubilee Pass. As you enter Death Valley, the highway makes a turn to the right and heads north. The ruins of the Ashford Mill can be seen off to the left after 33 miles. Visit the site if you wish, but there is not much left to see. This was once the site of a mill that processed ore from the nearby Golden Treasure Mine, often called the Ashford Mine, just five miles to the east. While the mine was located in 1907 at the tail end of the Greenwater excitement, it wasn't until 1914 that this mill was built. The name Ashford Mill is a misnomer, because the Ashford brothers neither built nor operated the facility.

The Ashford Mill around 1916
(Death Valley Museum photo)

The Ashford Mill ruins in 1956

While you are at the mill site, you cannot help but notice Shore Line Butte just to the west. The hill is made up of volcanic basalt and fanglomerate of the early Pleistocene Funeral Formation. The rocks themselves are not as interesting as what has happened to them. Late in the Pleistocene, after this hill was already in place, glacial melt water from the high Sierra flowed out of the Owens Valley into the China Lake Basin, then into the Searles Basin followed by the Panamint Basin, to eventually overflow down Wingate Wash into Death Valley. The result was ancient Lake Manly, a freshwater lake ninety miles long by six to eleven miles wide, with a depth of up to 600 feet. During that time, wind-whipped waves cut terraces into the shoreline. When the climate warmed up and the glaciers no longer fed Lake Manly, the lake cut new terraces as the water evaporated and the lake began to shrink in size. Ancient Lake Manly is long gone; however, these fossil beaches remain. Geologists call them wave cut terraces. There are at least ten of them here on Shore Line Butte. This same phenomenon can also be seen at Mormon Point south of Badwater, and again above Mushroom Rock.

On the eastern side of the highway opposite the road to the mill, a Class I desert road heads towards the colorful south end of the Black Mountains (N35°55.245 W116°40.860). This is the road that once connected the mine to the mill and, after resetting your odometer, it is where you will leave the pavement. The road forks after 0.7 miles (N35°55.677 W116°40.384); stay to the left (the right fork has been closed). Soon the road deteriorates to Class II. The reddish brown hills on the left are a mixture of Pliocene sediments, mostly conglomerates and other stream deposits. To the right in the Black Mountains, the rust brown rocks are part of a very old, highly faulted complex of Precambrian metamorphic rocks. Geologist Levi Noble, who pioneered geologic study in Death Valley in the 1930s, described the southern end of the Black Mountains as the *Amargosa chaos*. The term was very appropriate, and has stuck.

The road now ends at a camping area on the top of the alluvial fan, nearly three miles in off the highway. You are going to have to hike the last 1¼ miles to see the mine, but it is not a difficult walk. Leave your car at the road's end, and just walk around the hill and then descend into the wash. Walk up the sandy wash a short ways, watching for a rock cairn on the left.

On the hillside is the remnant of a once paved road, steeply climbing up the ridge to the east. Hike up the road a third of a mile to the ridgetop. From here it becomes obvious why the Ashford brothers chose this route when they built this wagon road. A giant piece of rock has rolled off the mountainside to come to rest like a big chock stone in Ashford Canyon. The former road over this low ridge bypasses this obstacle. Simply walk down the road back into the wash, and follow the wash up to the mine. From the end of today's road to the lower workings of the mine, it is an easy hike of about an hour. **Stay out of the underground workings. They are not safe!**

It is unclear when gold was first discovered in this little canyon in the Black Mountains, but it was probably during the Greenwater excitement of 1905. The Gold Key Mining Company had staked claims everywhere, but did not keep up their required annual assessment work. Brothers Harold, Henry and Louis Ashford refiled on some claims, whereupon Gold Key promptly sued them. The Ashford boys ultimately prevailed, but by this time it was 1910, and the legal expenses had taken all of their cash. They leased the property for $60,000 to self-styled Hungarian nobleman, Count Kramer. The Count in turn leased the mine to Los Angeles oilman Benjamin McCausland for $105,000. By this time it was 1914. McCausland and his son Ross blasted out a road, the remnants of which you see today. They brought in a lot of machinery, and installed a modern mill on a bluff on the east bank of the Amargosa River.

They worked the mine at a feverish pace from February to September of 1915. Some fifty men worked around the clock, mining the ore and trucking it five miles down to the mill. They had put about $230,000 into the venture, and had cleaned out about $100,000 of the best ore. McCausland defaulted on his lease from Kramer, causing Kramer to leave the Ashford brothers holding the bag. The Ashford's Golden Treasure Mine has never reopened.

The Ashford Mine when it was still operating
(Death Valley Museum photo)

22

Ibex and Saratoga Springs

Primary Attraction:	This outing features several attractions, including natural springs, sites occupied by paleo-Indians for thousands of years, old talc mines and their associated mine camps.
Time Required:	Saratoga Spring is a half-day outing out of Shoshone.
Miles Involved:	It is about 23 miles one way from Shoshone to Ibex Spring. Add another seven miles, if you choose to go on down to Saratoga Spring.
Maps:	1:100,000 Owlshead Mountains sheet; 1:24,000 Ibex Pass, Ibex Spring, and Old Ibex Pass Quadrangles.
Degree of Difficulty:	The dirt road portions are mostly Class I and II; only the last two miles into Ibex Spring have some Class III sections.

When you think of substances mined in Death Valley, you might well think first of borax with its visual images of heavily laden wagons being laboriously pulled across the desert by twenty-mule teams. Yet, there is another white colored non-metallic commodity in the Death Valley region that has been far more economically valuable than borax; it is common, everyday talc. In this outing, we will take a look at a place where talc was once mined.

From Shoshone, take State Route 127 south in the direction of Baker. Immediately upon leaving town, the highway passes through several miles of soft and easily eroded flat lying sediments. These are old lakebed deposits laid down in the bottom of ancient Lake Tecopa. Geologists estimate that Lake Tecopa covered some 85 square miles, and at its maximum could have been four hundred feet deep. Fossils and layers of volcanic ash within the sediments place the age of the lake at as much as three million years, meaning it was a body of water well before the beginning of the Plio-Pleistocene Ice Age. Curiously, it was probably the Ice Age that ended Lake Tecopa's existence, because with the added rainfall and melt water of the Sherwin phase of the early Pleistocene, Lake Tecopa filled to overflowing, breaching its southern shoreline like a bursting dam. A channel quickly eroded, causing the lake to drain into what is now Death Valley.

After passing the second left turnoff to Tecopa, you will notice several roads on the right going up to mines in the Ibex Mountains to the west. These are all talc mines, tapping into that great white resource found throughout the Crystal Spring Formation; but more about that later. The largest talc mines on the distant hillside are the Giant, the Eclipse and the Paddy's Pride. The oldest is the Eclipse, which opened in the 1930s. Pfizer operated the Mammoth and Bonny Mines from the 1950s through the mid 1970s.

Ibex Pass is crossed at a point 14.5 miles south of Shoshone. During the steep descent down the south side,

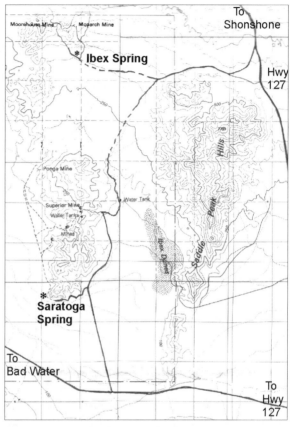

distant views of the Dumont Dunes can be had. A good road goes right up to these sand dunes. It is one of three dune areas in the California desert where the BLM permits unlimited use by Off Highway Vehicles.

Just before reaching the microwave relay facility, at a point 16.3 miles south of Shoshone, look for an unmarked dirt road going off to the right (N35°45.553 W116°19.37); this is where you leave the pavement. Reset your odometer here. The Class I road bypasses the electronic site and heads west. A mile from the highway, the road enters Death Valley National Park and gently descends a sandy wash. In the springtime when conditions are just right, this area comes alive with the yellow brilliance of the desert sunflower sometimes called desert gold *Geraea canescens*.

At a point 2.8 miles in from the highway, the main road seems to swing south and a side road goes off to the west; turn right here (N35°45.616 W116°22.233). Although this road was once paved to accommodate heavily laden ore trucks, barely a trace of the old asphalt remains. While the road is mostly Class II, the first Class III pitch comes within a quarter-mile, when you are crossing a wash. The next intersection is reached 5.1 miles in from the highway (N35°45.959 W116°24.24). The road going straight-ahead leads to Ibex Spring and the sprawling remains of the old mine camp around it. Remember, while exploring these old cabins: **be ever watchful for rodent droppings, and when you find them, avoid disturbing them. They could harbor the virulent Hantavirus.**

Modern man first set up camp here in 1883, with the erection of a mill to process silver ore from the Ibex Mine. That operation lasted eight years until the ore ran out. The mill shut down, and the camp was abandoned. The Greenwater excitement of 1905 brought in a new crop of prospectors and miners, and some congregated around Ibex Spring. That boom went bust as well, and peace and quiet once more descended upon Ibex Spring. In the 1930s, ceramic tile began to become very popular in home construction and the demand for talc, one of tile's major ingredients, rose. The extensive talc deposits in the Ibex Hills were opened up, and once again Ibex Spring became home to those working the nearby mines. The decaying remains of the structures you see today date back to the 1950s, when several nearby mines were going strong.

The road past the camp goes up the fan into a canyon where the Ibex, later called the Moorehouse Mine, was located. It operated from 1940 until the 1970s, and was the area's biggest producer.

The Moorehouse Mine was the area's largest producer.
(Death Valley Museum photo)

Ibex Spring itself may be a disappointment in that it is overgrown with mesquite, arrow-weed, willow, salt cedar, and other vegetation. Someone has even brought in a few palm trees. As a general principle, the NPS would like to eradicate these exotic species from our national parks. Here in Death Valley they certainly face a formidable task.

Talc miner's camp at Ibex Spring

At the intersection back a quarter-mile before reaching Ibex Spring, the road which heads north goes up to the Pleasanton, Mammoth and Rob Roy Mines. In all of these mines, the talc deposits are associated with the Crystal Spring Formation. These are the oldest layers of the larger Pahrump group of very old Precambrian rocks. Millions of years ago, the limestones and dolomites of the Crystal Spring Formation were intruded by a molten rock called diabase. Where this igneous rock came in contact with the sedimentary rock, a zone of metamorphic rock was formed, and with it came talc. These talc zones may be anywhere from a few inches up to 200' thick. The talc is often mined through a system of underground tunnels; however, large deposits close to the surface have also been mined by open pit methods.

Pfizer worked the Monarch and Pleasanton Mines in the 1960s. Cyprus Industrial Minerals purchased them in 1972, and worked them for only a year. They have remained closed since, although they still have ore reserves should the price of talc increase significantly. It is interesting to visit these mines, for many still have ore bunkers and loading facilities remaining. **Obviously, it would be foolish to enter any of the underground workings.**

Once you have had your fill of talc mines, and if you still have part of the day left, you might consider going on down the main road to Saratoga Spring. This was the road that went to the left at a point 2.8 miles west of Highway 127 (N35°45.616 W116°22.233). This Class II road heads south, occasionally through some soft sand, but it is usually not a problem. These sandy areas support a large population of the pretty, and at times very fragrant, sand verbena *Abronia villosa*, a member of the Four-O'Clock family. Its rose-purple flowers have an extended period of bloom from February sometimes into July.

Sand verbena *Abronia villosa*

It is 6.1 miles down to the well-marked turnoff to Saratoga Spring, and then another 1.3 miles to the parking area. Saratoga Spring is a very substantial desert water hole, with a reliable year around flow. The several acres of ponds support a unique pupfish *Cyprindon nevadensis nevadensis*, found nowhere else in the world. This tiny ice-aged species was trapped when ancient Lake Manly dried up. The surrounding marshes are home to many varieties of amphibians, reptiles, and assorted mammals. The water attracts birds of every description. Some are just passing through, while others stay here all year around.

Unfortunately, Saratoga Spring is also home to a species that is not wanted here. This is hornwort, an annual aquatic plant. Like the tamarisk thickets around Furnace Creek Ranch and the Russian thistle that seems to be everywhere, hornwort is an exotic plant, brought in by someone many years ago. It is National Park Service policy to attempt to eradicate these non-native plants.

Saratoga Spring has no doubt been in use by man since the Pleistocene Ice Age; however, most evidence of prehistoric man's occupation only goes back to the period of 1 AD to 1100 AD, when the so-called Saratoga Spring Culture existed in Death Valley. Traces of these peoples are found all up and down the valley, but because they were here in relatively large numbers, and because archaeologists first studied them here, they have been conveniently named by their locality.

The Saratoga Spring people were sophisticated hunters and gatherers, who had replaced the atlatl with the more accurate bow and arrow. Their arrowheads, knives, choppers and scrapers were of fine quality, as were their metates and manos. Pottery shards indicate that these people had trading relationships with the Basketmaker and later Pueblo peoples to the east. Shell beads found in Death Valley also show similar contact with Pacific coast tribes to the west. The Saratoga Springs people left rings of stone, suggesting they might have been "sleeping circles" or even makeshift houses. They also left curious rock alignments on the desert floor called geoglyphs. These are very difficult to date, and their purpose still mystifies archaeologists. The conventional wisdom is that they were for religious or mystical purposes, just like the petroglyphs pecked into rocks. What happened to these people remains unclear. The Shoshone peoples moved in about 1000 AD, and for a while the two cultures existed side by side. Some think the Saratoga people were simply absorbed by the newcomers.

Saratoga Spring

There are remains of two stone cabins at Saratoga Spring. These no doubt go back many years, perhaps more than a century to the 20-mule team borax days. I recall one cold and stormy night here at Saratoga Spring back in the 1950s, when I was roaming around this country in my surplus WWII G.I. Weapons Carrier. At that time, one of the stone cabins was still intact, complete with a roof. Rather than sleeping outside in the wind and rain, I threw my sleeping bag on the cabin floor and was quite cozy. I was not alone, however. As soon as I turned the lantern out, the cabin was alive with the scurry of little feet. Being unable to sleep, I decided to attempt to capture my hosts on film. I set up a camera and flash on a tripod in front of a few broken pieces of vanilla cookies, and turned out the lantern again. I did not have to wait long in the dark. Upon hearing a munching sound I depressed the cable release on the camera, and voila! Little did that packrat know his photograph would be appearing in a guidebook nearly sixty years later.

The author's roommate enjoys a cookie.

As dead as the desert may seem in the daytime to the uninitiated, nocturnal life abounds once the sun goes down. One of these nocturnal creatures is the packrat of the genus *Neotoma*. Packrats get their name from the curious behavioral pattern of collecting odd bits and pieces of material, which seemingly have no particular use, to put in their den. When gathering such an item, they often exchange it for another object. The unraveling of a packrat's nest often reveals expended .22 gauge shotgun shells, bits of bright shiny metal, and God only knows what. I have awakened in the morning to find things missing. I once found a Canadian nickel on a rock beside the campfire; I knew it had not been there the night before.

Known as middens, packrats' nests can have great scientific value. Scientists have found well-preserved nests in caves and rock shelters that have been radiocarbon dated as old as 45,000 years. The packrat selects one spot in his home in which to defecate and urinate, something it does often. During the animal's life, this perch is usually moist. Pollen from nearby plants will adhere to this sticky surface. Thousands of years later some paleobotanist like Dr. Ken Cole comes along, dissects the midden, and extracts the tiny pollen grains. From those, he can identify the dominant plant types, giving us a good look at what vegetation was growing here during the last Ice Age. These middens can also reveal ancient insects, and bird and small mammal bones. USGS geologist Robert Thompson found a packrat nest in Nevada that was lined with scorpion tails. That must have been one very aggressive packrat with attitude!

A typical packrat midden

From Saratoga Spring, it is but four miles south to the graded Harry Wade Road (N35°38.811 W116°23.496). From here, you can turn right, returning to State Route 178 after 25.7 miles. Or by turning left, State Route 127 is just 4.1 miles to the east.

Big Pine A Long Time Ago

Big Pine in the 1890s

Big Pine's Butler Hotel

Big Pine circa 1920
(Above photos courtesy of Richard McCutchan)

Chapter VI

Trails Out Of Big Pine

For the outdoorsman, Big Pine is synonymous with hunting and fishing in the High Sierra or possibly mountaineering in the Palisades. Thus, it may seem like a strange place to make a gateway to Death Valley National Park. However, with the passage of the 1994 California Desert Protection Act, which created Death Valley National Park and greatly expanded its boundaries to the west, Big Pine has indeed now become the jumping-off place for hundreds of square miles in the northwest corner of the park. Most of this parkland is roadless *wilderness*, but it remains closer to Big Pine than anyplace else. Since this isolated portion of the park receives relatively few visitors, the National Park Service has not yet established an information office in Big Pine, as they have in Beatty. Check with the Interagency Visitor Center in Lone Pine for up to date road information.

In addition to the backcountry excursions described herein, there are lots of additional opportunities for backroad exploring in the White and Inyo Mountains east of Big Pine. (Those routes are described in *Inyo-Mono SUV Trails*.)

Big Pine's roots go back to 1869. Once the Owens Valley Indian Wars were over, small farming communities began to develop up and down the valley, and Big Pine was one of them. The community got a big boost in 1877-78, when an irrigation ditch system better distributed the waters of the Owens River, and farms flourished. That all came to an end in 1924, as the City of Los Angeles acquired the water rights and the ditches dried up. Big Pine became relegated to being a bedroom community of its larger cousin Bishop, just fourteen miles to the north.

Nevertheless, 1200 people still call Big Pine home. It has a market, two sporting goods stores, four places to eat and four motels. It also has a couple of gas stations; your fuel tanks should be topped off before heading east. Take advantage of these services, for there will be none where you are going.

23

Steel Pass from the Eureka Valley

Primary Attraction:	A visit to "singing" sand dunes and lonely landscapes.
Time Required:	From Big Pine to the summit of Steel Pass and return will take the better part of a day.
Miles Involved:	It is 48 miles from Big Pine to the Eureka Dunes, from where it is another 15 miles to the summit of Steel Pass. If you elect to cross over into the Saline Valley and return from there, the round trip distance back to Big Pine is another 70 miles. **Do not under estimate your fuel consumption. Top off your tank before leaving Big Pine. There are no services anywhere along the way.**
Maps:	1:100,000 Last Chance Range sheet; 1:24,000 East of Joshua Flats, Hanging Rock Canyon, and Last Chance Range SW Quadrangles.
Degree of Difficulty:	The access roads to the Eureka Dunes are Class I or better. Beyond the dunes, it is a Class II road to the lower narrows in Dedeckera Canyon. Here, there are four rock ledges to be climbed: Class IV, III, III, and IV in that order. Once over these obstacles, it is all Class II to the summit, except for one more short, but steep hillside that has a Class III pitch.

One of the most lonely jeep trails that you are likely to find in the Death Valley area is the cross-country route between the Eureka Valley and the Saline Valley. It is not shown on many maps, and hence people may not realize such a road even exists. **You should not be attempting this route, unless you have another vehicle with you.** The route can be done in either direction; however, it might be a little easier going from south to north.

On the northern edge of Big Pine, take State Route 168 eastward, as if you were going into the White Mountains (N37°10.387 W118°17.401); reset your odometer as you leave Highway 395. After crossing the Owens River, you will come to the site of Zurich Siding on the old roadbed of the narrow gauge Carson & Colorado Railroad that went through here between 1883 and 1960. Soon a paved road to the left goes north to the "big ears" of the Cal Tech radio astronomy parabolic dishes pointed skyward. Here deep within the Owens Valley, sheltered by the High Sierra on one side and the Inyo Mountains on the other side, is a listening post for radio waves coming from deep space.

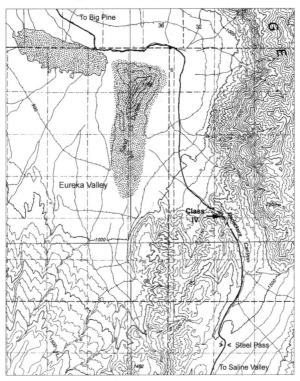

There is an intersection with paved roads on each fork 2.3 miles from Highway 395 (N37°11.096 W116°15.174). The left fork is State Route 168; go to the right on the Death Valley Road. It climbs into the Inyo Mountains, passing through a narrows known as Devil's Gate. At a point 13.6 miles from Highway 395, a dirt side road goes right to Papoose Flat in the heart of the Inyo Mountains; continue east on the paved road. In another 1.9 miles, the graded dirt Waucoba Saline Road turns off to the right (see Excursion #24). Keep left on the paved Death Valley Road to go into the Eureka Valley (N37°08.256 W118°03.197).

The crest of the Inyo Mountains is crossed 16.3 miles from Highway 395, and the road begins its descent into the Eureka Valley. The paved road stays just outside of the national park boundary as it goes through Little Cowhorn Valley, crosses Joshua Flat and drops down into the Eureka Valley. Once on the valley floor, the road makes a sharp turn to the right, and the pavement ends 31.8 miles from Big Pine. The next seven miles are graded gravel.

At one time it was possible to take a Class III road north from the big bend into Fish Lake Valley by way of colorful Horse Thief Canyon, where petroglyphs can be found. Another Class III route left at this curve to go northwest into Soldier Pass Canyon. Both of those routes were closed on October 31, 1994, with the passage of the California Desert Protection Act and the creation of the Piper Mountain Wilderness.

The graded dirt road heads southeast through a narrow BLM corridor that has national park land on either side. A graded road goes off to the left 38.1 miles from Highway 395 (N37°14.341 W117°47.356). It occupies a narrow corridor between the Piper Mountain Wilderness on the left and the Sylvania Wilderness on the right. This is the present day route into Fish Lake Valley, where it connects with State Routes 168 and 266.

At a point 0.6 miles beyond this intersection, 38.7 miles from Highway 395, a side road to the right goes south to the Eureka Valley Sand Dunes. This is the way to Steel Pass. If you continue straight ahead instead, you will pass the sulfur mining camp of Crater, and eventually enter the northern end of Death Valley. It is 38.4 miles from this intersection to the nearest gas pump at Scotty's Castle.

After resetting your odometer, turn right, and immediately enter Death Valley National Park. At a point 9.2 miles from the Death Valley Road, and just before reaching the dunes, the road turns to the east. Soon you will pass a small campground on the right. It is "primitive" by National Park Service standards in that it consists only of picnic tables and a vault toilet. Users are expected to carry out their own trash. No camping fees are being charged.

The Eureka Sand Dunes, a National Natural Landmark

The large natural sand pile is 680 feet high, 3.3 miles long, and 1½ miles wide, making it the highest dune in California. The U.S. Department of the

Interior designated these sand dunes as a Natural Landmark in 1984, when the Bureau of Land Management administered the area. The area was put into Death Valley National Park with the passage of the 1994 California Desert Protection Act. Driving and camping on the dunes is prohibited; however, you can walk out upon the dunes, which is something I would recommend.

This dune is one of only two sand dunes in California that are known to *bark* or *boom* when conditions are just right. (Other such dunes that exhibit this strange phenomenon are the Kelso Dunes south of Baker in the Mojave National Preserve Devil's Playground, and three localities in Nevada.) The *booming* or *roaring* sound can be generated when conditions are just right, by starting sand avalanches off the top of the dune. In order to achieve the effect, the sand grains must be (1) very dry and in very low humidity, (2) well sorted, and (3) of medium size.

These dunes have been forming here since the end of the Pleistocene glaciation. The sand contains five species of beetles that have evolved here independently of beetles elsewhere. They are now unique, found nowhere else in the world. This situation is similar to the evolution of the desert pupfish and minnows in Death Valley, and the Inyo black toad of Deep Springs Valley. Also present are three rare and endangered plants: the Eureka Dune Grass *Swallenia alexandrae,* the Eureka Evening Primrose *Oenothera avita eurekensis*, and the Nevada Oryctes *Oryctes nevandensis,* plus one rare plant, the Shining Locoweed or milk-vetch *Astragalus lentiginosus micans.* **Please do not disturb any insects or plants, while you are walking upon the sand.**

The Class I road continues eastward along the northern base of the dunes, and then turns south again to eventually circle the eastern end of the dune field. Ahead and to the east are colorful layers of brown strata in the Last Chance Range. These are old marine sediments of Cambrian and Ordovician age. Those layers with the conspicuous horizontal stripes are the Bonanza King Formation. Below it is the Carrara Formation; above it is the Nopah Formation. The oldest is 560 million years old, the youngest 500 million years.

Although the road crosses areas of powdery fine silt that turns into bottomless mud in wet weather, as well as traversing some sections of soft sand, the trail remains mostly Class I for nearly five miles beyond the campground. Then fourteen miles in from the Eureka Valley Road, the trail deteriorates to Class II. It is another two miles to Dedeckera Canyon.

Dedeckera Canyon was named after a plant discovered by the very accomplished amateur botanist Mary DeDecker of Independence. The California Native Plant Society considers the shrub July Gold *Dedeckera eurekensi* a rare plant. It is only found on north facing limestone slopes between 3,500 and 7,000 feet in the White, Inyo, and Panamint Mountains, including in this locality.

Your real backcountry adventure begins upon entering Dedeckera Canyon. You are in the canyon no more than ¼ mile when the lower narrows are reached. Here you will encounter four sections of bare bedrock ledges that you must climb up and over. These obstacles are less than fifty yards apart. Fortunately, each is only ten to fifteen feet long. At one time someone poured a bit of concrete here to make the going easier, but that has mostly washed out. The first ledge is Class IV, followed by two at Class III, and the last Class IV again. (The first rock ledge is rather narrow, and Loris considers it to be Class V. I rate all four ledges as only Class III for those coming down the canyon.) Short wheelbase 4WD vehicles, with high clearance and without running boards, should have no serious problems. **Drivers of wide or long wheelbase vehicles should get out, and first scout the way on foot.** Once these obstacles have been overcome, the road ahead is mostly Class II.

The Dedeckera Canyon narrows

The upper narrows are ¼ mile above the lower narrows, but they present no problems for vehicles. This is a good place to look at the very old Cambrian marine sediments of the Nopah Formation. Dedeckera Canyon was eroded out of the crushed rocks in a fault zone. The NPS would prefer that visitors not camp in Dedeckera Canyon, because of the sensitive botanic habitat.

Once you pass through the upper narrows, the canyon is left behind and the country soon opens up. Should you pass this way in the winter, the hillsides will appear to be rusty brown from the dry stems of the Wild Buckwheat

Eriogonum fasciculatum var. *polifolium*. The springtime is another matter. The many wildflowers found here range from the lowly carpet phlox to the tall stately Prince's Plume *Stanleya pinnata*.

The Class II road skirts around the western edge of a large Joshua tree covered flat to head for a gap in the lava-covered mesas. This dark basalt lava poured out of the earth during Pliocene times, covering many hundreds of square miles. The volcanism was not a one-time event, but occurred over a long period of time. Sometimes it was ash, rather than lava, that was ejected from the volcanic vents. The road passes such a layer of white ash at a point three miles above the upper narrows.

A layer of white volcanic ash is sandwiched between two layers of basalt lava.

You will encounter a short, but steep hill a mile beyond the outcrop of ash. Engage your four-wheel drive, and put your transmission in low range. If the road is dry, this Class III ascent should cause no serious problem. Once you are on top, it is only 1.5 miles across the broad flat to Steel Pass, seemingly named for a steel post that once stood here at the 4,500' elevation. A two pound coffee can holds a register in which people passing through can leave their names and comments.

Prior to the 1994 inclusion of this area into Death Valley National Park, Steel Pass saw relatively few backcountry travelers. When I first came this way in the 1960s, I doubt if the route over the pass saw more than a dozen vehicles a year. The summit register now suggests that figure has increased substantially. **This is still very lonely country; it is no place to face a vehicle breakdown. For this reason a party of at least two vehicles is recommended.**

If you elect to continue, it is 12 miles from Steel Pass to Lower Warm Springs in the Saline Valley. The first two miles below Steel Pass are Class III, as the route twists and winds its way through the boulder-filled alluvium. The remaining 10 miles to Lower Warm Springs is all a slow, but generally easy Class II.

24

The Saline Valley Road

Primary Attraction: Hot springs, sand dunes, gold mines, salt marshes, bird watching, old borax works and salt trams are all things to see along the Saline Valley Road.

Time Required: A minimum of two days should be allowed to properly see the sights of the Saline Valley.

Miles Involved: It is one hundred miles from Highway 395 in Big Pine to State Route 190. **No services of any kind are available along the way. Be sure your gas tank is topped off before you leave Big Pine.**

Maps: 1:100,000 Last Chance Range, Saline Valley, and Darwin Hills sheets; 1:24,000 Uhlmeyer Spring, Cowhorn Valley, Waucoba Spring, Pat Keyes Canyon, Lower Warm Springs, Craig Canyon, West of Ubehebe Peak, Nelson Range, Jackass Canyon, Lee Wash, and Santa Rosa Flat Quadrangles.

Degree of Difficulty: Although it has a washboard surface for many miles, the main Saline Valley Road is a wide graded strip that cannot even be considered Class I in difficulty. However, there are many side roads going off the Saline Valley Road that lead to interesting features. These side roads range in difficulty from Class II to Class IV.

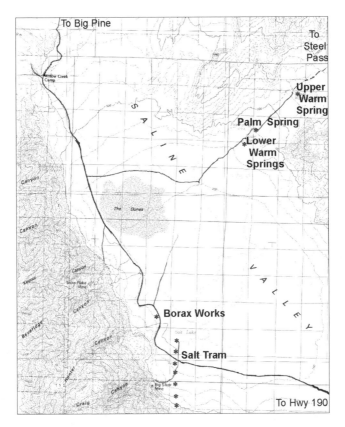

An enormous region of more than four hundred square miles, the Saline Valley was added to the newly created Death Valley National Park with the passage of the California Desert Protection Act late in 1994. This vast area is rich in archaeological and historical resources, has some interesting geologic features, and contains some very important wildlife habitat. Running through this enclosed basin is a rough road, occasionally maintained by the County of Inyo. Along this thin strand of graded dirt, access can be made to old gold mines, salt mines, borax works, sand dunes, hot springs, well-watered canyons, and salt marshes. The Saline Valley Road has a little something for everyone.

Your backroad odyssey begins on Highway 395 at the north edge of Big Pine. Here there is a U.S. Forest Service display describing the ancient Bristlecone pines of the White Mountains. There is also a campground. Reset your odometer as you leave Highway 395, and take State Route 168 eastward (N37°10.387 W118°17.401).

After crossing the Owens River, you will come to the site of Zurich Siding on the old roadbed of the narrow gauge Carson & Colorado Railroad that went through here between 1883 and 1960. A paved road to the left goes north to the "big ears" of the Cal Tech radio astronomy parabolic dishes pointed skyward. Here deep within the Owens Valley, sheltered by the High Sierra on one side and the Inyo Mountains on the other side, is a listening post for radio waves coming from deep space.

There is an intersection 2.3 miles from Highway 395, with paved roads on each fork (N37°11.096 W116°15.174). The left fork is State Route 168, the main access route into the White Mountains. Stay to the right on the Death Valley Road that climbs into the Inyo Mountains, passing through a narrows known as Devil's Gate. At a point 13.6 miles from Highway 395, a dirt side road goes right to Papoose Flat in the heart of the Inyo Mountains (see *Inyo-Mono SUV Trails*). Continue east on the paved road another 1.8 miles to where the graded dirt Waucoba Saline Road turns off to the right; this is 15.4 miles from Highway 395 (N37°08.256 W118°03.197). Those wishing to go into the Eureka Valley (see Excursion #23) should keep to the left on the paved road. Reset your odometer, and turn to the right on the graded Inyo County road for your visit to the Saline Valley.

A sign announces that it is 67 miles to the Hunter Mountain Road and 84 miles to State Highway 190. **Be forewarned: there are no services of any kind for the next one hundred miles**. A second sign announces that the road is not plowed in the winter. The 7,500' elevation here is the high point of the entire route. Keep in mind that if you do visit the Saline Valley during the winter months, there is the possibility that a storm could bury this road in deep snow at any time. The road at the southern end of the valley goes over a 6,200' high point that could also be closed by snow. Unwary drivers of conventional vehicles have found themselves stranded in the Saline Valley with no way out. Persons with four-wheel drive vehicles do have two additional options: they can exit over the Class III Steel Pass route that has a high point of 4,500 feet (see Excursion #23). A second option would be to go up the Lippencott Grade to the Racetrack (see Excursion #28). The high point on that route is 3,900 feet. In recent years, the NPS has taken a blade over the Lippencott road, and it may be passable to two-wheel drive vehicles having high clearance. However for 45 of the past 50 years, this route has usually been passable to 4WD vehicles only.

The graded Waucoba Saline Road begins a gradual descent as it heads to the southeast. The road forks 1.3 miles from the pavement; stay to the right, but both forks come together again in ¼ mile.

The road stays just outside the Death Valley National Park boundary as it skirts around the southern end of Cowhorn Valley, and remains so for the next four miles as it continues its gradual descent. Unfortunately, the road surface feels like you are driving over an old fashioned washboard. Then, a little more than six miles from the pavement, the graded road begins a series of steep switchbacks down into Marble Canyon just ½ mile below, and you enter Death Valley National Park.

Placer gold was discovered in the sandy gravel of Marble Canyon as early as 1882. Dry washers operated here regularly from 1894 until 1906, and again during the depression years of the 1930s. It was found that the richest gravels were on top of the bedrock, some 100 plus feet down. The shafts and mine headframes you see today date from this later era. The lode source of this gold may be close, but it has never been found.

One of the gold mines in Marble Canyon

The county road turns left and heads down Marble Canyon. After ¼ mile, a Class III side road climbs steeply up a draw to the south side to the Opal Mine. If you want to visit this old mine, there is an easier way to get there; stay on the county road going down Marble Canyon.

After descending Marble Canyon for 1.4 miles, the county road suddenly makes a right turn to climb out of the defile via Opal Canyon (N37°05.474 W117°57.871). The side road to the left continues down Marble Canyon, crosses Jackass Flats, and after seven miles eventually ends at an unnamed playa.

A half-mile up from the bottom of Marble Canyon, a Class II and III side road to the right goes to the Opal and Silver Spur Mines. They were minor silver and lead producers around the Turn of the 20th Century.

The Waucoba Saline Road continues to head south, gradually gaining altitude. The piñon-juniper forest is entered at Whippoorwill Flat, and for the next several miles there are some nice campsites along the road. Prior to October 31, 1994, you could camp here and have a cheery campfire. Camping is still permitted, but now that this is part of the national park, campfires are prohibited.

Today the piñon-juniper forest in the greater Death Valley area extends from 5,800 feet on up to 9,000 feet or more, but this has not always been the case. By examining 10,000-20,000 year old packrat middens in Death Valley, paleobotanists Phillip Wells and Deborah Woodcock, together with Geffrey Spaulding working in the Eureka Valley, found that at the end of the Pleistocene Ice Age, the juniper trees *Juniperus osteosperma* were growing much lower, perhaps down to 1,000 feet. They also found widespread evidence of the Whipple yucca *Yucca whipplei* that no longer grows anywhere in the Death Valley area. These finds substantiate the long held views that those times were cooler and somewhat wetter, but still provided a semi-arid environment. Interestingly, no pollen of the piñon pine was found. Scientists working throughout the Great Basin region have a wealth of evidence suggesting that these trees moved in during the mid-Holocene, 3,000 to 4,000 years after the Pleistocene ice had retreated.

It is curious to note that many of the juniper trees here are infested with mistletoe *Phoradendron juniperium,* a true plant parasite. However, the piñon trees growing just a few feet away have no mistletoe growing on them.

After reaching the 7,300' high point that some call North Pass, you begin the sometimes-steep descent of Whippoorwill Canyon. The piñon-juniper forest is soon left behind, and with that are the first distant views of the salt flats at the bottom of the Saline Valley, still nearly 25 miles away. The road crosses the upper Waucoba Wash drainage, goes over a notch in a ridge, and begins its long straight descent into the Saline Valley.

At a point nearly 17 miles in from the pavement, a Class II side road right heads up the alluvial fan to the base of the Inyo Mountains (N36°54.680 W117°54.461). If you have time for a little exploration off the main road, this might be the place to do it. By taking this side road to the right, you will come to a fork in 1.6 miles (N36°54.860 W117°56.251). The branch to the left will take you to the remains of the Blue Monster and Lucky Boy Mines. If you continue straight ahead, the road will deteriorate to Class III as you enter lower Lead Canyon, so named by miners who found that commodity here. If you bear to the right upon entering Lead Canyon, you will find the Bunker Hill Mine. All of these mines sought lead and silver. Return to the Waucoba Saline Road, but keep in mind that future odometer readings will have to be adjusted by the number of extra miles you have driven.

Continue south on the Waucoba Saline Road. A Class I side road 22 miles in from the pavement goes right a short distance to the private property surrounding Willow Creek Camp (N36°50.313 W117°55.106). The camp has served as the offices, shops, and living quarters for a number of nearby talc mines, including the White Eagle and Gray Eagle Mines. Those mines have operated on and off for many years; but even when they are closed, the camp remains occupied.

Now called the Saline Valley Road, our road continues its gradual descent for the next five miles, heading for the distant sand dunes. At a point 32 miles in from the pavement, an unmarked Class I side road goes off to the left (N36°47.069 W117°52.986). This is the dusty road to Lower Warm Springs, one of the premier attractions in the Saline Valley. (For a description of this road to Lower Warm Springs and points beyond, see Excursion # 25.)

The main Saline Valley Road forks 1.5 miles south of the Warm Springs turnoff. You may take either fork, as they soon rejoin. The branch to the left has one hundred yards or so of flour-like dust, but it gets you much closer to the sand dunes. Go left if you wish to visit the dunes.

The Saline Valley Sand Dunes

The main county road goes to the right. After ¼ mile, a Class II side road heads up the alluvial fan towards the Snow Flake Talc Mine, perched on the hillside high above Beveridge Canyon. This road becomes a rocky Class III after only a mile.

In this canyon is the site of Beveridge, one of the most remote ghost towns in the west. I have spent about a week camping and exploring around this old camp: once after a long 8-hour backpack over 10,668' New York Butte, and once after a 40-minute helicopter ride from the Lone Pine Airport. I can tell you without any reservation, the helicopter was easier! The site of Beveridge can also be reached by climbing up from the Snow Flake Talc Mine. The route from the Saline Valley is more strenuous than the Burgess Mine route (see *Inyo-Mono SUV Trails*) that goes over the top of the Inyos to descend to the camp. The Snow Flake Talc Mine route involves a dry trail less climb of some 3,000 feet in the most rugged country in the Death Valley region.

Continuing south on the Saline Valley Road beyond the Snow Flake Talc Mine turnoff, the "sand dune cutoff" comes in from the left after a mile (N36°43.992 W117°50.579). Here you can look to the right and see the Snow Flake Talc Mine road switch-backing 1500' up the mountainside. After another 1.5 miles, another miner's camp with its enormous junk pile lies hidden behind the mesquite thicket on the left. A side road to the right goes up to the mouth of Beveridge Canyon, where the year around stream disappears into the alluvial fan.

South of the Warm Springs turnoff at 36.4 mile, a large salt cedar tree marks the beginning of private property on both sides of the county road. A half-mile ahead, Artesian Road goes off to the left (N36°42.844 W117°50.037). This Class II road was once a very dusty alternative route to Lower Warm Springs. Most of that road has now been closed by *wilderness* designation, but that was no great loss. The road now stops at an artesian well two miles to the northeast.

A tenth of a mile south of Artesian Road, the crusty white ruins of the Conn and Trudo Borax Works can be seen on either side of the county road. Borax was found here long before similar deposits in Death Valley were exploited. Partners Conn and Trudo began extracting the borate minerals here in 1875. This was six years before Aaron Winters recognized the white substance in Death Valley, seven years before Isadore Daunet started the Eagle Borax Works, and nine years before Coleman and Smith started the Harmony Borax Works in 1884 and the Amargosa Borax Works in the following year. Conn and Trudo operated here continuously until 1907, hauling their product out by wagon via San Lucas Canyon, a route that has subsequently become hopelessly washed out.

Remains of the Conn and Trudo Borax Works

Continuing south on the county road, a fence on the left marks the beginning of the wildlife refuge established by the BLM and the State Department of Fish and Game in the days prior to the Saline Valley Salt Marsh being added to Death

Valley National Park. Continue on down the county road, and you will find a short side road entering the fenced-off refuge. The salt marsh is an excellent place to observe wildlife, particularly the birds, some of which live here all year around. Many more species simply stop and rest on their annual migration routes.

The abundance of wildlife did not escape the notice of prehistoric man either. Many archaeological sites have been found throughout the Saline Valley. Most were winter camps occupied only seasonally by small bands, but the vast number of sites found suggests a very long period of use, perhaps 2,000 years. Small bands of Shoshone have occupied the Saline Valley even in historic times.

Just beyond the end of the wildlife fence, roads leave the county road on the right and the left (N36°41.078 W117°48.940). To the right, a Class II road goes up the alluvial fan to the still privately owned Essex Mine, later called the Big Silver Mine. On the other side of the county road, a pair of tracks follows the old salt tram towers 0.7 miles down to the water's edge. The last fifty yards of this road can get very muddy, so park well back from the water.

Towers of the old salt tram

Salt of remarkable purity was extracted from the brine in the bottom of the Saline Valley during World War I. Test shafts sunk into the old lake bed revealed that the salt deposits were at least thirty feet thick. This tramline was used to hoist the product some 7500' up Daisy Canyon and out of the Saline Valley, to the 8,900' crest of the Inyo Mountains, and then down 5200 feet to a railroad terminal at the eastern edge of Owens Lake near Swansea. The tramline was 13 miles long and a masterpiece of engineering. It was added to the National

Register of Historic Places in 1974. What you see here are the last few towers at the eastern end. Many of the towers between the salt lake and the bottom of Daisy Canyon are gone. For the very ambitious, however, the old mule trail used in construction of the tram can still be followed up Daisy Canyon, where many of the towers still survive. For those less eager for exercise, the summit station can also be visited by taking a breathtaking Class III road along the Inyo Crest (described in *Inyo-Mono SUV Trails*).

The Saline Valley Road heads east along the valley floor for the next 17 miles, and then gradually turns south again as it climbs the bajada. Eleven miles beyond the salt tram, a 4' high rock cairn on the left marks the turnoff to the Lippencott Grade (N36°37.198 W117°38.933). This road will take you to the Racetrack playa and, from there, on to the Hunter Mountain Road or the road to Ubehebe Craters (see Excursion #28). In the last forty years the Lippencott Grade road has been closed by washouts more than it has been open, so it is best to check with the Rangers before attempting it. Nevertheless, it does make a potential escape route from the Saline Valley, should both ends of the county road be buried in deep snow.

The Saline Valley and the nearby Lee Flat area are still home to a population of feral burros, in spite of the best efforts of the BLM and the NPS to eliminate them. Four miles beyond the Lippencott Grade turnoff, a small area to the left is fenced off. Some years, back the BLM erected this burro exclosure to study the effects wild burros were having on the desert forage. As you can see, the plants outside the fence look pretty much the same as those protected on the inside. The empirical evidence at this exlosure pretty much supports the findings of NPS researchers Ralph and Florence Welles who, in the period from 1954 to 1961, tried to determine if the feral burros were having an adverse impact on the bighorn sheep populations. They observed healthy bands of each species living side by side in mutual habitat, and concluded the perceived burro impact was highly over-rated. Nevertheless, two decades after the Welles' study, the feral burro population had doubled. By the 1980s, the wild burro population reached the point that they could no longer be ignored by the BLM and the NPS. Further, the National Park Service is philosophically dedicated to the removal of all exotic species within the park. Resource managers won't be happy until the last of the remaining burros are rounded up or shot. The only drawback to the *final solution of the burro problem* is that it costs the government $1,500.00 for each and every burro disposed of. Full funding of the endeavor has been a problem, but the project moves forward, and soon Death Valley National Park will be burro-free.

Six miles beyond the Lippencott Grade turnoff, the county road enters Grapevine Canyon, and the geology changes dramatically. Gone are the Paleozoic marine sediments seen previously all along the eastern face of the Inyo Range. Here we find quartz monzonite, a silica-rich form of granite. Of early Cretaceous Age, this igneous rock is probably closely related to similar igneous rocks introduced in the Sierra Nevada about that same period of time.

Geology also played a key element in the formation of Grapevine Canyon. It was a series of faults that pushed the eastern flank of the Inyo Mountains upward in relation to the floor of the Saline Valley. That fault system turns at the base of Daisy Canyon and heads to the southeast, heading directly for the Panamint Valley sand dunes. Grapevine Canyon was eroded out of the broken and sheared off rocks along this fault zone. This same zone of broken rock also allows subsurface water to seep to the surface creating a series of springs. In the spring, particularly in wet years, there is a small stream that runs the entire course of the canyon. This water not only supports a thick jungle of grapevines, from which the canyon gets its name, but it also supports a wide variety of birds, reptiles, and mammals. As you drive along the road, you are likely to flush out dove, quail, and chukars. These birds all rely on that life giving trickle of water. There are precious few good places to camp in the Grapevine Canyon; but if you do, remember the policy requires that you do not camp within 200 yards of any water source.

The road up Grapevine Canyon is a bit steep in places, but it is good and most vehicles should have little problem. Near the top of this 4½-mile long canyon, an old corral reminds us that this was, and still is, cattle country. Grazing was not permitted in the old Death Valley Monument, but the BLM did have a few grazing allotments in lands outside the monument. When the new and greatly expanded Death Valley National Park was created on October 31, 1994, three pre-existing BLM grazing allotments where included in the park expansion. These cattlemen were able to retain their grazing permits within the new park. Thus it is that you may see cattle in Grapevine Canyon.

The top of Grapevine Canyon is reached 30.3 miles from the Lower Warm Springs turnoff and 78.4 miles from Big Pine, and we come to the Hunter Mountain Road at an elevation just a few feet short of 6,000 feet (N36°31.603 W117°32.807); some call this South Pass. The Hunter Mountain Road is also graded, and is often in better condition than the Saline Valley Road. By turning left, you can cross Hunter Mountain and eventually descend to Ubehebe Craters and the floor of Death Valley. By this route it is 52½ miles to the nearest gas pump at Scotty's Castle.

You will want to turn right to go to State Route 190. Proceed one tenth-mile, then stop, get out, and look over the edge; it is a grand view. Below is Mill Canyon, and beyond are the Panamint Valley sand dunes. Still further out, the entire length of Panamint Valley stretches to the south.

The road soon enters the piñon-juniper forest and, within a mile of South Pass, climbs to a 6,250' high point. From here, the rest of the way is all downhill. Five miles from South Pass, the road begins to cross Lee Flat with its enormous Joshua tree forest. Joshua trees *Yucca brevifolia* are closely related to other types of yuccas. Joshua trees are considered to be indicator plants of the Mojave Desert. They are widespread throughout the higher elevations in the deserts of Southern California, as well as Southern Nevada, and small portions of NW Arizona and SW Utah. They were supposedly so named by the Mormon pioneers entering Utah, who thought they resembled Joshua lifting his arms to heaven.

Pay close attention to the road ahead. This is open range where the cattle can roam freely. Cattle grazing is not permitted in most of our national parks, but when the new lands were added to the newly formed Death Valley National Park in 1994, the NPS inherited three grazing permittees from the BLM. Today, the only one left is the Hunter Mountain Allotment.

Lee Flat

Seven miles from South Pass, the first traces of asphalt begin to appear on the roadway, and the park boundary is reached in another mile. A mile and a half beyond the entrance sign, a side road to the left goes 1.2 miles over to the Lee Mines, Wonder Mine and Silver Reid Mine (see pages 197-198). Eleven miles from South Pass, and a little more than a mile beyond the turnoff to the Lee Mines, a side road to the right crosses the western edge of Lee Flat. It then descends into San Lucas Canyon before climbing again to an 8,200' high point at the old mining camp of Cerro Gordo.

For State Route 190, stay to the left on the now mostly paved road. The highway is but six miles to the south. Once at Highway 190 (N36°19.839 W117°42.912), you may find yourself low on fuel. You have two options: you can turn left, descend into Panamint Valley and proceed 63 miles to Trona, or go over Towne Pass to Stovepipe Wells. By going this way, the nearest gas pump is 12.7 miles at Panamint Springs Resort or 38 miles at Stovepipe Wells. By turning right, the nearest gas pump is 32 miles at Olancha or 35 miles in Lone Pine.

25

Steel Pass from the Saline Valley

Primary Attraction: Natural hot springs, suitable for bathing. You can also experience the true desert wilderness from the comfort of your car.

Time Required: The traverse of Steel Pass into the Eureka Valley is an all day outing.

Miles Involved: From Lower Warm Springs to the summit of Steel Pass is only fifteen miles. However, the distance from Big Pine to Lower Warm Springs, then over Steel Pass into the Eureka Valley and back to Big Pine again is 124 miles. **Do not underestimate your fuel consumption! Top off your tank before leaving Big Pine.**

Maps: 1:100,000 Saline Valley and Last Chance Range sheets; 1:24,000 Lower Warm Springs, West of Teakettle Junction, Saline Peak, and Last Chance Range SW Quadrangles

Degree of Difficulty: The Saline Valley Road to the Warm Springs turnoff is graded dirt, and while it has a washboard surface in places, it is a maintained road. The seven miles from the Saline Valley Road to Lower Warm Springs is all Class I. From there on, the next thirteen miles are Class II, with the last 2.3 miles to the summit being generally Class III. For those wishing to go on over the pass into the Eureka Valley, the route is mostly Class II, with only one short section of Class III descending a series of four rock ledges in lower Dedeckera Canyon.

One of the most lonely jeep trails that you are likely to find in the Death Valley area is the cross-country route between the Saline Valley and the Eureka Valley. It is not shown on many maps and hence people may not realize such a route even exists. **This is a route you should not attempt unless you have another vehicle with you.** The route can be done from either direction, with the Saline to Eureka Valley direction being a little easier on your vehicle.

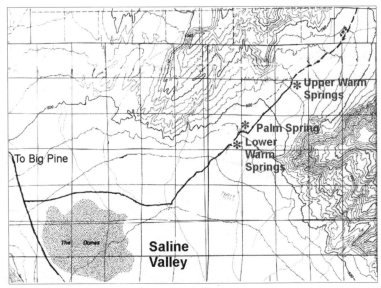

Our backroad outing to Steel Pass begins at the turnoff to Lower Warm Springs from the Saline Valley Road (N36°47.069 W117°52.986). This is 48 miles in from Big Pine, the last 32 miles of which are graded dirt.

Although not maintained by Inyo County, as is the Saline Valley Road, the Lower Warm Springs road is nevertheless Class I, making it passable to all vehicles, including motor homes and those pulling travel trailers. It heads due east, passing the northern margin of the Saline Valley sand dunes that cover about six square miles. These northern-most dunes don't shift much with the wind, because clusters of mesquite have stabilized them. An early morning stroll across the sand will reveal a wide variety of animal tracks left the previous night.

A cluster of mesquite and palm trees is reached after seven miles. An NPS sign says *Saline Warm Springs - Clothing Optional Use Area.* The main road stays to the left, but other turnoffs to the right go to campsites nestled amid the mesquite thickets.

The many acres of travertine terraces here suggest the warm springs have shifted around a bit during the last 10,000 years; however, they seemingly have always attracted man. Artifacts found on the elevated desert pavement nearby show that Native Americans camped here, at least during the winter months. In historic times, the springs attracted workers from nearby borate, silver and salt mines, and as early as the 1920s, even a few tourists. In the late 1940s and early 1950s, articles about the warm springs appeared in the pages of *Desert Magazine,* and the secrets of the Saline Valley began to get out. More and more people were finding their way in here. Citizens built improvements, piping the warm waters to concrete-lined pools where they could soak a weary body in relative comfort. *Al fresco* bathing has been a long-standing tradition at the warm springs, a practice that continues to this day. While the pools are technically a "clothing optional area", in practice many of the bathers are wearing only a big smile.

Lower Warm Springs was the home of a hippie colony of considerable size in the 1960s. In spite of their professed commitment to love and peace, these folks sometimes displayed hostility to "outsiders" and casual visitors. The Bureau of Land Management had so many complaints, they had to step in and assume more authority and control over the site. The BLM made it a more family friendly public spa, and permitted a permanent volunteer caretaker to look after things. Besides keeping the pool clean, he planted palm trees, constructed steel fire pits, and installed two outhouses (one of which has a solar-voltaic powered electric light!) The National Park Service generally did not change things when the area was included in Death Valley National Park late in 1994. Indeed, the caretaker has been provided with a radio transceiver for emergency use.

Prior to 1994 under BLM control, and under NPS management since then, camping at no charge has been permitted anywhere around Warm Springs, for periods of up to 30 days. That could change at some point in the future. The Park Service is considering the construction of walk-in campsites from a central parking area. With that, the charging of nightly camping fees seems sure to follow. Two of the attractive features at Lower Warm Springs are the dozens of palm trees planted in the last forty years and several hundred square feet of meticulously maintained green grass. The Park Service takes a dim view of "exotic species" running rampant in our National Parks, so there is reason to suspect this introduced flora, such as the grass and palm trees, might some day be torn out.

Fearing that the National Park Service had plans to tear out the soaking tubs, too, a group of users got together and formed an organization to keep a wary eye on the warm springs. They are the "Saline Preservation Association" (SPA). At the moment, the Park Service appears to be unwilling to anger the public and has no plans to restore the area to its pristine prehistoric condition. However, the construction of any new tubs will not be permitted.

The things that are not likely to change are the waters themselves. My field notes indicate that on December 14, 1969, I measured the water temperature at Lower Warm Springs at 112°F, with the bathing pool being 106°F. Twenty-nine years later, on December 19, 1998, I found the source spring to be 114°F, with the nearest pool 110°F, and the pool by the grass 106°F.

The road continues past the north side of Lower Warm Springs and heads in a northeast direction. The potholes increase in size, causing the road to deteriorate to Class II. Palm Spring is slightly more than ½ mile away. Its cluster of tall palm trees stands out like a green beacon in a sea of brown. Campsites around Palm Spring are plentiful, although they do not have many of the amenities of those around Lower Warm Springs. Missing are the mesquite thickets that provide both shade and privacy.

The source pool at Palm Spring has the hottest water of the three warm spring areas. It was measured at 123°F one cold December morning. The source feeds two widely separated bathing pools through buried pipes. The bath waters measured a more tolerable 108° and 106° respectively.

Palm Spring

The road continues beyond Palm Spring, still heading northeast across the creosote-covered alluvium. A cluster of mesquite trees on the left 1.5 miles above Palm Spring marks the location of yet another spring in this chain. Archaeologists have found the remnants of old Indian villages on the mesa tops in this area. It seems that ancient man was just as fond of soaking up the hot mineral waters as today's generations.

Judging from the many acres of travertine deposits and their thickness, hot springs have existed in this corner of the Saline Valley for thousands of years, possibly since the end of the Pleistocene Ice Age. One such travertine terrace is reached 1.8 miles beyond Palm Spring. The road briefly turns to Class III as it scrambles up the side of these water-borne mineral deposits.

Notice the Saline Range to your left as you make your way north. Most of these mountains are covered by three million-year-old basalt lava of Pliocene age, but ahead and to the left you can see the banded layers of the 500-million-year-old sedimentary rocks that form the core of these mountains. These are very old marine sediments of the Wood Canyon Formation, the Zabriskie Quartzite, the Carrara Formation, the Bonanza King Formation, and the Nopah Formation. All are of Cambrian age, a time when life on earth was limited to a few primitive organisms living in the sea.

Three miles above Lower Warm Springs is Upper Warm Spring. In historic times this spring escaped man made "improvements" such as soaking tubs and palm trees; it has always retained its natural condition. In the days before this area became part of Death Valley National Park, the BLM constructed a six-foot chain link fence surrounding a half-acre around the spring. The object was to keep wild burros from fouling the waterhole; it seems to have worked. Upper Warm Spring looks pretty much today as it did thirty years ago. And the 99°F water temperature seems to have changed little, too.

A mile and a half above Upper Warm Spring, the road leaves the bajada and enters the wash. The wheel tracks are not so distinct now, although the route remains Class II. On the bajada on either side of the wash are a variety of cacti, including prickly pear, cholla, and the round cottontop barrel cactus. The wash is a narrow open corridor between *wilderness* areas on either side. For the curious hiker, there are petroglyphs and other signs of early Indian evidence in these lava fields. **Remember the defacement and collecting of artifacts is a serious violation of Federal law.**

As barren as they may seem, the great lava fields of the Saline Range must have supported game animals in earlier times. Prehistoric Indians have left their petroglyphs in several places, seemingly magical symbols to ensure good hunting. At one such site, the author found a large basalt boulder, with a rounded depression, clearly a mortar in which seeds, piñon pine nuts, and other commodities were ground to a powder. At another site, random obsidian flakes behind a lava squeeze suggest ancient man used the site as a hunting blind, overlooking what was possibly a game trail.

Four miles above Upper Warm Spring, the road passes the toe of a lava flow coming out of the Saline Range. When this basalt poured eastward out of a crack in the earth's surface, it was a hot viscous, slow-moving mass. Geologists use an Hawaiian term "aa" to describe this type of lava flow. The fluid fast-moving type of flow is called "pahoehoe". Geologist B. Clark Burchfel of Rice University, who studied these mountains, found both types of lava flows.

A basalt lava flow near Marble Bath

The 1913 Ballarat quadrangle and 1957 Dry Mountain 15-minute topographic maps show a feature named *Marble Bath* some distance above Lower Warm Springs. I have searched for, but never found Marble Bath, and I have not talked to anyone who has. Indeed, I was never sure just what it was that I was looking for. The late Wendell Moyer, who knew the Saline Valley as well as anyone, shared my search and subsequent frustration. Dr. Moyer had a great sense of humor, however, and he took positive measures to respond to the Mystery of Marble Bath. He hauled an old bathtub to the place on the map, and filled the bottom with hundreds of children's blue playing marbles that he had ordered from Dow Corning on the East Coast. Thus, anyone looking for Marble Bath could find the landmark. Unfortunately, the NPS did not share his humor, and they removed it.

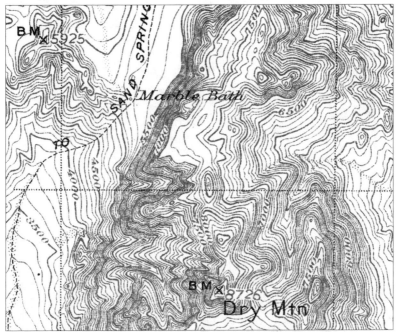

Marble Bath is shown on the 1913 topographic map.

The road leaves the wash 10 miles above Upper Warm Spring, and once again winds its way up the alluvial fan, deteriorating to Class III in the process. The route remains this way for a little more than two miles. Suddenly, a low ridge is climbed, and once the top is reached, the land falls away to the north. As anti-climatic as it seems, this is 4,500' Steel Pass, so named for a steel post once imbedded here. A two-pound coffee can holds a register in which people passing through can leave their names and comments.

Prior to the 1994 inclusion of this area into Death Valley National Park, Steel Pass saw relatively few backcountry travelers. When I first came this way in the 1960s, I doubt if the route over the pass saw more than a dozen vehicles a year. The summit register now suggests that figure has increased substantially. This is still very lonely country, and it is no place to face a vehicle breakdown. I know I was out here alone once, when I broke a rear axle near Marble Bath. I was eighty miles from my home in Bishop, and completely on my own. Fortunately I was able to able to limp back on the drive train to my front axle.

From the summit of Steel Pass, it is 14 miles down to the nearest graded road at the Eureka Dunes, and 50 miles beyond them to Big Pine (see Excursion #23).

Panamint Springs

This 1937 Frasher photo shows the store and gas pumps.

Panamint Springs Resort in the late 1940s

During a 1949 reenactment drive between Lone Pine and Death Valley,
this 20 mule team borax train stopped at Panamint Springs.
(Frasher photos from the author's collection)

Chapter VII

Trails Out of Panamint Springs

Panamint Springs is situated on State Highway 190, on an alluvial fan coming out of Darwin Wash. From its lofty perch 500' above the north Panamint Dry Lake, it commands a grand view of the northern part of the soaring Panamint Range and the distant sand dunes. There is no spring here, as the name would imply. Water is piped out of Darwin Canyon just to the west.

There was no settlement here when Herman Eichbaum built his toll road between Darwin Falls and Stovepipe Wells in 1925 and 1926. It would not be until 1937 that a local talc miner, Bill Reid, and his wife Agnes decided to develop a wayside stop on the road between Lone Pine and Death Valley. A niece of showman William "Buffalo Bill" Cody, Mrs. Reid was a colorful woman in her own right. When her husband died in 1946, she stayed to run the business at Panamint Springs for another 15 years.

The State of California had a Highway Maintenance Station here for many years, complete with employee housing. With the reorganization of that agency, CalTrans decided to close down many of these remote facilities. With the passage of the California Desert Protection Act in 1994, Death Valley was elevated to the status of a full national park, and in the process the western boundaries of the former national monument were pushed westward and now include Panamint Springs.

The western-style Panamint Springs Resort and RV Park offers the basics to a traveler: a restaurant with a reputation of having very good food and patio dining, a bar, motel rooms, RV sites with full hook-ups, tent campsites, showers, a mini-mart with limited groceries, gifts, propane, diesel fuel, and gasoline. The facility is open all year, and boasts that its 2,000' elevation makes it the coolest resort in the park.

26

The Big Four Mine

Primary Attraction: An abandoned mine, and a very challenging trail.

Time Required: This is a half-day excursion out of Panamint Springs Resort.

Miles Involved: The mine is only seven miles off State Route 190, and less than twelve miles from the Panamint Springs Resort.

Maps: 1:100,000 Darwin Hills sheet; 1:24,000 Panamint Springs and The Dunes Quadrangles.

Degree of Difficulty: This road has everything from Class I to Class V (with very little in-between!) **The last mile of road to the Big Four Mine is not for the inexperienced or the faint of heart**. While heavily laden ore trucks once plied this road, it was in a time long ago; never more.

The road to the Big Four Mine not only leads to yet another mine, but also provides hiking access to the Panamint Valley sand dunes, Lake Hill, and if you know where to look, some prehistoric geoglyphs.

From the Panamint Springs Resort, reset your trip odometer and take State Route 190 eastward down into Panamint Valley and across the north Panamint Dry Lake. You will pass the Panamint Valley Road to the right in 2.5 miles (N36°20.370 W117°25.388). Look for a wide graded dirt road heading north at a point 4.5 miles from Panamint Springs; turn left here (N36°20.515 W117°23.324).

The graded road is deceptively good for the first few miles as it approaches Lake Hill, prominent on the valley floor just to the left of the road. There is an interesting theory as to how this small mountain came to be here in Panamint Valley. USGS geologists Wayne Hall and Hal Stephens looked at the rocks on Lake Hill and found them to be largely Ely Springs dolomite with a little Eureka quartzite. These rocks of late Ordovician age sat on top of young Quaternary alluvium and were totally out of place, isolated from other rocks of the same age. In looking around to determine where they came from and how they got here, Hall and Stephens found identical rocks near the crest of the Panamint Range some 3½ miles to the east. They postulated that during the extensive faulting during the late Pliocene, an enormous piece of the mountain had broken off and

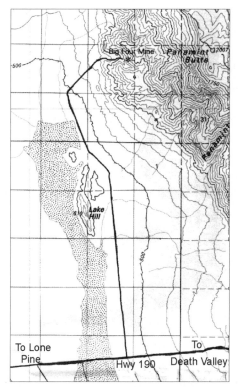

slowly slid nearly 5,000 feet down the mountainside to come to rest on the floor of the valley; thus, the origin of Lake Hill. While that theory may sound a bit far fetched, I can offer nothing better.

Lake Hill dominates the northern end of Panamint Valley.

Lake Hill was an island during the Pleistocene Ice Age, not just once, but several times. When the ancestral Owens River filled China Lake, the overflow went through Poison Canyon to create Lake Searles. When that basin filled to its natural capacity, the overflow went around the southern end of the Slate Range to fill Panamint Valley. The resulting lake at its maximum was some 56 miles long, up to 10 miles wide, and as deep as 900 feet in places. When the shoreline reached a point 1,910' above sea level, the water then flowed down Wingate Wash to create ancient Lake Manly in what today is Death Valley. The summit of Lake Hill is 2,030' above sea level. Thus when Lake Panamint was full, (during the Tahoe stage of the Wisconsin period) only the highest 1,020' of Lake Hill were above the surface of the water.

One should keep in mind that the water levels in Lake Panamint fluctuated greatly throughout the Pleistocene. Wave cut shorelines have been observed anywhere from 1,045' above sea level all the way up to 1,977 feet. You may well ask, "How could the water get as high as 1,977' above sea level when it spilled out of Panamint Valley at 1910 feet?" The answer is that the Panamint Mountains continue to be pushed upward, and what may have been 1,910' in the Pleistocene is now 1,977 feet.

But enough of this geologic trivia; Lake Hill is worthy of a climb if you don't mind a 500-foot ascent, walking all the way over rough rock. The climb to the summit can be done in an hour. Take your binoculars. To the southeast you can pick out a Holocene fault cutting across the alluvial fan. The western side of the fault has been raised with the resulting displacement having disrupted the drainage patterns on the alluvial fan.

If you are ever fortunate enough to fly low over Panamint Valley in a light aircraft, you might spot some prehistoric rock alignments known as geoglyphs. Although not as spectacular as the prehistoric intaglios found on the desert pavement near Blythe, or those of Nazca in Peru, the Panamint Valley geoglyphs are, nevertheless, a unique prehistoric resource that archaeologists have yet to adequately explain.

And speaking of archaeology, the northern end of Panamint Valley likely had more people living in it 9,000 years ago, or even 5,000 years ago, than live there today, even on holiday weekends during the peak of the winter tourist season. When anthropologist E.W. Nelson came through here in 1891, he found one hundred Indians living at the northern end of Panamint Valley, mostly at Warm Sulfur Springs and in the Panamint Dunes. Even as this ancient lake was drying up for the last time, early man inhabited its swampy shores. We know this, because excavations have uncovered crude Pinto Culture points going back 9,000 years.

Usually when we think of *archaeological digs,* our minds conjure up a series of strings laid out in a grid pattern of one meter by one meter, with the archaeologist carefully picking away with a trowel, a dental explorer, and a very fine camel's hair brush. Back in the 1960s, before Lake Hill was off limits to vehicles, I encountered a tractor digging trenches near the south base of the hill. When I asked the operator what he was looking for, I learned that a noted archaeologist was trying to reach the bottom of the alluvium that had washed down off Panamint Butte in the last several thousand years. Buried somewhere down there was the same layer of soil upon which these ancient occupants dwelled. She was looking for evidence of their times. That tractor destroyed my concept of meticulous excavations.

It is unlikely that you will find any Clovis points at Lake Hill, but keep in mind that the collecting of arrowheads, regardless of age, is prohibited in our national parks. Remember, too, that Lake Hill, like the Panamint Dunes, is now classified as *wilderness*. Vehicles must stay on the established roadway.

These guys grazing near Lake Hill seem to have escaped the park service roundup.

The roadway to Lake Hill is a good Class I, and a reasonably good Class II for a ways beyond. At a point 5.6 miles north of State Route 190, the roadway makes a distinct turn to the right. This is the closest point to the sand of the Panamint Dunes. A desert track once led over to them, but that route was closed by the BLM and, with the expansion of Death Valley National Park in 1994, that vehicle ban has been maintained. It is a four-mile walk one way to visit the dunes.

At this bend in the road, the route begins to climb the alluvial fan, and the road deteriorates as it does so. It remains a rough Class II for the next three-quarters of a mile, but becomes Class III as you pass between two mounds of basalt lava. It deteriorates further within another quarter-mile, to become Class IV in places as it goes up the rocky wash.

The canyon is soon entered. On the right is 280-million year old limestone of the Keeler Formation of Pennsylvanian and Permian age. On top of that is the only slightly younger Owens Valley Formation, also of Permian age. One minute your wheels are trying to gain a foothold on the white limestone on the south side of the canyon; a few minutes later, the wash has taken you to the brown Cambrian metamorphosed sediments of the Nopah Formation on the north side of the canyon. It is here that the road ends today. It is an easy half-mile walk up the wash to the remains of the Big Four Mine.

Also known as the War Eagle, the Big Four Mine was a lead mine with claims first filed in 1907. Not much happened until 1940, however, with the first ore being shipped out by truck in 1942. Between late 1944 and late 1952, records show that 470 tons were mined, containing 16.6 percent lead, 12.5 percent zinc, and 2.6 ounces of silver per ton. The mine is high on the left side of the canyon and worked in three levels. A series of ore shoots and an aerial cableway brought buckets of ore to the canyon bottom. Some of the bunkers remain; some have collapsed. A road to the middle level has been obliterated by a torrent of basalt lava washed down from the ridgetop. **You can hike to the upper workings, but the slope consists of steep loose rocks and is treacherous. As always, do not enter any of the underground workings.** If you want to see the ore they were mining, look at a small pile on the canyon bottom near the old mine camp.

Ore bunker at the Big Four Mine

27

Back Door to Darwin

Primary Attraction:	Interesting geology, old mines, and a rare desert riparian habitat.
Time Required:	This is a half-day excursion out of Panamint Springs Resort. Better yet, take all day and hike to Darwin Falls, and explore some of the side roads that lead to old mines on Zinc Hill.
Miles Involved:	This is a loop trip of 37 miles from Panamint Springs and return.
Maps:	1:100,000 Darwin Hills sheet; 1:24,000 Panamint Springs and Darwin Quadrangles.
Degree of Difficulty:	There is a little Class I, but the road is mostly Class II, with a touch of Class III in a few places.

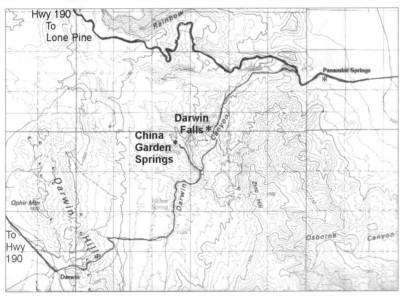

The century old mining camp of Darwin can be visited by a perfectly good six-mile long paved road off State Route 190. But if you had wanted to get about on paved roads, you would not have bought this book! So, I am going to take you to Darwin by the less traveled back door.

From the Panamint Springs Resort, head west on State Route 190 in the direction of Lone Pine. After exactly one mile, turn left onto the graded dirt road going up Darwin Wash and reset your trip odometer (N36°20.362 W117°28.773).

A young electrical engineer, Herman Eichbaum saw the tourist potential of Death Valley in the 1920s. He sold his successful tour business on Catalina Island to the Wrigley family, and in April of 1925 he petitioned the Inyo County Board of Supervisors for the right to build a scenic toll road through Death Valley. His petition was initially denied, but Eichbaum persevered. By September he was given the green light to build a toll road from Darwin Falls to the original Stovepipe Wells, just east of the sand dunes. Construction began in November, and a few days before Christmas the construction crew was on top of Towne Pass. A month later they were just starting across the dunes. Eichbaum's 38-mile long Death Valley Toll Road was officially opened to motorists on May 4, 1926. Some said it was a road to nowhere, because at the time it was still a full six months before the Stovepipe Wells Resort would open its doors for business. At one time the Darwin Wash road was asphalt, but today that smooth surface is but a distant memory. While technically the Darwin Wash Road cannot be considered any worse than Class I, the washboard surface is enough to rattle your teeth loose.

The old Eichbaum Toll road in Darwin Wash circa 1928
(Frasher photo from Death Valley Museum collection)

The road stays within the confines of the canyon bottom for the first few miles, passing through some interesting, though complex geology. At first the rocks on either side are a granite-like quartz monzonite; however, they soon turn into a highly metamorphosed basement complex of older rocks, capped by a much younger volcanic series. At a point 2.4 miles in from the highway, the last mile of road to Darwin Falls has been closed to help protect the wildlife that depends on this rare desert stream. You must walk this last mile from the small parking area (no overnight camping). It is a very pleasant walk, with a gain in elevation of only a couple of hundred feet. At the end of the trail is lovely Darwin Falls, the first of nine such falls in the next half-mile of the canyon. Beyond this first fall, the route is generally trailless, and the canyon has a couple of narrows, where some rock scrambling is needed to get over the waterfalls.

Darwin Falls

With the change in Death Valley from a monument to a park in 1994, together with its considerable expansion, the Saline Valley, the Eureka Valley and much of the Panamint Valley have been added to the Death Valley National Park. A bend in the park boundary was made to include Darwin Falls. The National Park Service has pretty much taken over where the BLM left off. Under BLM management, Darwin falls was an *Area of Critical Environmental Concern*, and so it remains under NPS stewardship. The area does not get as many visitors as Badwater or Golden Canyon, but the number of people walking into the falls is considerable.

While the road no longer goes all the way to Darwin Falls, it does not end either. From the parking area, a Class II road ascends a side canyon onto the western flank of Zinc Hill, a 5,000' ridge on this northern end of the Argus Range. The road is all uphill for the next three miles, and while four-wheel drive may not be absolutely necessary, many will feel more comfortable with its added traction.

The road passes an ore bunker 1.6 miles above the Darwin Falls parking lot (4 miles in from the pavement). A Class III road turns to the left here to climb even higher on Zinc Hill to the mines above. Another such jeep trail is a quarter-mile up the main road. With names like Empress, Wynog, and Darwin Zinc, the mines of this mountain have, over a 75-year period, produced much lead, zinc, copper and silver. A number of mines were accessible only by mule trail, the remnants of which can still occasionally be seen. An enjoyable day can be spent exploring the routes to these mines by suitable backcountry vehicle and on foot. **As always, stay out of the old mine workings. The shoring is bad, and to enter is foolhardy.**

A summit is reached 2.8 miles above the Darwin Falls parking area, and the road begins to drop back down into Darwin Wash on the other side. The route now returns to Class II in its descent. The road swings to the left at 6.3 miles, but a fork to the right goes down the canyon a mile to China Garden Spring. This was the site of an old ore mill, now largely in ruins. There is a nice spring here beneath the shade of several large cottonwood trees.

Layers of 300 million-year-old marine sediments near China Garden Spring

During Darwin's heyday, Chinese lived here growing vegetables that they sold to the hungry miners in Darwin; hence its name. It is possible to hike down the canyon to Darwin Falls, although there is no trail, and some rock scrambling is necessary to bypass several of the waterfalls. If you have any thoughts of doing this, you need to have Michel Digonnet's book *Hiking Death Valley*.

Back on the main Darwin road, the Class II road continues on up the canyon. Notice on the left how the layers of sedimentary rock have squeezed, twisted, and contorted. Miller Spring is reached 2.2 miles above the side-road to China Garden Spring. There was once a mill here that processed ore from the surrounding mines. The site remains in private hands. The deteriorating, but still paved road to Darwin is encountered a tenth of a mile beyond. From here it is only four miles to downtown Darwin.

Darwin gets its name from Dr. Darwin French, whose expedition came through this general area in 1860 while searching for the illusive Lost Gunsight Mine of Death Valley fame. In their quest for fabulous wealth, the French group somehow overlooked the silver-bearing veins all around Mount Ophir. Those minerals remained overlooked until October or November of 1874. Word of the strike soon got out, and men poured out of nearby Cerro Gordo and Panamint City to get in on the ground floor. By 1875 the town of Darwin was established, and within a year there were some twenty mines feeding two smelters operating in the vicinity. The population grew to seven hundred people.

By 1876, Darwin had a population of 1000 rowdy miners who supported the town's fifteen saloons. At that time, the Cuervo smelter was turning out 20 tons per day; the Defiance smelter, 60 tons per day; and the New Coso smelter, an astounding 100 tons per day! To fire these hungry furnaces, piñon wood had to be packed in on long mule trains from the Argus and Panamint Ranges. Other mules were hitched to freight wagons to carry the heavy ingots of silver, lead, and zinc for many miles south to the railroad in Mojave. An estimated $29 million worth of precious metals came from the mines of Darwin between 1875 and 1952. This does not include another $7 to $8 million more from other nearby mines just to the north and east.

In 1938, geologist V.C. Kelley wrote that Darwin reached its peak of 5,000 people in 1880. Historian Remi Nadeau says Darwin reached its zenith in 1876 just before the new discoveries at Mammoth City and Bodie siphoned off some of its population. Whatever the date, mines began to close as the most easily worked orebodies were depleted. Nevertheless, one mine or another seemed to be working more or less continuously until the start of World War II. That conflict spurred its own type of activity, as tungsten was found and mined beginning in 1941. The town got another economic shot in the arm in 1945, when the Anacoda Company acquired the consolidated Darwin Mines and reopened many old workings.

To this day, Darwin refuses to die. The post office established in 1875 closed a few years back, but the hamlet still retains its 93522 Zip Code. Today only about 50 people call Darwin home. Unfortunately when those people want to put groceries in their pantry, they have to drive 35 miles to Lone Pine. **Note: The buildings in Darwin are all privately owned. Look around the town if you wish, but please stay on the street and do not trespass on private property.**

From Darwin, there is a paved county road that goes north five miles to meet State Route 190. From here it is a return trip of 17 miles back to the Panamint Springs Resort.

If you are interested in learning more about Darwin's past, try to find a copy of the 1996 book *Darwin, California*. The author, Robert Palazzo, is a full time attorney and part time Darwin historian and resident.

The Darwin general store in 1908
(County of Inyo, Eastern California Museum photo)

28

Around Hunter Mountain

Primary Attraction: High mountain scenery, old mines and, if you are very lucky, you might see stones that mysteriously seem to move by themselves.

Time Required: This is a full day's outing, when the days are long. It would be better to camp along the way and make the circuit in two days.

Distance Involved: It is 53 miles from Panamint Springs to Teakettle Junction via Hunter Mountain and Hidden Valley. The return trip from Teakettle Junction back to Panamint Springs via the infamous Lippencott Grade is another 55 miles. **There are no services of any kind along the way. Top off your fuel tank before you start.**

Maps: 1:100,000 Darwin Hills and Saline Valley sheets; 1:24,000 Santa Rosa Flat, Lee Wash, Harris Hill, Sand Flat, Ubehebe Peak, and West of Ubehebe Peak Quadrangles.

Degree of Difficulty: Most of this route is Class I and II. The road below the Lippencott Mine can range from Class III at best to completely impassible, depending on conditions of the moment. Further, conditions can change instantly. Always check with the rangers before attempting the Lippencott Grade. The Hunter Mountain Road can be closed by snow in the winter. If you want to see the skating stones on the racetrack when snow closes the Hunter Mountain road, you should come up the Lippencott Grade from the Saline Valley, or come in by way of Ubehebe Crater.

Truly off the beaten path, this loop exposes the visitor to another aspect of Death Valley National Park that most tourists never see. The topography and scenery range from the piñon and juniper slopes of Hunter Mountain to the austere beauty of the Racetrack Playa to the Joshua tree covered landscape of Lee Flat. **Top off your gas tank before leaving Panamint Springs. You have 108 miles of back roads ahead with no services of any kind.**

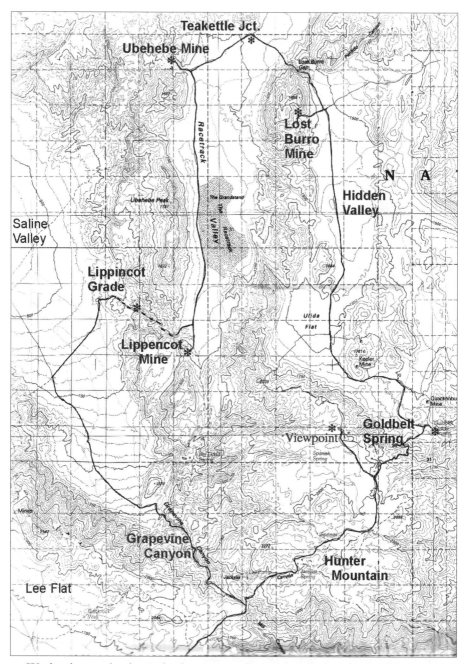

We begin our back road adventure at Panamint Springs, at an elevation of
1,900 feet, where after setting the trip odometer we head west on State Route 190.
After crossing the mouth of Darwin Wash, the highway climbs the spectacular

grade that circles the edge of Rainbow Canyon. These are relatively young Pliocene volcanic rocks, which rest unconformably upon much older Paleozoic limestones. The marine sediments can only be seen in a few road cuts near the top of the grade.

At a point 12.7 miles from Panamint Springs, a long ago paved road turns off to the right (N36°10.837 W117°42.912); this is the Saline Valley Road. A sign warns it is 85 miles to Big Pine, with no services along the way. Turn right here, noting your mileage as you leave the highway. The county road heads north across the southern end of Santa Rosa Flat. The elevation here is 5,000 feet, so we have already climbed 3,100 feet.

The road swings to the east after four miles, and then heads north again, crossing a low limestone ridge. On the other side of the ridge, 5.8 miles from Highway 190, a Class II side road to the right heads for the low hills a mile to the east. This was the site of the Lee, Wonder, Silver Reid, and other mines. This is an interesting side trip of slightly over a mile.

These low hills are composed of the Tin Mountain limestone of Mississippian age, and the slightly younger Lost Burro Formation of Devonian age. At some point in geologic time, hot solutions from deep within the earth forced their way upward into cracks and along layers in these sediments. Upon cooling, the minerals in the solutions were left behind. Those solutions contained concentrated amounts of calcite, quartz, barite and, of interest to the prospectors, silver, gold, lead, and zinc.

One of the first mines to tap into these orebodies was the Emigrant Mine (later called the Lee Mine). It was found in the 1870s, probably shortly after the big finds in Darwin in 1874. In his 1884 report to the U.S. Director of the Mint, geologist H.C. Burchard said this of the Emigrant Mine:

> *Emigrant mine with a shaft 100 feet in depth and lateral drifts which show a vein 4 feet wide, with a rich streak of gold and silver on both walls. Assay $200 per ton. The ore is sacked and shipped to San Francisco.*

Obviously, it would take pretty rich ore to be transported all the way to San Francisco for processing. A few years later, a mill was set up about seven miles to the northeast in what would become known as Mill Canyon. Still later, a mill was set up next to the mine; its stone foundations remain. When I first visited this mine in December of 1958, the old mill was in ruins; however, a leasee was operating the mine, with the ore going to Darwin for processing. From present day appearances, it does not seem that the mine has been worked in recent years. **There are still open shafts and holes, so watch your step and do not attempt to enter any of the underground workings.**

The Lee Mines in 1958

The Lee Mines in 1998

Returning to the Saline Valley Road, turn right to resume your loop around Hunter Mountain. A major unmarked intersection is reached 8 miles north of Highway 190. The left fork crosses the western edge of Lee Flat to descend into San Lucas Canyon, before climbing again to an 8,200' high point at the old mining camp of Cerro Gordo. For this excursion, you will want to keep to the right here on the Saline Valley Road.

Soon a second low limestone ridge is crossed and a sign announces you are entering Death Valley National Park. The road now crosses Lee Flat with its enormous Joshua tree forest. Joshua trees *Yucca brevifolia* are closely related to other types of yuccas and are quite widespread in the Mojave Desert. Indeed, they are found throughout the higher elevation deserts of Southern California and Southern Nevada and in adjoining small areas of Arizona and Utah. They were supposedly so named by Mormon pioneers entering Utah, who thought they resembled Joshua lifting his arms to heaven.

This area has been used for cattle grazing for well over one hundred years. Grazing was not permitted in the old Death Valley Monument; however, the BLM did have a few grazing allotments in lands outside the monument. When the new and greatly expanded national park was created, several pre-existing BLM grazing allotments were included in the park expansion. Those cattlemen were able to retain their grazing permits within the new park. Thus it is that you may see cattle on and near Hunter Mountain. Pay close attention to the road ahead. This is open range where the cattle can roam freely, but not everything out there with four legs is a cow. We have seen feral burros grazing among the cows. Perhaps they were trying to escape the wrath of NPS personnel who are committed to eliminating them from the park.

Once across the flat, the road begins to gently climb into the lava-covered hills to the east. During a scouting trip after an unusually wet El Niño winter, the roadsides were alive with a variety of wildflowers. In places the hillsides were covered with a yellow carpet of Fremont xeraside. There was also the tall stately Prince's Plume of yellow, the tiny gilia and everything in between. The orange mallow was common, as was the ubiquitous Indian paintbrush, some with a very crimson coloration. Mojave aster with its purple petals surrounding a yellow core was common. Even the Blue sage put on its best flowering face for us. But the wildflower that most attracted our attention was the bright orange of the Desert Mariposa lily. Never anywhere had we seen this unique species in such profusion.

As the road climbs, the Joshua trees give way to juniper and piñon trees. At a point 15 miles in from the highway, those riding on the right side of the car will have fleeting glimpses down into Mill Canyon and to the Panamint Valley Dunes beyond. Indeed, from some turns of the roadway you can look south down the entire length of Panamint Valley. The elevation of the road here is nearly 6,000 feet, while the elevation of the Panamint sand dunes below is about 2,500 feet.

A second major intersection is reached 15.6 miles in from the highway. Like the last one, this one is unmarked. The left fork makes a 4,000' descent of Grapevine Canyon into the Saline Valley. Again keep right on the road that now hovers somewhere between Class I and II. We will return via the left fork near the end of our journey.

We leave the Pliocene volcanic rocks at this intersection, and for the next 11 miles we will be in granite-like rocks called quartz monzonite. They have been potassium-argon dated at 134 million years, putting them into the Cretaceous Period. These rocks are closely related in composition and age to the granitic rocks of the Sierra Nevada.

If you come through here in the springtime, and are very lucky as I once was, you might see the variety of Mariposa lily that has pure white petals. Also watch for Ceanothus, a large shrub with fragrant white flowers found only in the park's higher elevations. It is a favorite browse for deer (yes Virginia, there are deer here on Hunter Mountain).

A quarter-mile beyond the intersection there is a small sandy basin to the left, where the dune primrose seems to thrive at a much greater elevation than is its normal habitat. If you look closely, you may barely make out an old overgrown wagon road contouring around the western side of the hill. By walking along this old trail a half-mile to the ridgetop, and then following the rusting 1½ inch pipe down to the bottom of the canyon, you will find century old Lee Pump overgrown with wild rose and grapevine. Only the top of the boiler protrudes above the thick jungle of vegetation. At one time this steam powered pump lifted water from Jackass Creek out of the steep canyon, where gravity sent it 7 miles down hill to the Lee Mines.

Our dirt road dips down into the canyon 17.3 miles in from the highway, and crosses tiny Jackass Creek. This desert watercourse originates at a spring of the same name just up the canyon. During the winter months, this rare desert stream will flow several miles down into Grapevine Canyon to join another stream that flows nearly to the Saline Valley. The Hunter Mountain Road can also be very icy here in the winter. **Use great caution when ice covers the roadway.**

The road reaches its 7,000' high point on Hunter Mountain 18.6 miles from the highway. There are some nice campsites among the piñon pines. At 22.3 miles, look for a cattle guard in a drift fence to the right. By going through this gap in the fence, and continuing south for nearly a mile, you will find an old log cabin that some think goes back to the early 1870s. History does not suggest it is quite that old.

William Lyle Hunter was a Confederate officer who came west in 1865 to start a new life. Hunter ran mule trains in and out of Cerro Gordo in the early 1870s, hauling ore and supplies. He established a ranch on Lee Flat to support his fifty mules. He married in 1875, and eventually had four sons and a daughter. He moved to the Owens Valley to ranch when the mines closed, and eventually became the Inyo County Clerk. His next to youngest son was Bev, who took to grazing cattle and collecting wild horses. In Lester Reed's book *Old Timers of Southeastern California,* Bev Hunter says this cabin was his, which would suggest that it was built around the Turn of the 20th Century. Remember: Mice and other small rodents sometimes get into these cabins. Their feces, urine, and saliva can spread a virus that may infect humans with a nasty and potentially fatal illness called Hantavirus Pulmonary Syndrome. **Avoid all contact with rodent droppings, and do not stir up any dust where there is evidence of mice and rats.** (Inhalation of the virus is a common way of transmission to humans.)

Log cabin off the Hunter Mountain road

Back on the main road, the route deteriorates to Class II as it leaves the piñon forest and begins its steep 2,000' descent to the Goldbelt Spring area. On the way down, good views can be had of the sand dunes near Stovepipe Wells, some 20 miles away to the northeast as the crow flies. A side road right 26 miles from the highway goes 1.2 miles to Goldbelt Spring.

Some writers have described Goldbelt Spring as if it were an honest to goodness mining camp in the mold of Greenwater or Ballarat; that may be a bit misleading. Goldbelt Spring is one of those desert water holes where sourdough prospectors have camped for well over a century, as they searched for, and sometimes found, mineral wealth in the nearby hills. At times, those who stopped here simply pitched a tent. Others seeking a more substantial shelter fashioned a cabin out of whatever building materials they could find. The residents of Goldbelt Spring were a long way from their source of supplies, and they seldom stayed for extended periods of time. A crowded day at Goldbelt Spring during the Greenwater excitement of 1906 might have meant six people were living here, and certainly no more than a few dozen at its peak.

Today's ruins at Goldbelt Spring seem to be remnants of a later era when talc miners set up camp here in the 1930s and 40s. Unfortunately the last four wooden structures have all collapsed, and the single "cousin jack" dugout is about to suffer the same fate.

I would recommend a scenic and enjoyable all day hike from Goldbelt Spring, down Marble Canyon to Cottonwood Canyon. The trick is to have someone pick you up at the bottom end (see Excursion #10). The distance is a long 14 miles, but it is all down hill. While there are springs along the way, carry plenty of water. Keep your eyes open for petroglyphs on the canyon walls. They are there, but easily missed.

Back track the 1.2 miles to the Hunter Mountain Road and turn right. The main road now is pretty much Class I, as it makes its way down the bajada. The road heads west, then north, then west again, before entering Ulida Flat to head north once again. Along the way, several roads turn off to the right leading to talc mines.

An unmarked crossroads is reached 11 miles from the Goldbelt Spring turnoff, or 37 miles from the highway (N36°43.750 W117°30.301). The Class II road to the right goes up to the tiny seep called Rest Spring, and beyond it to the White Top Mountain area where you can look down into Death Valley (see Excursion #15).

An easy Class III, the left fork goes 1.2 miles to the Lost Burro Mine. Here, a gold bearing vein one to four feet wide was found at the contact point where the Cretaceous granitic rocks forced their way up through the Tin Mountain limestone. The first claims were staked in 1907. Between then and 1912, the mine is said to have produced $85,000 in gold. Between 1935 and 1942, when gold mines were shut down by Presidential Order, the official output was reported at 255 ounces worth a mere $5,281. However geologist Jim McAllister looked at the size of the workings in the early 1950s, and estimated the output was more like 2,800 ounces worth something in excess of $100,000. Could the operators have been under reporting their income?

The mill built in 1917 has been salvaged for use elsewhere; however, the timber frame remains. There is a weather-tight cabin at the mine that can be used as an emergency shelter in a storm, if you don't mind sharing your quarters with the mice and packrats. **Remember my previous warning about mice having the ability to spread the Hantavirus through their feces, urine, and saliva. Avoid all contact with rodent droppings, and do not stir up and inhale any dust where there is evidence of mice and rats.**

The Lost Burro Mine

The main road continues north, where it slips through a little canyon known as Lost Burro Gap before entering the Racetrack Valley. While this canyon is only a mile long, the steeply dipping limestone rocks here represent 100-million years of the earth's history. First is the Hidden Valley dolomite of Silurian age. Mid-way through the canyon is the Lost Burro Formation of Devonian age, and finally at the lower end is the Tin Mountain limestone of Mississippian age. All three of these formations contain fossils of the primitive animals that lived in the sea at that time, but they are tough to find.

At a point 15 miles from Goldbelt Spring, 40.2 miles from Highway 190 (without any side-trips), yet another important intersection is reached (N36°45.606 W117°32.536). This is Teakettle Junction, so named for the variety of teakettles that people have placed over the years to adorn the sign. The graded right fork heads towards Ubehebe Crater some twenty miles to the north. To complete our loop, we will want to turn left on the Racetrack Valley Road, taking us in a generally southerly direction.

At a point 2.2 miles south of Teakettle Junction, a short Class I side road right goes over to the Copper Bell and Ubehebe Mines (N36°43.750 W117°30.301). If you elect to make this short side trip, the Copper Bell is to the left, the Ubehebe to the right.

Together with a partner John Porter, the same William Hunter who ran mule trains out of Cerro Gordo found copper minerals here in 1875. But because the site was so remote and the copper content marginal, they were unable to profitably mine it. The two mines changed hands after Hunter's death in 1902. During the Bullfrog and Greenwater excitement in 1906, two imaginative mining promoters, A.D. Whittier and Jack Salsberry, became involved. The Ubehebe Mining Company was formed and shares at $1.00 par value were offered for 15 cents. A man of unbridled enthusiasm, Salsberry claimed he had 50-million tons of 10% copper ore in sight, and that the estimated value was at least a billion dollars. He talked of building a smelter and railroad. Two miles northwest of the Racetrack playa, Salsberry laid out the town site of Salina City, later renamed Latimer, to flatter a major investor. Historian Richard Lingenfelter says Latimer never had more than 20 tents at its peak. (I have never been able to find the site.) Needless to say, the grandiose dreams and schemes of stock promotions never lived up to their promise.

Nevertheless, the Ubehebe Mine did turn into a bonafide mine, although it was not copper, but lead, zinc, and even a little silver that were the important commodities produced. Mining began in 1916, peaked in 1928, and continued off and on into the early 1950s. The tramline to the upper mines was down when I first visited the mine in 1958, but all of the structures were still in good condition. The underground workings looked like the last day the miners left them. Such is not the case today. **Stay out of the tunnels and shafts!**

This steam tractor transported ore to the railroad at Bonnie Claire.
(California Division of Mines & Geology photo)

The Ubehebe Mine in the 1960s
(Death Valley Museum photo)

Continue south another three miles on the graded road, and you will reach the northern end of the Racetrack Playa, a dry lakebed that isn't always dry. It is during those infrequent wet spells, usually in the winter, that wind-blown rocks and other solid objects move about on the playa surface, leaving tracks in the mud to mark their route of movement. The National Park Service has a sign that nicely explains the process. While this phenomenon has been observed elsewhere in the western United States, including the Bonnie Claire Playa east of Scotty's Castle (see Excursion #13), the best examples of skating stones have been recorded here. Geologist Paula Messina, who wrote her Ph.D. dissertation on this phenomenon, has tried in vain to be present when these stones moved. Alas, nothing moved an inch while she was watching. She did find that, in general, most of the objects moved in the direction of the prevailing winds, a north to northeast direction. But once in the middle of the playa, the tracks left by the objects were often very convoluted.

It should be noted that driving on the playa surface is no longer permitted. You may certainly walk out there, but please leave your car on the road.

These boulders really do move!

The Class I road continues south from the Racetrack. South from Teakettle Junction 9.5 miles, there is an intersection where a road turns off to the right (N36°38.487 W117°34.470). This is the upper end of the infamous Lippencott Grade, which makes a steep descent into the Saline Valley to the west. Before starting down, however, you may wish to continue on south another 1.4 miles to the site of the Lippencott Lead Mine.

Straight ahead, a Class I road continues 0.2 miles to an NPS campground whose only improvement is a pit toilet. Beyond here the road deteriorates to Class III, and continues on another mile to the Lippencott Mine.

The Lippencott Mine's earliest days are obscure, but probably go back to the years just before World War I. It was not until World War II, however, that the demand for lead prompted an extensive exploration of the orebody. During that period, lead from this mine was shipped to Santa Ana, California, where it was made into automotive batteries. Zinc and to a lesser degree silver became important byproducts after the war. **Warning: Stay out of the tunnels and underground workings.**

To complete our loop, we must turn right at the intersection 9.5 miles south of Teakettle Junction (N36°38.487 W117°34.470). The road into Panamint City was not considered particularly difficult 40 years ago, but the Lippencott Grade out of the Saline Valley was an extreme challenge. Boy, how times have changed! The park service has run a blade over the Lippencott Grade as a convenience to the backcountry ranger who patrols this area. **Be forewarned, however; it doesn't** take much to wash out the Lippencott Grade. It can be opened one week and closed the next. Save yourself some grief, and always ask the rangers about its present status. Unless you obtain recent information to the contrary, consider the route down to be Class IV, and the route up Class V. When in doubt, scout the road ahead on foot before attempting to drive it.

From top to bottom, the Lippencott Grade is 4.5 miles long. In that distance, the change in elevation is 2,000 feet. It is still easier to go down the road than up it, but today those differences should not deter you if you want to make the ascent.

The main Saline Valley Road is reached 16.5 miles from Teakettle Junction. This is a good graded road receiving occasional maintenance by the Inyo County Road Department. There are many interesting features in the Saline Valley.

By turning right you can see the old salt tram, rest your weary bones in hot springs, or possibly take the jeep trail over Steel Pass to come out in the Eureka Valley. By staying on the county road you can also eventually come out onto Highway 395 at Big Pine. To return to Panamint Springs, you must turn left here. At 2,200 feet, this is very near the low point on this circle tour. It is a climb of nearly 4,000 feet up Grapevine Canyon to rejoin the Hunter Mountain Road, where we kept to the right so very long ago.

Once on the Saline Valley Road, it is six miles to the lower end of the canyon. In the springtime, particularly in wet years there is a small stream that runs the entire course of the canyon. This water not only supports a thick jungle of grapevines, from which the canyon gets its name, but it also supports a wide variety of birds, reptiles, and mammals. As you drive along the road, you are likely to flush out dove, quail, and chukars. Remember that this is within the park, and camping within 100 feet of flowing water is prohibited.

At the top of Grapevine Canyon, 27 miles from Teakettle Junction, we rejoin the road we came in on. By turning right we retrace our route 15.6 miles back to Highway 190, and from there it is another 12.7 miles back to the Panamint Springs Resort.

29

Osborne Canyon

Primary Attraction: Interesting geology and an abandoned mine are the main features of this excursion. Osborne Canyon, Lookout Mountain, and Snow Canyon can be combined for several days worth of four-wheeling outside of the national park, where the restrictions of what you can and cannot do are less onerous.

Time Required: Osborne Canyon is a half-day outing from Panamint Springs.

Distance Involved: The off highway portion is 9 miles one way.

Maps: 1:100,000 Darwin Hills sheet; 1:24,000 Panamint Springs Quadrangle.

Degree of Difficulty: The first four miles of dirt road are Class I or better. The remaining five miles are generally Class II or III, with a few short sections of Class IV.

Osborne Canyon is somewhat unique in this part of the Argus Range in that the prospectors who scoured these mountains in the 1860s and 1870s overlooked its mineral resources. It would not be until the early part of World War II that the operators of the Surprise Mine exposed the lead and silver minerals, and established a mine camp in this little visited canyon.

There are three ways to reach the entrance to Osborne Canyon, all of which are washed out and a bit confusing. I shall describe the easiest route. From Panamint Springs, go east on State Highway 190 for 2.6 miles, and then turn right onto the paved road to Trona (N36°20.372 W117°25.388). At 10.1 miles there is a graded dirt road on the right, with a sign reading *Minnietta Mine* marking the turnoff (N36°14.953 W117°21.170). (If you are coming from the direction of Trona, this turnoff is 6.5 miles beyond the Wildrose Canyon Road.) Reset your odometer here as you leave the pavement.

This graded road deteriorates slightly to Class I after three miles or so. You will reach the Nadeau Shotgun Road coming from the left 3.6 miles in from the highway (N36°14.269 W117°24.678). Veteran desert freight hauler Remi Nadeau built this road in 1876. It was called the Shotgun Road, because it cut straight across the bajadas of the Argus Range as if it had been fired from a shotgun. Stay to the right following Nadeau's old road to the north. A side road goes left to the Minnietta Mine at 3.9 miles (N36°14.524 W117°24.754). The Minnietta Mine is a worthy side trip (see Excursion # 37), but to find Osborne Canyon you will want to continue straight ahead.

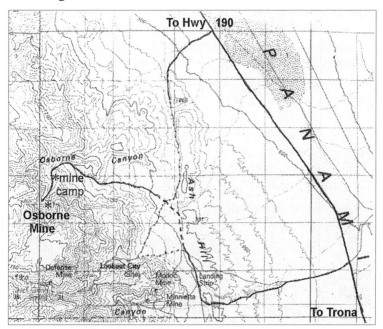

The road forks a tenth of a mile farther on; my recommendation is to stay right, continuing north along the western base of Ash Hill. This fork is washed out in places, but generally no worse than Class III. This was a reasonably good road at one time, but El Niño storms over the past 50 years have brought down a lot of new alluvium, making the boulder strewn route much more difficult.

If you pass this way in the springtime, on your right Ash Hill often puts on a vivid display of purple phacelia. It seems to thrive on the soils derived from this olivine basalt rock. Later, in the summer, cottontop cactus clusters on the left display their colorful flowers.

Yet another intersection is reached six miles in from the pavement (N36°16.053 W117°25.515). It can easily be recognized by the presence of a tractor-loading ramp. The left fork heads south up a boulder strewn wash to rejoin the Stone Canyon Road into Lookout after 1.5 miles (see Excursion #30). From the 2400' elevation, the right fork heads west up the wash into Osborne Canyon. The rough Class II road climbs nearly 2,000 feet in the next 3½ miles.

As you begin to make your way up the road, the rocks at either side of the canyon are varieties of impure limestone, part of the Keeler Canyon Formation.

Suddenly, they change from Paleozoic marine sediments to well-weathered igneous rocks of Jurassic age. While looking like granite to the layman, these younger rocks are technically a leucocratic quartz monzonite. They are a part of the Jurassic pluton that forms the igneous core of the Argus Range, and may be related to similar rocks in the Sierra Nevada.

The canyon forks 3 miles up Osborne Canyon from the tractor-loading ramp. The road swings to the left following the south fork. In a tenth of a mile, a couple of stone buildings are clustered on a bench to the left above the wash. This is the Surprise Mine Camp. The mine itself is another half-mile up the canyon. While you are looking around the old buildings, remember: **Mice and other small rodents infest these structures. Their feces, urine, and saliva can be the source of the Hantavirus, which can infect humans with the sometimes-fatal Hantavirus Pulmonary Syndrome. Inhalation is a common method of transmitting this virus. Avoid all contact with rodent droppings, and do not stir up any dust where there is evidence of mice.**

The Surprise Mine Camp

A quarter-mile beyond the Surprise Mine Camp, the quartz monzonite ends as the Carboniferous marine sediments reappear. First there is the Lee Flat limestone on both sides of the wash. Then, on the left, comes an exposure of the Perdido Formation, followed by the Tin Mountain limestone. Notice how the once flat lying layers have been tilted upwards, twisted and contorted by the forces of metamorphism. The road ends at a lonely ore bunker just beyond this interesting outcrop.

These layered rocks have been metamorphosed by heat and pressure.

The Surprise Mine

J.L. Osborne located the mining claims of the Surprise Mine in 1942. Osborne and his partner Slater tapped into several chimney-like orebodies of lead and silver minerals imbedded in the layers of steeply dipping and faulted Tin Mountain limestone. The principal minerals mined were galena (lead sulfide), cerrusite (lead carbonate), anglesite (lead sulfate), and pyromorphite (lead chlorophosphate). Silver and zinc minerals are also often associated with lead, and this was the case here, too, although here it was the lead that paid the bills. Of the several tunnels, the main adit goes into the hillside 160 feet. Off it is a stope from which 210 tons of ore were extracted in 1942. The main period of operation was in the years 1947-1951, when A.L. Foss worked the mine. There was no mill on the property. The ore was shipped by dump truck 55 miles to Keeler, from where it was transported by rail to the smelter. The total production is thought to have been around 700 tons. The mine seems to have last been worked in 1953, although the present owners still keep their claims valid. **Please respect the owners' property.**

When I first visited the site in June of 1958, the 1300' tramline connecting the mines high on the hillside with the lower ore bin still swayed in the wind. That cable is still there, but it now lies on the ground. From the road's end, it is a short, but steep hike up the hillside to the mines. **Caution: the underground workings are not safe. Do not enter!**

30

Lonely Lookout

Primary Attraction:	A forgotten, historic old mining camp perched high on a mountaintop in the Argus Range. This entire excursion is outside of the national park.
Time Required:	This is an all day outing if you like to stop and look around.
Miles Involved:	It is 18.5 miles from Panamint Springs to Lookout.
Maps:	1:100,000 Darwin Hills sheet; 1:24,000 Revenue Canyon and Panamint Springs Quadrangles.
Degree of Difficulty:	The dirt road portions range from graded gravel to a little Class IV at the Stone Canyon narrows. The Class III sections total two miles.

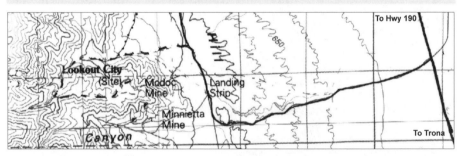

You don't need to be a ghost town buff to have heard of such old mining towns as Calico, Bodie, and Randsburg. These places are easily accessible in the family car, and are popular destinations for weekend trips. For every one of these well-known places, there are dozens of other camps forgotten by everyone except a few western historians. Lookout is one such camp, practically unknown to everyone and seldom visited, except by a hardy few in backcountry vehicles.

To reach Lookout from Panamint Springs, go east on State 190 for 2.6 miles, and then turn right onto the paved road to Trona (N36°20.372 W117°25.388). Go another 7.5 miles to a graded dirt road on the right. A sign reading *Minnietta Mine* marks the turnoff (N36°14.953 W117°21.170). (If you are coming from the direction of Trona, this turnoff is 6.5 miles beyond the Wildrose Canyon Road.) Note your odometer reading here as you leave the pavement. After following this graded road for three miles or so, it deteriorates to Class I. You will reach the Nadeau Shotgun Road coming from the left 3.6 miles in from the highway (N36°14.269 W117°24.678). Veteran desert freight hauler Remi Nadeau built this road in 1876. Stay to the right following Nadeau's old road. After 0.3 miles, a road goes left to the Minnietta Mine, a worthy side-trip (see Excursion #37), but to go to Lookout you will want to continue straight ahead.

A tenth of a mile farther the roads fork; either fork will take you to Lookout. The left fork is the most direct route, but it has one tricky Class III portion. The right fork makes a circuitous loop to the north and is a moderately challenging Class III. This route bypassed the Modoc Mine, a property that was once fenced off. If you pass this way in the springtime, it might be the preferred route, as the western side of Ash Hill on the right often puts on a vivid display of purple phacelia. In the summer, the abundant cottontop cactus clusters also display their colorful flowers. If you do choose this route, stay to the left at the tractor-loading ramp 1.9 miles to the north.

By turning left at the third road junction, you will find the most direct route to Lookout. In 0.4 miles you will come to concrete foundations marking the last remnants of the once very substantial Modoc Mine Camp. The mostly Class III road continues on, skirting the northern base of Lookout Mountain. A mile more and you will see a tunnel and ore bunker on the left. To the right, a road comes from the north; this is the northern loop route described previously. By coming through the Modoc Mine, you have made a shortcut saving two rough miles.

The road soon enters Stone Canyon, and deteriorates to Class III as you proceed. The canyon narrows in another 1.6 miles, with white marble exposed on both sides. A short Class IV pitch is encountered, but once you are on top, the road improves to Class II for the next quarter-mile. If you are looking for a sheltered campsite, look along here.

The canyon forks slightly more than a mile in from the mouth of Stone Canyon. The right fork goes over to the Defense Mine and dead-ends; keep to the left here, starting up the switchbacks. Loose boulders have rolled down onto the roadway from the slope above. You will have to carefully pick your way around these, as some are too big to move. **Drivers of long and wide vehicles could have a little trouble here.** It is but 0.4 miles of easy Class III to the top of the ridge, where there is a three-way intersection (N36°14.536 W117°27.214).

The right fork is the original stage road built in 1877. It continues up the canyon and goes to Darwin; however, the Navy has installed a locked gate that prevents through travel. This road crosses part of the China Lake Naval Weapons Center where unauthorized travel is prohibited. The middle branch dead-ends at a mine; take the left fork to go to Lookout. It doubles back to the top of the ridge, and approaches Lookout from the west. A bulldozer has been brought across this section in recent years and the rest of the way is a very pretty Class II. There are nice views of Telescope Peak and the entire Panamint Range. There is one last fork 0.9 miles beyond the three-way fork; again stay left. Lookout is but a quarter-mile farther.

The road to Lookout

Silver was discovered on the eastern slope of the Argus Range overlooking Panamint Valley in May of 1875. The newly formed mining district was called the Lookout District, because of its fine view. A town of the same name sprang up near the diggings on top of a barren and windswept ridge. At first the ore proved to be so rich in silver that it could be sacked and carried by mules across Panamint Valley to Panamint City, then a thriving community of 1000 people. New prospects on Lookout Mountain developed into viable mines, and in less than a year the production of this spunky little camp attracted the attention of San Francisco mining speculators, including Senator George Hearst. The Senator and his associates bought the Modoc and other promising mines, and the boom in Lookout began.

When Remi Nadeau's mule teams started hauling in supplies in 1876, among the first cargo were two large ore reduction furnaces that would permit silver to be smelted at the mines. By the fall of 1877, these two furnaces were turning out more than 300 silver-lead bars every day from ore averaging $200 per ton. As happened elsewhere, the bullion was cast faster than it could be hauled away, and large stockpiles of ingots built up. By 1877 the insatiable appetite of the furnaces had consumed everything nearby that would burn. At that point, a road was built across Panamint Valley to the piñon-covered slopes of Wildrose Canyon, where ten kilns were constructed of stone to supply the furnaces of Lookout with charcoal. At the same time, another road was built to the west across the Argus Range. A tri-weekly stage connected Lookout with Darwin and Panamint City by May of 1877. By this time Lookout boasted of some 30 to 40 houses, with three saloons, two general stores, and a livery stable.

Lookout City around 1877

The Modoc furnaces on Lookout Mountain
(County of Inyo, Eastern California Museum photos)

The camp remained active through the 1870s, but gradually the more accessible orebodies were exhausted, and the miners began to drift away to more promising camps. The mountaintop metropolis faded into history, although the mines of Lookout Mountain have experienced several short-lived revivals. Although the richest ore is worked out, even now each major increase in the price of silver brings renewed activity in the Minnietta, Carbonate, Defense, and Queen of Sheba mines.

The elements, vandals, and bottle hunters have all taken their toll on the windswept site of Lookout. Nevertheless, the stone walls of about forty buildings remain in various stages of ruin. Judging from the number of broken champagne bottles, life in Lookout must have been mighty tolerable in spite of its isolation. The foundation of a wagon scale once used to weigh ore shipments can still be seen on the north side of Main Street. At the eastern end of town, an ancient boiler lay rusting in the sun for many years. Today Lookout's only inhabitant is a cactus wren, who each spring builds her nest in the protected shelter of a doorless safe.

It seems a paradox that the Wildrose Charcoal Kilns, only one small chapter in the Lookout story, are visited by tens of thousands of tourists each year. Yet the town and its mines that built them, just a few miles away, are seldom heard of, much less visited.

Camp at Lookout if you wish, but please do not utilize the remains of the buildings for firewood. In the 50 years since I first visited the site, I have noticed a lot of deterioration. Help save what is left for the next visitor to enjoy.

Lookout today

31

Snow Canyon

Primary Attraction:	The canyon offers two old gold and silver mines, and all the challenging trails a four-wheeler could want. This area would make a great weekend destination for any 4WD club.
Time Required:	The two old mine camps in the bottom of Snow Canyon are a little more than an hour out of Panamint Springs, but budget much of the day if you elect to visit the mines high on the mountainside.
Miles Involved:	It is 18 miles from Panamint Springs to the Golden Lady Mine Camp.
Maps:	1:100,000 Darwin Hills sheet; 1:24,000 Revenue Canyon Quadrangle.
Degree of Difficulty:	It is a Class I or better road to the mouth of the canyon, then Class III to the two mine camps. Climbing the ridge to the mines is mostly Class III and IV, with a few Class V ruts to overcome.

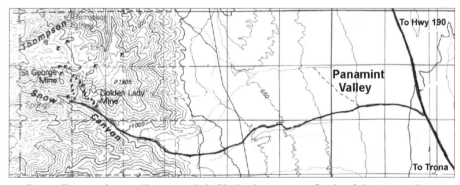

Snow Canyon is a well-watered defile in the eastern flank of the Argus Range, where wild burros intuitively seek refuge from the government bureaucrats trying to round them up.

To reach Snow Canyon from Panamint Springs, go east on State 190 for 2.6 miles, and then turn right onto the paved Panamint Valley Road to Trona

(N36°20.372 W117°25.388). Go another 7.5 miles to the graded Minnietta Road on the right (N36°14.953 W117°21.170). Note your odometer reading, but continue south on the highway. At a point 3.2 miles south of the Minnietta Road, look for an unmarked Class I road to the right (N36°12.265 W117°20.189). (If you are coming from the direction of Trona, this turn-off is 3.2 miles beyond the Wildrose Canyon Road.) Reset your odometer, and turn right.

The desert road, mostly Class I and II in spots, heads westward gradually climbing the bajada formed by alluvium coming out of Thompson, Snow, and Wood Canyons in the Argus Range. The old Nadeau Shotgun Road (see Excursion #37) is crossed 3.7 miles from the pavement (N36°11.828 W117°23.922). By turning to the right, you can return to the Minnietta Road just three miles to the north. For Snow Canyon simply cross the Nadeau Road, and continue westward.

Yet a second crossroads is reached after another mile; the BLM has posted the roads to the left and right as closed, because the lands on either side of the Snow Canyon Road are part of the *Argus Range Wilderness*.

Our desert road drops down into the wash coming out of Snow Canyon 5.5 miles from the paved highway. The ascent on the other side is Class III. Soon the road improves to Class II again and remains that way for 0.6 miles, when it again crosses the wash and briefly becomes Class III. Extensive stone walls on the right 6.9 miles in from the pavement mark the beginning of the Golden Lady Mine Camp. A tenth of a mile beyond, a fork to the right climbs to the mill site and on up to the mines high on the north wall of Snow Canyon. It was near this intersection that the mine had its living quarters. There are rock walls of a half dozen structures, plus two corral enclosures made from the same rock. If you wander through the bushes just east of the intersection, the circular stone ruins of the mine's first arrastra can be found.

The Class II road climbs steeply to the mine's mill site. There is plenty of flat ground here for a large group to camp. Little remains of the mill, save for some stone foundations and crumbling red brick indicating the site of small reduction furnaces. Above the millsite, a steep and badly rutted Class IV road climbs the mountainside 1000 feet or more to the various workings of what was once the Golden Lady Mine. **Use extreme caution if you use this road.**

The rocks in the bottom of Snow Canyon are the same Cretaceous granite that makes up much of the Argus Range. But the rocks where the ore was mined, high on the canyon's north wall, are the same Carboniferous limestone formations as those containing the Modoc, Minnietta, and other mines of Lookout Mountain.

History does not easily recall exactly when the Golden Lady Mine was discovered. It was in those heady days of the early 1870s when Panamint and Lookout were booming. In spite of its name, more silver than gold was produced.

The Class III Snow Canyon road continues up the canyon 0.4 miles from the Golden Lady Mine Camp to the somewhat younger St. George Mine camp. Here, too, is ample flat ground where a small group might make camp. None of the buildings are left at the camp, except for the powder magazine dug into the hillside. **It is unsafe to enter!**

Beyond the mine camp, the Class III road continues up the canyon a quarter-mile to a fork. The right fork heads steeply up a side canyon to the north to ascend to the mines high above. The left fork circles around to the mill site and the bunkers, which once collected the ore brought down the mountainside by aerial tramline.

The St. George Mine was originally known as the Merry Christmas Mine, because the first of its two systems of quartz veins was discovered in December. The quartz revealed free gold when crushed to a fine sand. Other associated metals included a variety of sulfide minerals, iron pyrite, chalcopyrite and arsenopyrite. The common copper mineral green malachite can also be found along the road between the mill and the mine where it has spilled off heavily laden ore wagons. Like its neighbor the Golden Lady, the St. George Mine produced more silver than gold.

A small seasonal stream reaches as far down the canyon as the St. George mill site in wet years. During these periods dove and quail are very abundant here in Snow Canyon. Although they are seldom seen, the night air is alive with the sounds of hoot owls. More conspicuous are the small bands of feral burros that also inhabit the canyon.

The road ends at the mill site, and here the *Argus Range Wilderness* begins. Those so inclined can hike up the canyon for a mile or more before the going gets really steep.

The mill site of the St. George Mine

Bygone Ballarat

Ballarat in the 1920s

Ballarat's adobe walls
(Searles Valley Historical Society photos)

The author took this photo of Ballarat in the 1950s.

Chapter VIII
Trails Out of Ballarat

The ghost town of Ballarat may seem to be a strange hub to use as a base for outings, because it has little in the way of services. Nevertheless, it is centrally located in Panamint Valley, and all of the west side canyons of the Panamints are readily accessible from Ballarat.

The year was 1893. The excitement of Panamint City had already died down when Charles Anthony and John Lamphier began to stake claims in Pleasant Canyon. They generated little attention until three years later, when Henry Ratcliff found a promising lode in the summer of '96. At the same time, James Cooper staked some claims farther up the canyon. The word got out, and once again dusty prospectors appeared from nowhere, and headed up the western canyons of the high Panamints.

In less than a year, the Ratcliff Mine was going strong, and it became obvious that a town was needed to house the two hundred miners. There simply wasn't enough room in Pleasant Canyon, so a few of the mine buildings were moved down to the alkali flats at the mouth of the canyon. An 80-acre town site was laid out, and the land was subdivided into lots. Thus was born the town of Ballarat, named after a world-famous Australian gold camp. Ratcliff's employees lived in Ballarat and commuted the six miles to work each day by wagon. By June of 1897, there was sufficient need to establish a post office at Ballarat.

The Ratcliff Mine operated successfully from 1897 to 1903, producing nearly a half-million dollars in gold. It was by far the largest and most productive mine in Pleasant Canyon. After the Ratcliff ceased operation in 1905, the World Beater Mine opened just a half-mile up the canyon. Ballarat had a renewed lease on life. As all mines eventually do, the diggings in Pleasant Canyon also shut down. The big rush to Skidoo came in 1906, and the miners moved north a few miles. But the long supply route from Mojave still ran through Panamint Valley, and Ballarat's existence was prolonged a little longer. Finally in 1917, Ballarat's last saloon closed its doors for good.

Ballarat's most famous person was Charles Ferge, known best as "Seldom Seen Slim". He came to Ballarat in 1913, and never left. Although he liked to project the image of a recluse, he enjoyed pulling the odd tourist's leg. I can recall that when I was a kid, Slim came into Ted Lang's service station in Argus, showing large square iron pyrite crystals to city slickers en route to the first Death Valley 49ers' encampment. Slim passed it off as gold, but even at age eleven, I knew better! Slim died in 1968, and is buried in Ballarat's Boot Hill. So interesting and well known was he that his funeral was featured on national television.

Left to right: Seldom Seen Slim, Walter Sorensen,
Chris Wicht, and Fred Grey on Thanksgiving Day, 1935
(County of Inyo, Eastern California Museum Photo)

The buildings of Ballarat were made of two materials: wood or sun dried adobe bricks. After Ballarat's decline, the wooden buildings were dismantled for use elsewhere, leaving only the adobe structures. As infrequent as it is here, a century of rain has taken its toll, and every year there seems to be a little less left of old Ballarat. In recent years, there has been a small general store in Ballarat (no gasoline) and a small waterless campground, where a very nominal fee is charged.

32

Jail Canyon

Primary Attraction:	An old miner's camp in a remote canyon.
Time Required:	This is a half-day round trip out of Ballarat or Panamint Springs Resort.
Miles Involved:	It is 13 miles from Ballarat (or 25 miles from Panamint Springs) to the end of the road at the Jail Canyon miner's camp.
Maps:	1:100,000 Darwin Hills sheet; 1:24,000 Jail Canyon Quadrangle.
Degree of Difficulty:	Once off the Indian Ranch Road, it is mostly Class II, with only a few Class III sections across the wash.

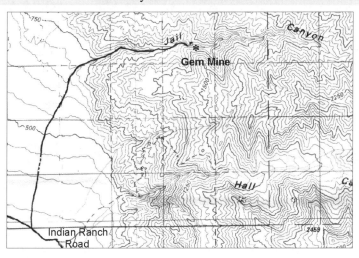

One of the most spectacular four-wheel drive routes in the entire Death Valley region was once the route from Jail Canyon over the ridge into Hall Canyon on the western slope of the Panamints. *Wilderness* designation has closed that road, and today you can go only as far as the abandoned miner's camp in Jail Canyon. Nevertheless, the road into Jail Canyon makers an interesting excursion in this little visited part of the Panamint Range.

From downtown Ballarat, go north on the graded county Indian Ranch Road. At a point 7.7 miles north of Ballarat, look to the right for an unmarked road that heads north and starts to climb the alluvial fan; turn right here (N36°08.677 W117°14.033). Ahead you will see white-looking sand and gravel that washed out of Jail Canyon during a flash flood. This material cut across the jeep trail in several places, but the route has been re-established. Death Valley National Park is entered two miles up from the Indian Ranch Road (N36°10.677 W117°14.033). A mile beyond that, a closed track once turned off to the left to go into Tuber Canyon and the site of the O.B. Joyful Mine that is now in the *wilderness*.

Jail Canyon is entered 2.7 miles above the Indian Ranch Road. A few short Class III portions will be encountered in the next mile or so. You will also encounter a giant boulder, the size of a house, in the bottom of the wash. Was this boulder washed down the canyon by a flash flood, or did it roll off the hillside above? What do you think?

This house size boulder rolled down to the canyon bottom from the ridge on left.

Finally, an old miner's camp is reached 5.4 miles from the Indian Ranch Road. This is the site of the Corona Mine, which prior to 1949 was known as the New Discovery Mine, and before that the Gem Mine. Bedrock has forced underground water flowing down from the very summit of Telescope Peak to rise to the surface here. There are a couple of structures left, leaning badly, and possibly collapsed by now. Also here are the ever-present piles of rusting cans, vehicles, and machinery so typical at these old mines.

The geology here is of very old Precambrian metamorphic rocks that were later intruded by Cretaceous granite. Hot mineral solutions making quartz veins occurred at the contact of the two rock types. These quartz veins contain gold, silver, lead and zinc. It was these veins that were discovered by Jack Curran in 1899, who called his find the Gem Mine. Curran had no money to build a mill, but Ballarat merchant Charles Weaver did. Curran gave a half interest to Weaver for his three-stamp mill. With the building of a waterwheel at the spring, Weaver's mill did the trick, and they were soon making monthly shipments of bullion.

The history of the Gem Mine becomes somewhat obscure after 1900. The waterwheel and original mill were destroyed by a flash flood in 1901. When Geologist R. J. Samson visited Jail Canyon in 1931, the Gem Mine was still being worked. When I first came through here in 1957, I found a man named Troster living here. He said he had owned the claims for many years, but he was doing no serious mining.

Look up to the precipitous south wall of Jail Canyon. At one time the steepest jeep trail in the Death Valley region switch-backed up the canyon wall (it climbed 1,000 feet in one half-mile). It went on over the ridge into some prospects in Hall Canyon. It was a thrilling ride with some of the hairpin turns so sharp, even short-wheelbase vehicles had to back up and maneuver around them. Alas, this masterpiece of engineering was closed to vehicles with the expansion of the park, but you can still hike the road. The trail starts in a wash 0.2 miles below the Corona Mine Camp.

Jail Canyon is not the sort of place you would want to drive all the way from Los Angeles just to see. But after you have explored the other canyons on the western slope of the Panamints, this one should go on your list, too.

This cabin at the Gem Mine Camp has subsequently collapsed.
Stay out of structures like this to avoid possible exposure to the Hantavirus.

33

Rogers Pass via Pleasant Canyon

Primary Attraction:	Pleasant Canyon has lots of history and old mines galore, all mixed in with plenty of high Panamint scenery.
Time Required:	The loop trip up Pleasant Canyon, over the ridge into Middle Park, and then back to Ballarat by South Park Canyon can be done in a single day. There is so much country to see here, however, that taking two days would be even better.
Miles Involved:	It is only 12 miles from Ballarat to Rogers Pass. Add another 20 miles to return to Ballarat via South Park Canyon (see Excursion #34).
Maps:	1:100,000 Darwin Hills sheet; 1:24,000 Ballarat and Panamint Quadrangles.
Degree of Difficulty:	The entire route is usually no more difficult than Class III. **Winter snows can bury the roads above Stone Corral anytime between December and March.**
Remarks:	In recent years, the willows have been spreading their branches over the roadway in the lower canyon, where they could possibly scratch the paint of a passing vehicle.

Like Surprise Canyon just to the north, the Pleasant Canyon road takes you high onto the piñon-covered slopes of the Panamint Range. Unlike Surprise Canyon, however, you can climb up one canyon, cross over a ridge, descend into an isolated valley, cross another pass, and descend by yet another canyon to make a complete loop. Like many of these outings, the condition of the route can vary greatly from one month to the next. Between December and March, it is a good bet that deep snow will make the high elevation portions of this loop impassable.

Our journey back through time and into the high Panamints starts in Ballarat. A sign in downtown Ballarat points east to the Pleasant Canyon Road. If you are in doubt, ask at the general store. Reset your odometer, and follow the graded dirt road northeast out of town (N36°02.882 W117°13.442). (This is not to be confused with the Indian Ranch Road, which starts northwest out of Ballarat). It will soon turn eastward if you are on the correct road. A Class II road turns off to the left in a half-mile (N36°02.976 W117°12.893). This road goes into Jackpot Canyon and ends at a spring. Keep right on the main road, and soon you will be in Pleasant Canyon.

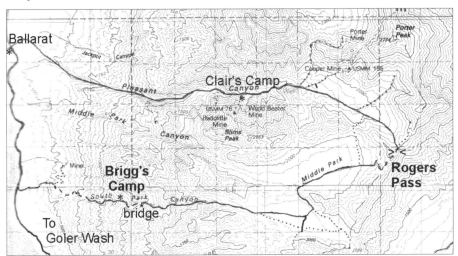

Bedrock in the canyon bottom 2.5 miles from Ballarat forces buried water to the surface. For the next mile up the canyon, this stream will be your constant companion. Indeed, sometimes the streambed is the road. On occasion, water and mud can produce Class III sections in the roadway, but often the route is no worse than Class II.

The streambed is lined with cattails and Desert Willow *Chilopsis lineras*, the latter sometimes attempting to overgrow the roadway. The Paiute Indians made good use of both of these plants. The slender willow twigs were used for baskets and sometimes for medicinal purposes, while the cattails were used as an absorbent in babies' diapers.

Four miles from Ballarat, a 1750' long aerial cableway goes up the steep south wall of the canyon to the Anthony Mine. One of the oldest mines in the canyon, it was found in 1893 by Charles Anthony. In its century long history, it was originally known as the Anthony Mine, later the Knob Mine, and most recently the Gold Bug. Over the years, the mine's quartz veins have produced both gold and lead.

Another half-mile up the canyon, a similar aerial cableway goes up the north canyon wall to yet another mine. It is interesting to note here that while the barrel cactus appears in great numbers, they are all growing on the steep canyon wall, and none are growing on the south side of the canyon. They obviously prefer the dry, well-drained soils, and warm sunny exposures of the canyon's northern slope. The more moist and shady south wall of the canyon is preferred by the creosote bush.

Clair's Camp is reached 6 miles from Ballarat. Between 1897 and 1903, this was the camp and mill site for the Ratcliff Mine that is perched high up on the canyon's south wall. Again, it was an aerial cableway that lowered the ore 500 vertical feet to the canyon bottom, where it could be crushed and milled. This was the mine found by Henry Ratcliff in 1897, and the one that turned out to be the richest in Pleasant Canyon. During the five-year period between 1898 and 1903, it produced 15,000 tons of ore, which by some estimates were worth up to a million dollars.

Walter Delos Clair, an energetic entrepreneur with homes in Los Angeles, Bishop, and Sylvania, Nevada, bought the mine and mill site in 1912. He reasoned that the ore milling methods employed by Ratcliff were inefficient, and the ore dumps below the mill site should still contain a lot of gold. Clair was no dummy, and history proved him right. He installed a cyanide mill, and operated it until World War II, when President Roosevelt's Executive Order closed all the nation's gold mines. W.D. made a relatively good living here during the years of the Great Depression. The cyanide plant supported not only himself and his wife Kate, but also the families of Vere and Donald, his two married sons who worked the plant alongside him. Some 20,000 tons of the old tailings were put through a cyanide mill between 1928 and 1942, recovering about $5.00 per ton in gold that had been missed the first time. W.D. died in December of 1942, and eventually Kate and her boys moved away. In 1949 the Clair family leased the old Ratcliff Mine. This time gold was not the principal mineral being sought, but rather galena (lead) and scheelite (tungsten).

W.D. Clair (photo courtesy of Earl Clair)

I came up Pleasant Canyon for the first time in the mid 1950s. By that time the Clairs had only a caretaker living here. A locked gate blocked further travel up the canyon. Fortunately, the gate could be opened with the offering of a few tin cans: one containing Prince Albert tobacco and a couple more of Lucky Lager beer. In recent years the property has been sold to a corporation in Arkansas, the caretaker is gone. The gate is still there, but it is unlocked. It has been many years since Clair's Camp has seen any maintenance, much less heard the steady pounding of the ore mill.

One can prowl through the deteriorating buildings, but do be watchful for nails protruding upward from pieces of wood, and be ever mindful to avoid any place where there is evidence of mice and rodent droppings. The mine's main kitchen and mess hall building was made of earthen walls. Here, too, the lack of upkeep has taken its toll. Stay well away from the redwood water tank; it is leaning badly and looks like it could fall over at anytime. The remnants of two boilers can be seen at the mill. The steam from them powered an engine, which drove a wide belt that turned the ore crusher. In its 100-year history, the mill here has utilized several types of devices to crush the ore. The last mill used was a 4' x 6' Marcy ball mill. It is still there, although badly vandalized. Prior to that, a 20-stamp mill was utilized. Some of its remains lie on the junk pile.

Clair's Camp

The canyon opens up a bit after passing Clair's Camp. Soon another aerial cableway goes up the south side of the canyon. This, too, brought ore down from the Ratcliff Mine.

A mile above Clair's Camp on the left side of the road was a miner's camp, burned a few years ago to cover the murder of its caretaker. On the right, a short steep side road climbs up the hillside a half-mile to the mill site of the World Beater Mine, another important producer in this canyon. When I wrote the first edition of *Death Valley Jeep Trails* in 1968, I took a picture of two friends standing here beside the enormous 10-stamp mill. Unfortunately, nothing remains of the mill today, except for its stone foundations. The mill was being dismantled in preparation for a move to Tonopah when a worker's cutting torch accidentally set it on fire. The actual tunnels and shafts of the World Beater Mine are high on the slopes above. Once again, it was an aerial cableway that brought the ore down to the mill.

The author took this photo of the 10-stamp mill at the World Beater Mine in 1968 before it was accidentally burned during dismantlement.

Passing the lonely wooden structure at the World Beater Mine camp, the road soon enters the piñon-juniper forest. By this time you have risen some 4,500 feet since leaving the mud flats at Ballarat. The shrub with the yellowish-green stems is ephedra, commonly called Mormon tea. Boiling a handful of stems in water can produce a passable cup of tea. The Indians are said to have drunk this solution to cure intestinal ailments. Some say it is an acquired taste; others add sugar to counter the bitter taste left by its high tannic acid content. Try it if you wish, but it should be noted that **ephedra contains the drug epinephrine, a cardiac stimulant about which the FDA has issued a health warning. Do not drink tea made from ephedra if you have any kind of cardiac problem. Prolonged consumption may also cause personality changes and other psychiatric disorders!**

A water trough is passed on the left two miles above Clair's Camp, and just ahead is the new park boundary (N36°01.885 W117°07.708). An old stone corral was built at the site of a reliable spring, and hence its name. This corral was used as a reference point when some of the earliest mining claims were staked. It is thought to have been built by Paiute Indians who came here in the fall to collect piñon nuts. At one time, water was piped from this spring all the way down to the World Beater Mine camp.

On the left, a Class III side road leaves the main road here (N36°02.031 W117°05.844). It climbs nearly 1,300 feet in a little more than a mile to pass through a 7,145' gap in the ridge and go to the site of the Porter Mine, found by Henry "Harry" Clay Porter. Harry was 36 years old when he left the coalfields of Pennsylvania to come to California. He turned to prospecting in 1899. In 1902 he and his partner Wade Richardson set out on a two-year search for the Lost Mexican Mine, and they may have actually found it. They sold their find, which they called the Mountain Boy, for $10,000 and went their separate ways. With his grubstake renewed, Harry continued to prospect in the Panamints. He found a quartz vein showing wire gold in 1908, and developed this lode into the Mountain Girl Mine. Everyone else simply called it the Porter Mine. Harry remained here for the next 41 years, going down the canyon to be with his friends at Clair's Camp or Ballarat only when the winter snows got too deep. He died at the ripe old age of 86, and is buried in Bishop.

The side trip to the Porter Mine is interesting, but impassable in the winter and early spring when snow lingers longer on the north side of the pass. The view north down into the roadless Happy Canyon basin and beyond to the summit of 11,049' Telescope Peak is quite nice. Henry knew how to pick them.

Still Class II the main road continues on ahead. In a tenth of a mile, on the left are the remains of a steam powered four-stamp mill operated by Bessie Hart during the 1905 period. Ore from Bessie's own mine could not put beans on her table, but her custom milling for others did pay the bills. There is a story that Shorty Harris once proposed to Bessie after seeing the quantity of air she could pump through the blacksmith's bellows down in Ballarat. History does not record her exact answer, but Shorty died a bachelor in 1934.

Also on the left is a Class III side road (N36°01.995 W117°05.699) that goes up the hillside 1½ miles to dead-end at the Cooper Mine, found in 1896 by James Cooper. From different sides of the same ridge, both the Porter Mine and the

Cooper Mine tap into the same system of quartz veins that have invaded this very old pre-Precambrian rock. Specimens of the ore can be found along the road. **Timbers shoring up the tunnels are rotting. Stay out of the underground workings.**

The road forks at a point 0.8 miles above Stone Corral. Take either fork; they both go a half-mile ahead and rejoin again. There is another fork 1.7 miles above Stone Corral. Hidden in the trees here is a weather-tight cabin that is kept unlocked by the National Park Service. Like several other cabins in the Panamints, this one can be used by backcountry travelers as an emergency shelter. Please do not use any of the food or water, unless it is an emergency! **Warning: Mice and other small rodents sometimes get into these cabins. Their feces, urine, and saliva can be the source of the Hantavirus that can infect humans with a nasty illness called Hantavirus Pulmonary Syndrome, which can be fatal. Avoid all contact with rodent droppings, and do not stir up any dust where there is evidence of mice and rats. Inhalation of the virus is a common method of transmission to humans.**

At this intersection, the right fork makes a steep ascent of 600 feet in a half-mile to cross a pass in the ridge and descend into Middle Park. My recommendation would be to stay left on the main road. It continues up Pleasant Canyon another 1.3 miles. The first mile remains mostly Class II, with the last 0.3 miles an easy Class III. Then, 12 miles from Ballarat, the road suddenly reaches a saddle on the crest of the Panamint Range. The air is clean and crisp up here, and likely to be cool even in August. Here on this ridgetop, a sturdy metal sign reads:

Rogers Pass
El. 7140

Wm Manly & Jn Rogers crossed this pass on the way to get supplies for 49ers trapped in Death Valley. Later, as they led the Bennet & Arcane families to safety, they came here to view the land ahead, looking back, one said, "Goodbye Death Valley!" The date was Feb. 14, 1850. It is believed they crossed the Panamints via Butte Valley & Redlands Cy. They crossed the Slate via Fish & Isham Cyns, then to Providence Spring at Great Falls in the Argus Range. Up Wilson Cy & across the valley to Indian Wells Spring on the way to a Spanish ranch near Newhall. All this party survived. Erected Jan '92 ET Conf. Trona Chapter

(See Excursion #39 for more about the "Escape Trail".)

The road forks on the saddle, with branches going up the ridge to the left and the right. To the left, a very rocky Class IV road climbs steeply northward towards an antenna site 1000' higher. To the right, a Class III route climbs the ridgeline to the south, and descends again to another saddle. By turning right, Middle Park is but a couple of switchbacks down the hillside to the west, and South Park is over the low divide to the south from there. It is nearly twenty miles from Rogers Pass back to Ballarat via the Class II and Class III roads in South Park Canyon (see Excursion #34). **Another word of warning: In South Park Canyon, just above Briggs Camp, is a narrow bridge spanning a chasm in the cliff-side where a portion of the mountain slid away. The Inyo County Road Department engineers have examined this bridge and have rated it at no more than 6,000 pounds maximum. If your backcountry vehicle exceeds that weight, turn back. Do not attempt to cross the bridge!**

The road down South Park Canyon will be remembered for its steep grades and spectacular narrows. This circle tour can be done from either direction, but the grades going up South Park Canyon are more severe than Pleasant Canyon. Once you are back down and out of South Park Canyon, it is 6.7 miles back to the starting point in Ballarat.

Cacti favor the sunny south facing slopes of Pleasant Canyon.

34

Rogers Pass via South Park Canyon

Primary Attraction:	Offering old mines and high Panamint scenery, in combination with Pleasant Canyon, the loop trip made makes an interesting camping outing for your family or 4WD club.
Time Required:	The loop up South Park Canyon, over the ridge into Middle Park, and back to Ballarat by way of Pleasant Canyon can be done in a single day; however, there is so much country to see, two or even three days would be better.
Miles Involved:	It is nearly 20 miles from Ballarat to Rogers Pass by way of South Park Canyon, and another 12 miles back to Ballarat by way of Pleasant Canyon.
Maps:	1:100,000 Darwin Hills and Ridgecrest sheets; 1:24,000 Ballarat, Manly Fall, Manly Peak and Panamint Quadrangles.
Degree of Difficulty:	In the lower canyon, loose gravel, large rocks and steep grades make the route mostly Class III, with several short areas of Class IV. **Water flowing down the road at Colter Spring often freezes during the winter months, making the road so slippery as to be impassable.**
Remarks:	Because of restrictions on a bridge ahead, the loop through to Pleasant Canyon cannot be completed if your vehicle weighs more than 6000 pounds.

The excursion up South Park Canyon to Roger's Pass with a descent via Pleasant Canyon (or visa versa) is one of the most scenic and historically interesting rough-road journeys in the Death Valley country.

From downtown Ballarat, note your odometer reading and start south on the oiled Wingate Road in the direction of Goler Wash. In just a half-mile you will pass Post Office Spring, where it is thought that the second Jayhawker Party camped after their perilous escape from Death Valley in 1850. The site got the name, not because a post office was ever here, but because local outlaws, in cahoots with certain stagecoach drivers, used the site to stash cash here. The stage driver would pick up the cash, and in turn leave groceries on the return trip.

Stone ruins near Post Office Spring in 1965
(Searles Valley Historical Society photo)

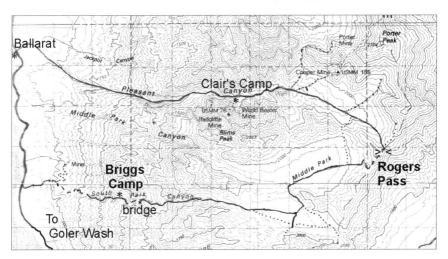

A side road goes left 3.9 miles south of Ballarat (N35°59.998 W117°13.234). Although it is not marked, this is the way to South Park Canyon. The Class II road climbs steeply through the fanglomerate of the mesa. Because traction is poor, many will engage their four-wheel drive within a half-mile of leaving the oiled road, but the grades become gentler once you top the mesa, and the road improves to Class II again. Stop for a moment at one of the several vantage points. The views down upon Panamint Valley are quite nice.

A second set of steep Class III zigzags are encountered two miles above the oiled road. They are only a half-mile long. At a point 2.8 miles above the oiled road, 6.7 miles from Ballarat, you enter South Park Canyon and immediately the very old metamorphic rocks in the canyon walls close in upon you. The loose gravel in the wash makes it a Class III road for the next half-mile, with at least two Class IV sections and one steep Class V grade. The latter is 7.5 miles out of Ballarat, and can be easily avoided by a short bypass to the left. The canyon opens up and the road improves 7.8 miles out of Ballarat. It is mostly Class II from here on to the crest.

At a point 8.1 miles from Ballarat, a side road to the left steeply makes its way up the north wall of South Park Canyon. This Class III road leads to the Suitcase Mine, whose lower workings are but a half-mile above the canyon bottom. In gaining access to their claims, the miners had to carve a series of four switchbacks so severe that the drivers of most vehicles with four wheels will have to see-saw around the hairpin turns. Although this mine is nearly a century old, it has obviously been worked in recent years. This side trip is well worth the effort, as the views down into Panamint Valley are breathtaking.

One of the cabins at Briggs Camp

A cluster of buildings adjoining a spring and old mill site is reached 8.8 miles from Ballarat. Today the site is called the Briggs Camp, although its history seems to go back long before Harry Briggs ever came to the Panamints, well over a half-century ago. Indeed, the two cabins at the camp are in better condition today than they were 20 or 30 years ago. The C. R. Briggs Corporation allows free use of the cabins on a first come, first served basis, providing the property is duly cared for. The public seems to have reciprocated by maintaining the structures and keeping them stocked with emergency food, bedding, and other amenities of rural life. The fig tree next to the upper cabin has thrived, and other landscaping has added to the comfort of this remote outpost. On occasion Bighorn sheep wander through the camp, sampling the tasty green grasses and shrubbery. **Remember: Mice and other small rodents sometimes get into these cabins.**

Their feces, urine, and saliva can be the source of the Hantavirus that can infect humans with a nasty illness called Hantavirus Pulmonary Syndrome, which has proven be fatal in nearly half the cases reported! Avoid all contact with rodent droppings and do not stir up any dust where there is evidence of mice and rats. Inhalation of the virus is a common way of transmission to humans.

A short distance above the Briggs Camp, South Park Canyon narrows once again. This time the bedrock has created a series of dry waterfalls so high and so severe that no animal, much less a vehicle, could ever get over them. To bypass this impassable section of canyon bottom, the early miners carved a road out of the south canyon wall. Although marginal, this road was adequate for nearly 75 years. However, an El Niño driven storm in 1983 caused a portion of mountainside to slide away, severing the already precarious road. Passage through South Park Canyon was thus interrupted for a decade until 1994, when miners fashioned a crude but effective bridge out of old utility poles. Inyo County road engineers were less than enthused with the results. They permitted the structure to remain, but limited the weight to 6,000 pounds.

At a point 0.3 miles above the Briggs Camp, the BLM has placed a sign that reads: *Narrow bridge ¼ mile ahead, Max. Wt. 3 tons GV, No turn around.*

The infamous bridge

The reader would be well advised to heed the warning. **If your fully loaded vehicle weighs more than 6,000 pounds, go no farther!** Not only could you and your vehicle end up in a crumbled mass of metal 400' below in the bottom of the wash, but your actions could once again sever the road through South Park Canyon for another decade. This is no place for a 7,000-pound Hummer!

The road enters the wash again a tenth of a mile beyond the bridge, this time above the dry waterfalls. The canyon opens up, and once again the road improves to Class II. In another tenth of a mile, a side road right goes to the Thorndike's Honolulu Mine high on the south ridge.

The Honolulu Mine was discovered in 1907. At first, the richest ore was brought out on the backs of mules. It was not until 1924 that John Thorndike built the steep, twisting road up South Park Canyon. He then built a 2,150' tramway from the mine to the canyon bottom, from where he hauled the ore out by truck. The property was last worked between 1942 and 1944, when 1300 tons were taken out.

As a footnote to history, John Thorndike had more on his mind than just mining. He had long dreamed about building a tourist hotel on the summit of 11,049' Telescope Peak. Those plans never materialized for obvious reasons; however, in the 1930s he and his wife did erect a few tourist cabins at 7,500 feet, just below Mahogany Flat. Some of these cabins were still standing when I first climbed Telescope Peak in the 1950s. Alas, Thorndike's Resort did not turn into a second Furnace Creek Inn. The cabins have been subsequently torn down, and the site turned into a public campground.

The South Park road continues up the canyon. Notice the cinnamon roll-like swirls of highly metamorphosed rock on the left 0.2 miles above the Honolulu Mine road. In the springtime it is in this area that nature puts on a grand wildflower display. Bright crimson Indian paintbrush, orange mallow, yellow broom, purple phacelia, white prickly poppy, and long stems of blue lupine all tint nature's pallet.

At 5,700 feet, Coulter Spring sends its life giving water flowing across and down the road 10.6 miles from Ballarat. In December, January, and February, daytime temperatures in the shady areas are often insufficient to melt the blanket of ice. Under those circumstances, the roadway becomes treacherous and often impassable. Coulter Spring also marks the boundary of national park lands N35°59.666 W117°08.162). From here on into South Park, the roads improve to Class I and II.

Slightly more than 11 miles out of Ballarat, the first piñon pines begin to appear. Soon South Park Canyon opens into a treeless basin nearly three miles long by a half-mile wide; this is South Park. The road forks 11.7 miles from Ballarat. Both forks run east up the valley and rejoin after 1½ miles. Take the left fork as it is sometimes less dusty. After going only a tenth of a mile, a crossroads is reached.

To the right, a road runs south crossing the dusty landing strip to come to a dead-end in a couple of miles at some prospect holes. If you chose to take this road to the right, look for several side roads going off to the left. They go eastward up the valley to a 6,500' vantage point where the views are outstanding. Some 3,000 feet below lies Butte Valley and beyond; looking down Anvil Spring Canyon is the white floor of Death Valley. A little to the right and 1000' below is Striped Butte with its unique bands. By looking still farther to the right, you can see the road leading to the summit of Mengel Pass (see Excursion # 9).

To go on to Middle Park and Rogers Pass, you will want to stay to the left at this crossroads. The main road will soon take you past an abandoned mine camp. The main cabin has burned, and what is left is an unsightly collection of rusting machinery and refuse. On the hillside above the camp is the tunnel and the air compressor building. The rusting artifacts suggest that this mine is of more recent vintage than those far below in South Park Canyon. What appears to be a perfectly straight road running for nearly a mile down South Park is actually a crude airstrip installed to provide easy access to this mine.

It was not mineral wealth that attracted geologist Julia Miller to study this area. It was the very old Precambrian rocks. She found evidence of very old glaciation of the Proterozoic Kingston Peak Formation. This is not the recent Plio-Pleistocene glaciation that started a mere 2.7 million years ago that we are talking about. The traces of glaciation in the Kingston Peak Formation occurred one half-billion years ago!

South Park

The road continues past the mine camp, doubles back to the northwest and soon tops a 6,400' ridge. Spread out below you to the north is Middle Park, a similar basin having an elevation nearly identical to that of South Park. The main road descends from the pass 0.2 miles, and then forks. The Class II main road goes right, heading east through Middle Park. In 1.2 miles, a side road goes north to cross the ridge into Pleasant Canyon. My recommendation is to continue east another mile to the crest of the range, and from there turn left, taking a Class III road up the ridge a half-mile to drop down onto Rogers Pass. This is the more scenic route. To complete the loop from Rogers Pass, it is but 12 miles down Pleasant Canyon to Ballarat (see Excursion #33 for that route description).

35

Mengel Pass via Goler Wash

Primary Attraction: Typical canyon scenery of the Panamints, and the only through pass over the southern half of the range still open to vehicles. Along the way is a bit of history, both old and new.

Time Required: The ascent of Goler Wash can take a few hours, or a few days. It all depends on the road conditions of the moment.

Miles Involved: It is 26 miles from Ballarat to the summit of Mengel Pass. Add two miles for a side trip to Barker Ranch.

Maps: 1:100,000 Darwin Hills and Ridgecrest sheets; 1:24,000 Ballarat, Manly Fall, Manly Peak, and Anvil Spring Canyon West Quadrangles.

Degree of Difficulty: I have seen Goler Wash when it was no more difficult than Class II, and I have seen it when it was mostly Class IV and V. The roadbed has been washed out and rebuilt many times over the years. How you may find it is anybody's guess. Since the El Niño rains in the winter of 1982-83, the road has been mostly Class III, but with at least four sections of Class IV and sometimes Class V. When it is bad, the four dry waterfalls are generally rated Class IV coming down the canyon going in an east to west direction. Under these conditions, if you choose to go up Goler Wash, expect all four of these bare rock waterfalls to be difficult, with two and possibly three to be Class V. **At best, the road through Goler Wash can be negotiated by any high clearance vehicle, but at its worst, Goler Wash should be attempted only by experienced four-wheelers in short wheelbase vehicles. It is recommended that you first inquire about the current condition of the canyon.**

Sooner or later, all backcountry explorers of the Death Valley region will go over Mengel Pass, a low notch in the Panamint Range that separates Death

Valley and Panamint Valley. The roads on either side can be challenging, but there is scenery and history in each mile driven.

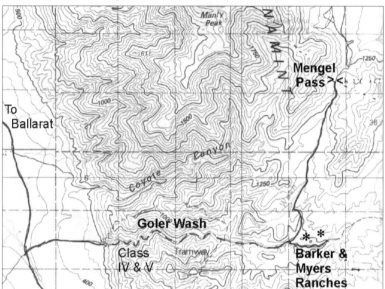

From downtown Ballarat, note your odometer reading, and start south on the oiled road in the direction of Goler Wash. South of Ballarat 3.9 miles, a side road goes left to South Park Canyon (see Excursion #34). At a point 7.7 miles from downtown Ballarat, you will pass the entrance to the C.R. Briggs Mine operated by the Canyon Resources Corporation. In the late 1990s this mine was one of the five top gold producers in California. It is a new mine, with 1997 being its first full year of operation. In 1998 the mine produced some 80,300 ounces of gold. It has reserves of an additional 653,000 ounces in sight and, unlike many of the mines in the Panamint Range that have played out, this one should be around for a long time.

A crossroads is reached 15.3 miles south of Ballarat; turn left heading up the alluvial fan (N35°51.476 W117°10.781). You will enter Goler Wash and its canyon within two miles. Note your odometer reading as you enter the canyon. Within 0.4 miles, in the narrowest parts of the canyon, there is a series of four dry waterfalls that must be ascended. Each is slightly different, ranging in difficulty from Class IV to V. Suddenly the road has become very interesting, immediately turning from Class I to Class V, with no transition in between. **Warning: proceed with great caution. Scout the road ahead on foot, before attempting to drive over these ledges.** (Coming downhill from Mengel Pass, I would rate them all at Class IV.) Once over the fourth section of bedrock, the road improves to a much more manageable Class III.

Goler Wash

The rock walls of an old forgotten miner's cabin are on the right 1.7 miles into the canyon, followed in 0.3 miles by a tramline on the left going up to the Lestro Mountain Mine. This was a gold mine tapping into a 5' quartz vein high on the canyon's wall. Some 600 tons of ore came down this tramline in 1940, on its way to the Golden Queen Mill near Mojave. The road improves to Class II three miles into the canyon, and the Lotus Mine camp can be seen on the right. The mine itself is actually high on the south ridge at the upper end of a 2,800' tramline. Quartz veins that yielded up to $50 per ton in gold can be found at the contact between a highly metamorphic andesite and limestone bed. Four tunnels with a combined length of nearly 1000' tapped the mineralized zone. Two aerial trams were utilized to bring the ore down from the ridge. This is the mine that Carl Mengel owned until 1935. The present owners of the Lotus Mine still pay their annual fees to the BLM to retain ownership of the claims.

Some careful boulder dodging will have to be undertaken above the Lotus Mine. Vehicles with a short wheelbase should have sufficient maneuverability, but long pickups could encounter some problems. Drivers of SUVs with low running boards should utilize a spotter on foot while twisting through the boulder patch. The new park boundary is reached 4.3 miles inside the canyon. (The boundary was on the summit of Mengel Pass prior to 1994.) The canyon forks a tenth of a mile beyond (N35°51.619 W117°05.836). The left fork reaches the summit of Mengel Pass in 3.4 miles.

You might want to make a short side trip to the right before ascending the pass. The road swings to the right, abruptly drops down into the wash, and then makes its way eastward under the spreading branches of cottonwood trees. This is Sourdough Spring, so named by Bill and Barbara Myers who lived just up the wash between 1932 and 1960. They claimed the name idea came from Carl Mengel, whose idea of a good breakfast was sourdough pancakes and fried liver. A half-mile above Sourdough Spring is the Barker Ranch, built by Bluch and Helen Thomason after Bluch retired from the Los Angeles Police Department. The property was sold to Jim and Kirk Barker after Bluch died. Just beyond the Barker Ranch is the Myers Ranch.

The Barker and Myers Ranches are places that received quite a bit of notoriety and national press back in 1969. In the very first edition of *Death Valley Jeep Trails* written in 1969, I said, *During the past year these isolated retreats have been inhabited by a small band of 'hippies', doing whatever hippies do.* Little did I know that these squatters were Charles Manson and his murdering gang. It was at the Barker Ranch that Charlie was arrested, although at the time his role in the Tate-LaBianca murders was not yet known. (See Appendix F for additional details.)

Charlie moved his band into Barker Ranch sometime in 1968. Mrs. Arlene Barker, who owned the property and whose granddaughter Cathy Gillies was one of Manson's followers, gave permission for Charlie to camp there. She thought he meant for only a few days. Manson had other plans. Not only did Charlie move his brood into Barker Ranch, but he had also made plans to kill Mrs. Barker to obtain title through Cathy. By a stroke of luck, the three creeps he sent to do the job had a flat tire in Panamint Valley and never completed the task.

Barker Ranch has once again returned to the peaceful anonymity it once enjoyed. The house is open and owned by the federal government. The visitor is free to go in and look around. It looks quite comfortable, although someone has filled the toilet with cement to prevent its use. The house could be used as an emergency shelter should a sudden storm arise, but you would not be alone. **Mice and other small rodents have infested these cabins. Their feces, urine, and saliva can be the source of the Hantavirus, which can infect humans with a sometimes fatal illness called Hantavirus Pulmonary Syndrome. Avoid all contact with rodent droppings, and do not stir up any dust where there is evidence of mice and rats. Inhalation of the virus is a common way of transmission to humans.**

A few ghosts might join you, too. One person who was close to the Manson gang says that there are three bodies buried eight feet deep somewhere on the Barker Ranch. They have never been found.

The Barker Ranch, where Charles Manson was apprehended in 1969

The road continues up the wash 0.3 miles beyond Barker Ranch to Myers Ranch. Bill and Barbara Myers settled in Goler Wash in 1932, building themselves a comfortable house complete with such amenities as flush toilets, a swimming pool, an orchard, and of course, a garden. They raised three children there: Charles, Pat and Corky. The Myers family reluctantly moved to Fresno in 1960, so that their children could have a better education. Much to the distress of the Myers family who still owns the property, the ranch house burned in 1999. **Please respect any KEEP OUT signs that may be posted.**

At one time a faint Class III road went on past Myers Ranch to steeply climb an unnamed pass, then continue on down into Wingate Wash, where it was an easy descent into Death Valley. That entire route has been closed to four-wheelers by wilderness designation. Vehicle travel beyond Myers Ranch is now prohibited.

Back down the canyon below Sourdough Springs, the main Goler Wash road goes to the left at the fork. The road is mostly Class II for the next 2.5 miles. After leaving the sandy wash, however, the last 0.9 miles is a steep Class III. On the summit is a monument containing the ashes of Carl Mengel, a single blanket prospector who lived just over the pass at Greater View Spring. (For a description of the route on the other side, see Excursion #9.)

36

Reilly Was a Company Town

Primary Attraction: A well-preserved mining camp reminiscent of Inca ruins in the high Andes Mountains of South America.

Time Required: This is an easy half-day trip out of Ballarat.

Miles Involved: From downtown Ballarat to downtown Reilly is only 10.5 miles.

Maps: 1:100,000 Darwin Hills and Ridgecrest sheets; 1:24,000 Slate Range Crossing and Maturango Peak SE Quadrangles.

Degree of Difficulty: The dirt road portions are mostly Class II, with only the last mile having a few Class III sections.

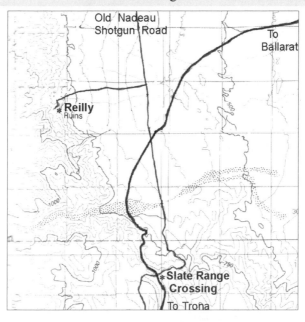

Reilly is another obscure mining camp that never made it into the spotlight during its heyday, and as such has been largely forgotten and overlooked by most historians. Its obscurity and the sturdy stone walls of its buildings have helped to preserve its heritage.

From downtown Ballarat, head west on Ballarat Road for 3.5 miles to the Trona Highway (N36°02.016 W117°16.907). Turn left toward Trona. The new (paved) Nadeau Road is passed after 3.8 miles (N36°00.219 W117°19.972). Just 0.4 beyond, look for the old Nadeau Road crossing the highway; it is not marked (N35°59.827 W117°20.255). Turn right here. This is the Nadeau "Shotgun Road", a wagon road built by Remi Nadeau in 1877 for his freight wagons going to Lookout. Proceed north for 1.1 miles, where a road to the left begins to climb the bajada (N36°00.772 W117°20.410). Leave the old Nadeau Road by turning left, and proceed up the bajada for 1.6 miles. The first left turn takes you to the town site of Reilly. The second road left, 0.1 miles beyond, takes you to the mill site. The third road left, 0.1 miles further, goes a quarter-mile up the canyon to one of Reilly's mines.

As a spinoff from the silver strikes at Darwin and Lookout, prospectors were searching every nook and cranny of the Argus Range. Two brothers by the name of Wibbett are supposed to have found some promising silver veins here in 1875. Little mining took place until 1882, when a promoter by the name of Charles Anthony brokered a deal with New York investor Edward Reilly, who bought the claims. Reilly formed the Argus Range Silver Mining Company and sold stock. With money from stock sales, Anthony had capital for running day-to-day operations. Reilly set about building a ten-stamp mill and began to block out ore in late 1882.

To accommodate the employees, who at one time numbered as many as sixty, Anthony put up a boarding house, a large general store, corrals and livery stable. He also built a fine house for himself. If Reilly wanted to profit by the ore, Anthony wanted to profit off Reilly's employees. A post office opened on January 22, 1883, even before the mill was operating. There was no water at the camp, so Reilly spent an additional $40,000 to run a pipeline over from Water Canyon, five miles to the south. Before a single ton of ore was crushed and processed, Edward Reilly had spent $200,000.

Because of numerous delays, the mill did not get into operation until September of 1883. Ironically that is also the month the post office closed its doors. Nevertheless, between October of 1883 and February of 1884, the Anthony Mill, as it came to be called, turned out bullion valued at $21,500. This was a far cry from the $200,000 that had been put into the venture. The mine operated another year, and the mill even longer, doing custom milling for other nearby mines. In the end, nobody got rich, not the stockholders, not Edward Reilly, not even Charles Anthony.

Today the mine works are crumbling and unsafe to enter. The mill is gone, leaving only its massive stone retaining walls. The camp of Reilly survives, in part. Remaining are the stone walls of some 23 structures, one with part of its roof still on. Many of these cabins were large enough for a bed and little else.

In spite of their small size, these modest workers' lodgings have survived a lot longer than Charles Anthony's fine wooden house.

Only stone walls greet the visitor to Reilly.

Timeless Trona

Trona in the twenties before the streets were paved.

In the 1940s, the American Potash and Chemical Company was the largest employer in the Searles Valley and owned the entire town of Trona.

Austin Hall in downtown Trona contained the market, drug store, post office, and pool hall, with a roofless movie theater in the center. (Searles Valley Historical Society photos)

Chapter IX

Trails Out of Trona

Most visitors bound for Death Valley zip right on through Searles Valley, not realizing there is some interesting country to be explored here. Having grown up here in the late 1940s and early 50s, I know better. Trona lies tucked away in Searles Valley between Mojave and Death Valley. Its reason for being lies in the white mineral deposits of the "dry" lake surface. They have been mined since the 1870s when John Searles and his brother began mining borax here. Dozens of chemicals have been extracted from those evaporate deposits, including potash, soda ash, glauber salts, lithium, and the mineral trona itself.

Sixty years ago Trona and West End were "company towns" totally owned by the American Potash and Chemical Company and The West End Chemical Company respectively. By the late 1950s the companies decided they wanted to produce chemicals, not act as landlord over a municipality. The homes and businesses in the town of Trona were sold off piecemeal to the highest bidder. The employee housing at West End was bulldozed away. Kerr McGee bought out "AMPOT" and, eventually, there was a consolidation with the West End Chemical plant at the south end of the valley. Kerr McGee ran the facilities for a number of years, followed by North American Chemical Company until the mid-1990s, when IMC bought the operation.

John Searles
(SVHS photo)

Searles Valley had a population of 5,698 in 1960. By 1990 the population had dropped by 48% to 2,740. The 2000 census revealed that the population has dropped a little more, but the downward trend seems to have stabilized. While Trona, and its southern suburb Argus have clearly seen better days, they nevertheless remain viable communities where some basic services are still available. There are two gas stations, two markets, a hardware store, an auto parts store, and a motel (in Pioneer Point, one mile north of Trona).

The Searles Valley Historical Society operates the Old Guest House Museum at 13193 Main Street. It is in a building dating from 1912. The museum is open Mondays, from 9 a.m. to noon, and Saturdays, 11 a.m. to 1 p.m. The Society also operates History House at 83001 Panamint Street. Built around 1920, it is one of the oldest houses still left in Trona, and is furnished in the period of the 1940s.

37

Remi Nadeau's "Shotgun Road"

Primary Attraction:	Follow portions of the first two wagon roads built in Panamint Valley to service the rich silver mines in the Panamint and Argus ranges.
Time Required:	You can follow the old Jacobs Road from Trona over Slate Range Crossing, and then follow the Nadeau Road to the Minnietta and Modoc Mines in half-day, if no side trips are taken. Some of these side trips are interesting, so plan on spending all day.
Miles Involved:	From the old West End Quarry road in Searles Valley to the Minnietta Mine Road in Panamint Valley is some 23 miles.
Maps:	1:100,000 Ridgecrest and Darwin Hills sheets; 1:24,000 Slate Range Crossing, Maturango Peak SE, Maturango Peak NE, and Revenue Canyon Quadrangles.
Degree of Difficulty:	The road is nearly all Class II, except where the road crosses a wash and might be Class III. **This road is not suitable for long wheelbase vehicles having a long overhang behind the rear axle.**

One of Remi Nadeau's mule teams
(Courtesy Remi Nadeau IV)

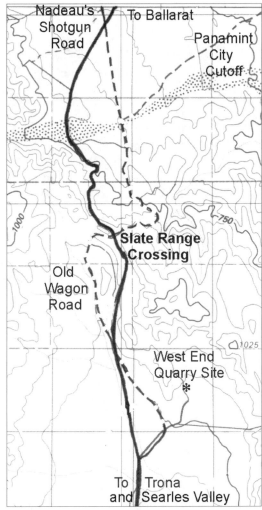

Although the emigrants of 1849 and 50 passed through Panamint Valley after escaping Death Valley, there was to be no wagon road for more than two decades after their passing. That all changed in 1873 when Richard Jacobs and his partner Bob Stewart found a ledge of silver high in Surprise Canyon in the Panamint Range. The following year Jacobs went to Los Angeles in order to raise the capital needed to develop his mine and to build a road to it. Jacobs was a smooth talker. He argued that his rich lode of silver would make everyone rich, and unless the folks of Los Angeles built the road to his mines, the citizens of San Bernardino or Bakersfield would do it. The movers and shakers in Los Angeles responded, and Jacobs had the money to build 60 miles of new road. Several hundred Chinese laborers were engaged, and work began in June of 1874.

The old wagon road supported by rock retaining
walls is as useable today as it was in 1874.

The new road left the Bullion Road to Cerro Gordo near Indian Wells, and
went east through Poison Canyon. Once in Searles Valley, it headed north to a
low pass at the western end of the Slate Range. The south side of Slate Range
Crossing was relatively easy. The northern slope required several miles of cut
and fill, but it was quickly overcome as well. By August of 1874, the road
between Los Angeles and Panamint City was established. One of the first items
to be carried over it was a ten-stamp mill going to Jacob's mine. Three years
later, French Canadian Remi Nadeau would build his "Shotgun Road" cutting
off from the Panamint Road at the northern base of Slate Range Crossing to the
mines of Lookout Mountain (see Excursion #30).

The silver booms in Cerro Gordo and Panamint City in the 1870s treated
Remi Nadeau quite well. But Remi was not mining silver; rather he was hauling
it. Nadeau had arrived in Los Angeles driving a team of oxen in 1861. He decided
to go into the freight hauling business. He borrowed some money from another
French Canadian, Prudent Beaudry, bought some mules and wagons, and set off
to seek his fortune. It just so happened that Prudent's brother, Victor, was half
owner of a very productive silver mine, high in the Inyo Mountains at a place
called Cerro Gordo. The mine's smelter was turning out bullion faster that it could
be hauled away. In December of 1868, Nadeau was awarded a contract to carry
silver bullion from Cerro Gordo, 200 miles south to the railroad in downtown
Los Angeles. In order to keep up, Nadeau increased his transport capacity to 32
teams of twelve to eighteen mules per team, with each team pulling two wagons.
Nadeau's teams moved some 700 tons of bullion in 1870 alone.

By 1874 it became obvious that with a population approaching 2000, Panamint
City would become another Cerro Gordo. In 1875 the twenty working mines in
the Darwin area supported a town of 700 people, including 78 businesses and

two smelters. 1875 was also the year that the mines of Lookout Mountain in the Argus Range were discovered and showed great promise. All of these mines needed their bullion hauled to market. The return trips would bring in machinery, supplies and building materials. Remi Nadeau was in the right business, at the right place, at the right time. Nadeau set about building roads for his freight wagons, and soon most commerce in Inyo County moved through the hands of his teamsters.

In the spring of 1877, Nadeau built his "Shotgun Road" from the bottom of the Slate Range grade to the Modoc Mine, thus cutting many miles off the previously more circuitous route. As soon as that road was completed, he shifted his crews to Wildrose Canyon, where yet another road was built to the base of Lookout Mountain, this one to transport charcoal from the ten newly erected kilns.

The booms at Cerro Gordo, Darwin, Lookout, and Panamint City all faded in time, but Remi Nadeau's mule drawn freight wagons still plied the roads of Inyo County until 1883, when the Carson & Colorado Railroad came into the Owens Valley. Being unable to compete with the railroad, he then moved his teams to the flourishing new camp of Tombstone in the Arizona Territory, where he sold the business. Nadeau returned to Los Angeles to build a fine four-story hotel at the corner of First and Spring Streets. Not only was it the tallest building in Los Angeles at the time, it was also the first with a mechanical elevator, and it remained the finest hostelry for years to come.

Remi Nadeau
(Photo courtesy of Remi Nadeau IV)

When I was a youngster, Jacob's old Panamint Road could be picked up at Pioneer Point just north of Trona. However, man's activities of the last fifty years have obliterated it there. To find the old road used by Nadeau's teams, go north out of Trona in the direction of Death Valley. While passing the Trona High School gymnasium at the north end of town, note your odometer reading. The paved Homewood Canyon Road goes off to the left 8.2 miles to the north. In another 2.5 miles a paved road turns off to the right. This road goes to the old West End Chemical Company limestone quarry that operated in the 1960s; turn right here (N35°55.276 W117°19.794). The old Nadeau Road can be seen fifty feet east of today's paved road. After 0.4 miles, the Nadeau Road makes a left turn and crosses Quarry Road. This is where we will pick up the old Panamint Road (N35°55.559 W117°19.444).

The West End Limestone Quarry in 1956

Follow the dirt tracks to the northwest as they skirt the base of a low limestone hill. The route is generally Class I, with a few Class II portions at minor washouts. The old Panamint Road crosses the highway to Death Valley 1.1 miles from Quarry Road (N35°56.315 W117°20.074). Resetting your odometer, cross the asphalt and pick the road up on the other side.

The Panamint Road forks in 0.3 miles; stay left on what appears to be the more traveled route. Within a hundred yards the road forks again. Take either fork; they soon rejoin. The road deteriorates to Class II as it starts up a small wash 0.6 miles from the highway crossing. Old campfire rings and scattered pieces of bottles and tin cans 0.8 miles in from the crossing suggest that this spot has been utilized as a layover for many years. Nadeau's muleskinners probably made it a regular stopping point on their long journey.

A crossroads is reached north of the old campsite at the 1.6-mile mark. Go straight ahead up the hillside. The top of Slate Range Crossing is but 0.4

miles ahead. At the summit, the Nadeau Road once again crosses the highway (N35°57.592 W117°20.110) and starts down into Panamint Valley. Still Class II, the roadway begins its descent across the pink volcanic rocks of Tertiary age. From this lofty vantage point, there are good views down into Panamint Valley. To the north, Nadeau's Shotgun Road can be clearly seen cutting across the bajadas like a laser beam. As you work your way lower, the rocks soon change from pink to dark basalt. Along the way, the stone retaining walls holding up the road seem just as well built today as they were 130 years ago.

It is only 3.5 miles to the bottom of the grade. There are fifty yards of Class III road as you cross the sandy wash coming out of Water Canyon about ½-mile ahead. On the other side, a fork goes off to the right; this was Jacob's original road of 1874 to Panamint City. The road straight ahead is Nadeau's wagon road of 1877. Some say it was called the *Shotgun Road*, because it was surveyed straight across the desert as if one was looking through the barrel of a shotgun.

The Shotgun Road

The modern highway is crossed once again at the 5.2-mile point (N35°59.825 W117°20.256). Note your odometer reading. A BLM sign identifies the route as "P03". Almost immediately on your left a Class II side road goes up the hill 1½ miles to a kitty litter mine, inactive since the 1980s. (There is a lot of flat ground here in the event you are looking for a campsite.)

Needless to say, the Shotgun Road goes straight ahead! In spite of the fact that the Shotgun Road cuts across the grain of the drainage coming off the Argus Range, the road is no worse than Class II. The next side road to the left comes after another 1.2 miles. This goes to the old mining camp of Reilly (see Excursion #36).

Continue north to 3.6 miles, where the next major road to the west climbs the fan 2.4 miles to the Onyx mine. Here in marble and limestone is a band of onyx some three to seven feet wide. The onyx quarried here was various hues of brown, cream, red and even green. Some was beautifully banded, some mottled and some cloudy; it would polish very nicely. The deposit was worked first in 1925 and for about fifty years since. When I first visited the site in the 1950s, the resident caretaker would sell specimens by the pound to rock hounds. The Searles Valley Gem & Mineral Society would come away with boxes of it. When I last visited the site in 1998, the camp was in ruins, and it looked like there was none of the good stuff left.

Beyond the Onyx Mine Road, Nadeau's Shotgun Road crosses a deep wash where a stone causeway had to be built. It remains today just as it was in 1877. In the next 3.5 miles, the Nadeau Road crosses four more roads; simply continue heading north. When you have traveled 8.3 miles since leaving the pavement, you will come to the paved new Nadeau Road, which goes to a limestone quarry at the base of the Argus Range. Turn left on the asphalt surface. Stay on the pavement for 2.5 miles; then make a right turn to put you back onto the Old Nadeau Shotgun Road.

The next five miles are a rough Class II, with a few Class III sections encountered when crossing gullies and washes. Eventually, the soil turns sandy and the road surface improves. At a point 6.5 miles from the new Nadeau Road, the Shotgun Road reaches the graded Minnietta Road coming in from the right. From this junction you have several options. The road on the left goes one mile to the Minnietta Mine. Largely overlooked in the Lookout Mountain excitement of the 1870s, the discovery of argentiferous galena in limestone did not occur here until the turn of the 20th Century. Between 1902 and 1949, the Minietta Mine produced significant amounts of lead along with some silver. The ore produced between 1948 and 1952 also contained some zinc and a little gold. The mine closed in the spring of 1957. The underground workings are extensive and on three levels. Remember, however: **Stay out and stay alive!**

If you wish to return to the pavement, turn right. The Trona-Wildrose Highway is but 3.6 miles to the east. If you continue straight ahead for a mile, another side road to the left will take you to the site of the Modoc Mine in ½-mile, and on to the old Mining Camp of Lookout after another 6 miles (see Excursion #30). All of these sites were ore shipping points for Remi Nadeau's mule drawn wagons.

If you continue straight ahead to the north after this second junction, you can access Osborne Canyon (see Excursion #29).

The Minietta Mine in its heyday during WWI
(County of Inyo, Eastern California Museum photo)

The Minietta Mine today

38

The Arondo Mine

Primary Attraction:	A visit to an old gold mine, with the chance of wild burro sightings along the way.
Time Required:	This is a half-day excursion out of Trona.
Distance Involved:	The mine is 30 miles round trip from Trona.
Maps:	1:100,000 Ridgecrest sheet; 1:24,000, Slate Range Crossing Quadrangle.
Degree of Difficulty:	The road in to the mine is no worse than Class III, and there is not much of that.

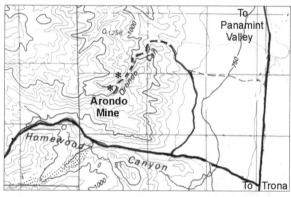

The Arondo Mine, sometimes spelled "Orondo", is situated in a canyon of the same name, on the eastern flank of the Argus Range at the north end of Searles Valley. It is a pleasant destination for a few hours or a full day.

From Trona take the Death Valley Road north out of town. As you leave town, note your odometer as you pass the Trona High School gymnasium (the large building on the left with the arched roof). Proceed north past Pioneer Point and the Valley Wells recreation complex. At a point 8.2 miles beyond the gymnasium, the paved Homewood Canyon Road heads west towards the Argus Range (N35°53.095 W117°19.958). Turn left here, and go west up the cholla-studded bajada. Just before entering Homewood Canyon, a graded dirt road turns off to the right (N35°57.509 W117°21.563). A sign reads *Inyo County Dump*; reset the odometer and turn right here. Pass the refuse transfer point on the left in 0.2 miles. The road continues on, although it deteriorates to Class I.

Notice the small spot of black basalt lava on the left. In this area the Argus Range is generally Mesozoic granite and quartz monzonite, but, in places such as this, it has been intruded by much younger Tertiary lavas. This little spot of basalt is a reminder of that recent volcanism.

The rough road goes north along the base of the mountains, cutting across the grain of the bajada. The dominant desert shrub here is the ubiquitous creosote. The cholla cactus so common along the Homewood Canyon Road is nowhere to be seen. Another very common plant along the trail here is the desert trumpet or bladderstem *Eriogonum inflatum,* a plant 12 to 18" high with a section of swollen stem near the top.

At a point a mile north of the pavement, the desert road deteriorates further to Class II. Look for a quail guzzler on the left. The California Department of Fish and Game placed these small cisterns throughout California's deserts. The infrequent rains are collected in aprons that channel the water down an inclined ramp, making water available to quail and other desert wildlife long after the rains have passed.

The road swings to the west and enters Bruce Canyon. The Class II road forks 2½-miles from the Homewood Canyon Road. The right fork continues up Bruce Canyon a half-mile where it dead-ends. A well-worn burro trail continues up Bruce Canyon another mile to Rock Spring. For the Arondo Mine, you will want to keep to the left up Arondo Canyon, a side canyon to the south. The reddish brown soil in the bottom of the wash is distinctly different from the light brown soils on the hillsides. That is because the dirt in the bottom of the canyon is actually the fine waste material that came from the two ore mills more than a mile up Arondo Canyon.

As you ascend Arondo Canyon, you will see an occasional barrel cactus on the hillsides. Wherever they are found, they seem to prefer the well-drained gravel hillsides to the sandy washes.

Soon the road deteriorates even further, to an easy Class III. At a point 3.7 miles from the paved Homewood Canyon Road, there is a fork in the road and an enormous tailings pile. These are the lower workings of the Arondo Mine. The Class III right fork goes up a side canyon another 0.4 miles to dead-end at the "middle workings", the site of a second mill site. The mill has burned, leaving only a huge pile of fine waste that was left over after the ore was crushed and the gold extracted. **Warning: Stay well away from the large open shaft; it is very dangerous to attempt to even peer down into it.**

The left fork remains Class III as it passes a shaft and continues to climb up the canyon bottom. It is another mile to the upper workings of the Arondo Mine. The early history of this mine remains obscure, but it is thought to go back to the 1890s. The property was worked intermittently from 1901 to 1941, and again by several leasees during the period of 1946 to 1950. The gold ore is found in a shear zone in the granitic rocks. While the ounces of gold per ton were relatively low, the gold that was present was in a free state, easily extracted by the cyanide leaching process.

When I visited this site in 1959, the main shaft still had its steel headframe, hoist house and several other outbuildings. In the last fifty years the headframe has been dismantled, the buildings have collapsed, and only the sturdy ore bunker remains. A protective screen covers the shaft. **Do not attempt to enter any of these old workings; the supporting cribbing is old and rotting.**

The Arondo Mine in 1959

The Arondo Mine in 1999

39

The Escape Trail

Primary Attraction: This little known route over the Slate Range provides an alternative route from Trona to Ballarat, while providing some nice scenic views and a bit of history along the way.

Time Required: Budget much of the day for this outing.

Miles Involved: The one-way distance from downtown Trona to downtown Ballarat via the route described is about 37 miles, of which only six miles are on paved roads. The return distance from Ballarat back to Trona is another 30 miles.

Maps: 1:100,000 Ridgecrest and Darwin Hills sheets; 1:24,000 Trona East, Copper Queen Canyon, Manly Fall, and Ballarat Quadrangles.

Degree of Difficulty: Most of the dirt road portion of this route is Class I and II, with only a half dozen miles being Class III.

Remarks: The various accounts of the emigrants passing through the Death Valley country, even those written by the participants themselves, are confusing and often contradictory. It will drive a sane person crazy trying to figure out who camped where, on what date, and the route taken to get there. Thus, it is not surprising that armchair scholars disagree with those who have actually put their boots on the ground and trod many of these same places. The definitive work on the subject is *Escape From Death Valley* written by Leroy and Jean Johnson in 1987. A less authoritative book offering many different conclusions is *Death Valley 49er Trails,* written by B. G. Olesen and published in 2004.

This excursion tells the story of, and looks at the route taken by, several groups of California bound emigrants who wandered into Death Valley and later "escaped" by crossing the Panamint Range into Panamint Valley, only to face even more hardships while crossing the Slate Range into Searles Valley. Two of those emigrants, a Mr. Fish and a Mr. Isham, survived the escape from Death Valley, only to perish while crossing the Slate Range.

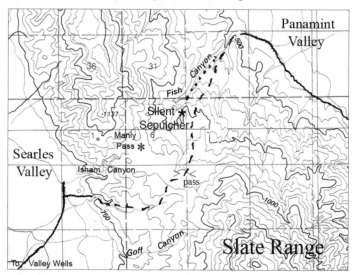

It would be more correct historically to take this trail going west from Panamint Valley to Searles Valley, the direction the escapees from Death Valley were headed; however, I have chosen to describe the trail in the opposite direction so that you might keep the stunning views of Telescope Peak in the windshield before you.

In late September of 1849, nearly 500 men, women and children in 110 wagons with about 1,000 horses, oxen, and cattle gathered at a rendezvous point at Hobble Creek, Utah territory. The group initially came together to be led by "Captain" Jefferson Hunt, who had made the overland journey to California two years previously, and was willing to lead the emigrants to California via the "Spanish Trail" for $10 per wagon.

Trouble seemed assured right from the beginning when opinions differed, and the group threatened to break up before the first wheel had turned. At least two hand-drawn maps that promised a "shortcut" saving hundreds of miles were produced. Although no one present had actually taken these presumed shortcuts, most were willing to gamble by going into unknown territory, rather than endure the known perils of a longer route with long sections without water and grass for the animals. Various factions of "short cutters" formed. These splinter groups often adopted colorful names for themselves, such as "Bugsmashers" and "Jayhawkers". Ultimately Hunt's San Joaquin Company, (a name soon to be corrupted to "Sand Walker Company") would start the long journey down the

Spanish Trail with only a few wagons under his leadership. A few weeks later, however, many of those short cutters would backtrack and return to Hunt's route, following his tracks into Southern California. Their journey was difficult, but not nearly as perilous as that of most of the emigrants who continued looking for the shortcut. In a matter of weeks, those blazing new trails were soon spread out in a string 200 miles long. Some were walking, and some were riding in wagons drawn by horses, mules, or oxen. Some, like the family of James Welsh Brier, a Methodist minister, his wife Juliet and three sons, had to abandon their wagon and continue their journey on foot.

In December of 1849, the first of these short-cut seeking emigrants wearily trudged down the sands of Furnace Creek Wash into the great depression in the earth's surface that we know today as Death Valley. The first contingent arrived on December 2nd. Among the last to straggle in on December 23rd were the Bennett and Arcan families, consisting of Asabel Bennett, his wife Sarah and three children, together with Jean Arcan and his pregnant wife Abigail and their three children. With them were also two young men: John Manly, age 29, a friend and former neighbor of the Bennetts, and John Rogers, age 25, whom Manly had met along the trail. The snow-capped peaks of the Panamint Range lay ahead of them all.

Exhausted, these weary travelers broke up into even more factions. Some, like the Bennett-Arcan party and the Harry Wade family, turned south and headed down the great trough of Death Valley. Others, like the "Mississippi Boys", the Jayhawkers, and the Brier family, tried to go around the Panamints to the north. Both faced incredible hardships far worse than those they had already encountered.

Under the leadership of Captain Town, the mostly single men from Mississippi and Georgia turned north at Furnace Creek, and entered Panamint Valley after ascending what is today known as Emigrant Wash and Towne Pass. Tagging along with that group was the previously mentioned Brier family and several other men, including William Isham, a popular fiddler around the evening campfire and teamster employed by another emigrant named Fish. Upon reaching the floor of Panamint Valley, most of the southern boys turned west, but the Jayhawkers, including "Old Man Fish" and his teamster William Isham, and the Brier family proceeded south down Panamint Valley. Upon seeing a low spot along the crest of the Slate Range, they turned west to cross the mountains there. In their weakened state, the group could not make the crossing in a single day. They stopped near the top and camped for the night. The Reverend Brier called the campsite *The Silent Sepulcher*. What was the good preacher thinking when he named this place the Silent Sepulcher? Was he thinking of the women returning to the empty tomb on Easter morning as described in John: 20 19-20?

Did he recognize the poor physical condition that Fish and Isham were in, and was he thinking this would be their tomb? Or was he thinking that this narrow canyon might be the burial place for them all?

The next day it was all they could do to reach the top of this low pass. Old Man Fish tried to proceed by clinging to the tail of an ox. He collapsed near the pass, and died a few hours later. Fish's companion, William Isham, made it across the Slate Range, but shortly thereafter he died of acute dehydration. Both men died on January 13, 1850.

Meanwhile, the Bennett-Arcan party chose another route. They turned to the south from Furnace Creek on January 6th seeking another way over or around the Panamint Range. They skirted the salt flats on the western floor of Death Valley, going from one brackish spring to the next. Lingering about a day behind the Bennett-Arcan party was Harry Wade, with his wife and four children. (The Wades were to blaze a route up Wingate Wash, and eventually rejoin the Spanish Trail near present day Barstow. Of all those who entered Death Valley, the Wades were the first to reach Southern California and the only group who did not abandon their wagon along the way.) After one unsuccessful attempt to get over the high Panamints, the Bennett-Arcan party was too weak to go on. Manly and Rogers volunteered to proceed on foot, in order to scout a route, secure provisions, and return. In the meantime the Bennett and Arcan families would make camp there at a small spring, and wait for the boys to return. Manly and Rogers left on January 15th carrying $60 in coin with which to buy provisions and horses for the return trip. Leroy and Jean Johnson, who have spent many years studying the route, hiking the canyons, and researching libraries, are convinced that once Manly and Rogers left the group's camp, they ascended Warm Springs Canyon to the crest of the Panamints at a place now called Rogers Pass (see page 232). They then headed down Middle Park Canyon. Once on the floor of Panamint Valley, they too turned south heading towards the low spot on the crest of the Slate Range.

On the second night of the boys' rescue mission, they camped at the same place the Reverend Brier had been five days previously, the place Brier called *The Silent Sepulcher*. Unlike Brier, who had managed to coax a quart of water out of the sandy alluvium, Manly and Rogers found no water there. The pair reached the crest (today's Manly Pass) on January 18th, and descended another drainage on the west (Isham Canyon), where they followed the Jayhawkers route south and west towards the Argus Range. Although on foot, Manly and Rogers made the long journey to Rancho San Francisco in only 16 days. After securing the needed supplies and animals, they immediately turned around and returned by the same route over the Slate Range. However, they rode their three newly purchased horses so fast on the return trip that two of them died along the way.

The trip back over the Panamints took them up Redlands Canyon and down Warm Springs Canyon. Upon reaching Salt Well, they found that the Bennett-Arcan party was not there where they had left them! The emigrants had moved their camp a few miles to the north. Manly and Rogers caught up with them on February 9th, only 26 days after they had left on their rescue mission.

This four-wheeling adventure follows the route the Jayhawkers, the Briers, Mr. Fish and William Isham took over the Slate Range as they left Panamint Valley, the same route used by Manly and Rogers in their great rescue mission, and the same route the Bennett-Arcan party ultimately used in their escape from Death Valley.

Our historical odyssey across the Slate Range begins at the roadside rest on Highway 178 on the southern edge of downtown Trona. When I grew up here during the late 1940s into the mid 1950s, this particular part of town was dominated by a series of two-story wooden bunkhouses that served as the bachelor living quarters for the men employed by the American Potash and Chemical Company. In the intervening years, those buildings have all been torn down. A few were replaced by more modern structures but for the most part, those old dormitories are now vacant lots.

From the roadside rest stop, reset your trip odometer to zero, and head north on the highway in the direction of Death Valley. In three miles the highway enters Inyo County, and the character, color, and composition of the roadway changes. North of the roadside rest 5.4 miles, turn to the right onto Valley Wells Road (N35°49.734 W117°20.317). Follow the road as it circles to the north around the tree lined recreation complex. Valley Wells got its start after World War I as a reservoir for the fresh water pumped from nearby wells, en route to the plant in Trona. It was converted to a swimming pool a few years later, when the plant managers decided they needed a warm weather recreation place for employees and their families.

Valley Wells in the 1920s after it was converted to a swimming pool. Some thirty years later, the author would spend many summer days cooling off here.
(Searles Valley Historical Society photo)

At 5.9 miles, follow the Class I dirt road as it proceeds eastward along the line of utility poles. A side road to the right at 7.6 miles (N35°50.656 W117°18.479) goes to the Ophir Mine, seen ahead in the distance at the base of the Slate Range. Still privately owned, this mine was a lead, zinc and silver producer, extensively worked in the 1940s. At one time, it was owned by the Gold Bottom Mines (see Excursion #40).

To follow the Escape Trail, stay to the left on the main road. A tenth of a mile farther, a road from the Ophir Mine goes left back towards the highway; keep to the right here, still following the Class I road as it passes a gravel pit and crosses a wash. After still another tenth of a mile, the foundations of an ore mill are passed on the left, and now the road swings more to the east. Look for a BLM sign designating Road P68 going off to the left in the direction of Isham Canyon 7.9 miles from downtown Trona (N35°50.738 W117°18.156). Turn to the left here; this is the "Escape Trail" over the Slate Range. Isham Canyon, the next canyon to the north, has become the playground of hard-core rock crawlers interested in pushing their 4x4s to the extreme limits. We will choose a less brutal route, BLM Road P68.

BLM signs such as this mark the route of the "Escape Trail"

The road will soon deteriorate from Class I to Class II. A mile more and you will find yourself starting up an unnamed canyon. The last time we took this trail was a fine spring day in early April. Upon stopping to look at the white showy flower of the Prickly poppy, we noticed a few "Army worms" crawling across the sandy wash. As a kid growing up in Trona, I can vividly recall one spring, perhaps in 1950, when these critters came crawling out of the Argus Range by the millions. They were crossing the highways in such numbers that unsuspecting motorists were losing control of their vehicles, because their tires had crushed so many they made the asphalt slippery. It is an old wives tale that Army worms appear at intervals of only every 17 years. Folk tales are often wrong, as in this case the length of time between appearances of this harmless little critter. An Army worm is actually nothing more that the larvae stage of the White lined sphinx moth *Hyles lineata*. When conditions are just right, and this does not happen every year, they hatch in great numbers, particularly in the Searles and Indian Wells Valleys. In their adult state, these moths are attracted to bright lights after dark, and may be seen circling around your gas camping lantern at night.

Army worm *Hyles lineate*

There is a major fork in the road 9.7 miles from downtown Trona (N35°50.827 W117°16.544). Stay to the left on BLM Road P68. After another 0.7 miles, there is a steep Class III section that climbs up and over a ridge. The short descent to the wash below is also Class III. Once down in the wash, follow the road to the right and gradually ascend the wash. It was in this area where we found Brittlebush and Western Mojave-aster to be in full bloom. The aster is a food plant for Neumoegen's Checkerspot, one of the more common desert butterflies.

Brittlebush *Encelia farinosa*

At an elevation of nearly 3100', the crest of the Slate Range is reached when your trip odometer reads 11.4 miles. From the summit there are wonderful views to the northeast into Panamint Valley and of 11,049' Telescope Peak, which dominates the distant skyline. On the other side of the crest, the road now descends the spine of a ridge with more great views all the way down.

The downgrades are steep for the next 1½ miles, so you will want to make the descent in lower gears to save your brakes. The bottom of the steep grade comes at the 13.4-mile point. In the bottom of Fish Canyon, there is a large metal sign on the left commemorating the rescue and escape from Death Valley by William Lewis Manley and John H. Rogers, who went for help and supplies, returning month later to lead the Bennett-Arcan Party to safety. The Trona Chapter of the Escape Trail Conference erected the large steel sign and monument in 1988. The sign points up the canyon to the Reverend Briar's *Silent Sepulcher* and the Fish gravesite. As long as you have come this far you might as well make the side trip of 0.9 miles up Fish Canyon to see these little visited places. You cannot turn up the wash here where the sign is posted, but you can by continuing down the canyon another 0.2 miles, then follow the tracks as they make a sharp left turn at the 14.0-mile point (N35°53.534 W117°14.994). Follow the Class III tracks up Fish Canyon and before long, the colorful volcanic rocks close in on both sides as the canyon narrows. The road ends in slightly less than a mile, and you will have to walk the last ¼-mile to find the next two metal signs.

The Fish Canyon "Narrows"

The first sign tells you that you are at the site of Reverend Briar's *Silent Sepulcher*. The sign does not say so, but the Briar party and the Jayhawkers including Old Man Fish and William Isham camped here on the night of January 12, 1850. This is where the Reverend Brier dug a hole in the sandy alluvium, and in about an hour's time, coaxed about a quart of water from the sand. Four days later, Manly and Rogers camped at this same place on the night of January 16th, while on their outbound rescue mission to Southern California. A month later, after they had returned with supplies and were leading the Bennett-Arcan party to safety, they stopped here again. (Manly later wrote that they had passed the dead body of "Old Man Fish" barely covered with brush. A decade later, in 1860, Manly returned to the Slate Range and found Fish's bones scattered about.)

Admittedly however, these events came and went over 150 years ago, leaving very little to see then, much less today. The events are recorded and preserved only by these large steel panels. One such panel commemorates the late Reverend Leonard L. Collard, founder and president of the Escape Trail Conference, an organization dedicated to preserving the "Escape Trail" and its history.

Driving in here in a four-wheel drive vehicle, with an ice chest full of drinks and snacks, it is a little difficult for folks in the early 21st Century to appreciate the despair and suffering experienced by those emigrants of the mid 19th Century. Yet here in Fish Canyon, the spirits of many were at rock bottom as they crossed these mountains, with two simply giving up and welcoming death.

Fish Canyon is a dead end (no pun intended) so when you have seen what little there is to see here, you will have to backtrack the 0.9 miles down the canyon. Upon reaching the road again, your trip odometer should now be reading 15.4 miles.

Continue following the Class II road down Fish Canyon. Ahead and across Panamint Valley, the workings of the Briggs Mine can clearly be seen along the western base of the Panamint Range. At 15.8 miles, BLM Road P168 turns to the right at the mouth of Fish Canyon. The road becomes even more rocky for the next 1½ miles. A 'T' intersection is reached with BLM Road P17 at 17.5 miles (N35°53.896 W117°13.098); go to the right. The road heads south to circle east around the mud flats and salt pan at the southern end of Panamint Valley.

At 21.5 miles on your trip odometer, yet another 'T' intersection is reached with a wide graded road. This is Wingate Road, also known as BLM Road P52. A right turn will take you up Goler Wash to Mengel Pass (see Excursion #35). Most day-trippers will want to turn to the left. From here it is about 15 miles north to Ballarat, 18½ miles to the highway, and a total of 30 miles back to Trona.

40

The Gold Bottom Mine and Beyond

Primary Attraction:	This is an opportunity to see the Searles Playa close up, to visit an old mine, and to get a good look at an old Pleistocene beach.
Time Required:	This is an easy half-day trip out of Trona.
Miles Involved:	It is only 9 miles from downtown Trona to the Gold Bottom Mine.
Maps:	1:100,000 Ridgecrest sheet; 1:24,000 Trona East Quadrangle.
Degree of Difficulty:	It is an easy Class I road to the lower workings, and Class III to the upper workings. If you continue on to the overlook into Copper Queen Canyon, the last quarter-mile is Class IV.

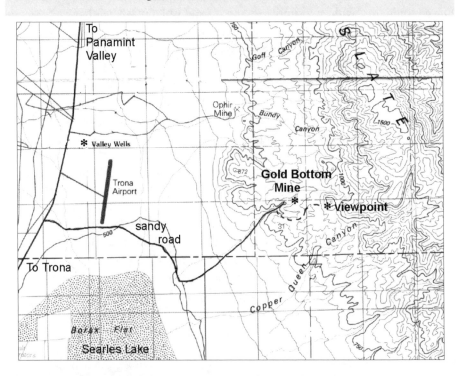

Originally called the Copper Queen Mine, the Gold Bottom Mine lies just inside Inyo County near the northern end of Searles Dry Lake. It is in very old Precambrian rocks on the western slope of the Slate Range. The Death Valley bound visitor can easily visit the site as a two-hour side trip off the Trona-Panamint Valley Road.

Take the paved highway north out of Trona as if you were going to Death Valley. Note your odometer reading as you pass the Trona High School gymnasium. At a point 2.7 miles north of the school (0.9 miles into Inyo County), look for a wide graded desert road heading east (N35°48.339 W117°20.864). (If you come to the Trona airport road, you have gone 0.9 miles too far north.) Turn east here, and soon you will be passing the south end of the Trona airport runway. There is a little soft sand here, but it should present no problem.

The road skirts the north end of Searles Lake, the fourth in a chain of six Ice Age lakes fed by the ancestral Owens River on its way to Death Valley. When the high Sierra was covered with glacial ice, the Owens River began its journey at Lake Russell (today's Mono Lake Basin), where it flowed south across Adobe Valley and the Owens Valley, picking up volume from the many smaller streams that fed into it. The smallest in this chain, Lake Owens drained to the south. This mighty river must have sent up an enormous cloud of mist, making an awesome roar, as it leaped off the hard basalt cliffs at Fossil Falls. China Lake was the next basin, and then the water turned east to enter Searles Valley by way of today's Poison Canyon. At its peak in the Tahoe Stage 75,000 years ago, Ancient Lake Searles was 32 miles long, up to 15 miles wide, and 800 feet deep.

Between the many ice advances in the late Pleistocene, there were interglacial warm periods when the mighty rivers stopped flowing. Without a continuing source of water, lakes like Searles pretty much dried up. The dissolved salts and other minerals became concentrated as the water evaporated. With each renewed wet and dry cycle, successive layers of silt and minerals were deposited on the lake bottom. It is these evaporate minerals that are being extracted today.

Borax was known to be here as early as 1862; however, no serious efforts were made to extract this "white gold" until 1873, when John and Dennis Searles hired a few Chinese laborers and opened a small plant near present day Trona. The operation prospered, and by 1890 some 50 workers and 50 draft horses were turning out up to 100 tons per month. By 1913, long after the Searles brothers had died, the Trona Borax Company bought out the Searles' interests. They sank brine wells in the lake bottom, and extracted a wide variety of minerals including potash, soda ash, salt cake, lithium carbonate, glauber salts and the mineral trona. Eventually, these holdings became the American Potash and Chemical Company, affectionately known to locals as AMPOT. A competing operation began at the south end of the lake, and this became known as the West End

Chemical Company. Both companies developed "company towns" adjoining their plants for their workers. This was the Trona that I grew up in during the late 1940s and 1950s. My parents and I lived in a company house, shopped in the company grocery, drug and department stores, and frequented the company owned movie theater, community center and bowling alley. In the Trona of that day, only the post office and school were not operated by the company.

AMPOT eventually sold out to Kerr McGee, and West End sold out to Stauffer. The company town at West End was torn down, and the one at Trona sold off piecemeal to anyone who wanted to buy a house and lot. North American Chemical Company bought out both companies' operations a few years back, giving them control over the entire lake. In the middle 1990s, IMC bought out North American, and they currently operate the plant. At the current rate of production, the estimates are that there are sufficient reserves to last another 150 years.

Normally, Searles Lake is not a bone dry playa. It often has enough water in its center to cover a few acres. During wet years however, the amount of standing water may be sufficient to cover hundreds or even thousands of acres, although I have never seen it high enough to cover this road.

This photo of Searles Lake was taken in March
of 1940 after an unusually wet winter.
(Searles Valley Historical Society photo)

As you go eastward beyond the playa surface, you will see some tracks going off through the sand on the left, but stay to the right on the main road. Straight ahead you will notice horizontal lines on the hillside, particularly if you come this way in the early morning light. These are wave-cut terraces left by Pleistocene Lake Searles. We will visit one of these ancient beaches on our way to the upper workings of the Gold Bottom mine.

At a point 3.1 miles from the highway there is an important road junction. The right fork continues south along the eastern shore of Searles Lake to come to a locked gate, marking the boundary of the Naval Air Weapons Station's *Range B*. While there is some interesting country down there, including Layton Pass, unauthorized travel is strictly prohibited by the Navy. Trespassers are treated as spies endangering national security. (If you are somehow able to prove that you are not an agent of a foreign power, then you are simply cited for trespassing and must appear before a Federal magistrate.) **Do not enter the Navy base!** You definitely want to keep to the left at this fork in the road (N35°47.319 W117°18.092).

In slightly more than a mile, the still generally Class I road will take you into a small canyon. Notice the horizontal layers of sand on the hillside to the left within a quarter-mile. These are remnants of Ancient Lake Searles, probably deposited during the Tioga Stage of the Wisconsin Period, a mere 20,000 years ago. Although I have found no mega-fossils here, it is deposits like these, at the edge of the old lake, which make good places to look for the remains of large Pleistocene vertebrates: creatures like mastodons, *Camelops*, a llama-like camel, and *Equus,* an early form of large horse. All have become extinct in the last 10,000 to 50,000 years. It's fun to look, but remember that the collecting of such fossils is permitted on BLM administered lands only with a permit.

A half-mile into the canyon, the wash makes a sharp bend, and a side road right climbs the steep hill out of the wash; this is the road to the upper workings. We will want to go there, but for the moment, let's keep to the left and visit the main mine site just around the corner.

Although few records were kept in its early days, the Gold Bottom Mine was one of four important hardrock mines in Searles Valley. (The other three were the Ruth and Arondo Mines across the valley in the Argus Range, and the Ophir Mine just two miles to the north of the Gold Bottom Mine.) It was lead, not gold or copper, that was the important commodity sought here at the Gold Bottom Mine, in spite of its various names. Silver and gold were byproducts, and were recovered along with the lead in the milling process. The first claims were staked in the 1880s, and some ore was produced before 1900. The lower workings were developed in 1916, and worked intermittently until 1943.

The important mineralization has taken place here in the very old and highly metamorphosed rocks of Precambrian age. Gold, silver, and lead were recovered from orebodies that were as large as 5' wide and 200' long. An estimated $900,000 to $1 million were taken out of the ground here. The mill site was outside of the canyon, down by Searles Lake. It is said that the narrow gauge railroad operated by the old Trona Borax Company once came over here.

In his book *Pete Aguereberry,* author George Pipkin says that Jean LeMoigne (see Excursion #10) worked for wages in the Gold Bottom Mine during World War I. Conditions in the mine were so bad that Jean came down with lead and arsenic poisoning, as did many of his co-workers. As if that were not enough, Pete also broke a leg before leaving the mine for good.

As a teenager in the 1950s, I learned all about hardrock mining here, through exploring the 7,500' of underground workings. At the time it was like an industrial museum, displaying a wide variety of underground features, including adits, shafts, winzes, raises, stopes, drifts, crosscuts, and the like. In those days the mine had been abandoned only ten years previously, and the ladders and shoring were still in good condition. Such is not the case today, however. **Under no circumstances should the underground workings be entered. Their danger cannot be over-stated. Six of the many claims here are patented, meaning this is private property where the owner's rights should be respected, even though the site appears to be abandoned.**

It has been my observation that this sheltered and warm south-facing canyon has all the conditions needed for wildflower seeds to germinate early. Among the species seen in bloom as early as January are sand verbena, desert trumpet, chorizanthe, eriastrum, blazing star, four O clock and the lesser mohavena.

To visit the upper workings, drive back a tenth of a mile to the bend in the canyon, and turn left on the Class II road steeply climbing out of the wash. Soon there are good views of Searles Lake. You can see all the way to the Trona Pinnacles at the south end of the valley. Look around at the soil, which consists of rounded rocks. This was a Tioga stage shoreline 20,000 years ago. There may have been more sand between the cobbles then, but it is easy to imagine the waves lapping up on the beach here.

The road deteriorates to Class III as it ascends a layer of dark basalt lava, just above the marine terrace. The road forks just a half-mile from the bottom of the wash. The right fork goes a short distance to the upper workings. The left fork passes a couple of prospect holes (get out and look for malachite and other greenish colored copper minerals) and then goes on another two miles to dead-end on a rounded granite hilltop overlooking the badlands of Copper Queen Canyon. The last quarter-mile is a steep Class IV pitch, with very poor traction. The views of the Slate Range and of Searles Valley are quite good from this lofty perch.

The author took these photos of the Gold Bottom Mine in 1952.

Appendix A

A Glossary of Geologic and Mining Terms

Adit: a horizontal tunnel.

Alluvial Fan: the cone-shaped deposit of sand and gravel washed out of a canyon.

Andesite: a brown, reddish, or gray volcanic rock with a mineral composition equivalent to granite.

Arkostic: having a significant amount of feldspar.

Arrastra: a crude animal-powered device in which gold ore is crushed.

Ash: very fine rock particles thrown out by explosive volcanic eruptions.

Bajada: the slope of sand and gravel where two or more alluvial fans have coalesced.

Basalt: a hard black volcanic rock, sometimes containing gas bubble holes.

Batholith: a large mass of igneous rocks still deep within the earth.

Bedrock: solid rock exposed at the surface of the ground.

Breccia: angular fragments of volcanic rock held together by finer material.

Bunker: a hopper-like structure in which ore is stored while awaiting transport or processing.

Cinder Cone: the accumulated pile of ash and cinder at the mouth of a volcano.

Collar: the rim surrounding the top of a shaft.

Conglomerate: a sedimentary formation of various rocks having a wide variety of particle size and shape.

Dike: an intrusion of molten igneous rock into a crack or joint.

Dolomite: a metamorphic form of limestone, containing magnesium carbonate and calcium carbonate.

Epoch: a unit of geologic time within a "period" (example: the Pleistocene epoch of the Quaternary period of the Cenozoic era).

Era: the largest subdivision of geologic time (example: Mesozoic era).

Fanglomerate: conglomerate deposited and cemented together, as in an alluvial fan.

Fault: a crack in the earth's surface with one side moving in relation to the other side.

Feldspar: a very common rock-forming mineral containing silica and aluminum oxides.

Galena: lead sulfide, a common ore of lead.

Glaciation: the formation and movement of ice masses.

Glory hole: a pocket of very rich ore.

Gneiss: a very hard, often banded metamorphic rock.

Granite: a coarse-grained igneous rock containing quartz, feldspar and mica as the principal minerals.

Granodiorite: an igneous rock of similar composition as granite, except it contains more plagioclase feldspar than granite.

Headframe: the structure over a shaft, which supports a pulley, used to hoist ore buckets.

Ice Age: a long period of cold climate, where snowfalls on the land accumulated vast areas of ice because precipitation exceeded melting. Ice ages have occurred as early as the Precambrian and as recently as the Holocene epochs.

Igneous rock: molten rocks formed deep within the earth that have been forced to the surface.

Iron pyrite: a crystalline form of iron sulfide, sometimes called "Fools Gold" which can be mistaken for gold by the untrained.

Lava: magma that comes to the earth's surface by volcanic action.

Limestone: sedimentary rock of calcium carbonate formed in the sea bottom by the accumulation of shells and other organisms.

Lode: a vein or deposit of valuable minerals in solid rock.

Magma: deep-seated molten rock.

Marine Terrace: a flattened natural terrace on a hillside originally formed by wave action on the shoreline.

Metamorphism: the alteration of older igneous or sedimentary rocks by great heat, pressure, or chemical changes, resulting in the changing of the original rock into something different.

Metasediments: sedimentary rocks that have been subjected to great heat and pressure causing them to become metamorphic rocks. Their original sedimentary composition may no longer be recognized.

Mine: a place where a mineral commodity has been extracted and processed for its economic value.

Mining claim: The mining law of 1872 permits a person who finds valuable minerals on Federal land to claim the right to mine it. Each lode claim measures 1500' long by 600' wide. Each placer claim covers 20 acres. Multiple claims are permitted. Improvements must be performed annually. In recent years more restrictions have been imposed on the staking of mining claims.

Monzonite: a granite-like igneous rock rich in both plagioclase and orthoclase feldspar and ferro-magnesium minerals, but having little quartz.

Obsidian: a black volcanic glass that has formed by very rapid cooling of volcanic lava.

Orebody: a sufficient concentration of valuable minerals to warrant the expense of mining.

Quartz: a common rock-forming mineral of silicon dioxide often found in a crystalline state.

Quartzite: a metamorphic form of sandstone.

Quartz latite: a volcanic rock rich in feldspar and quartz.

Quartz monzonite: a granite-like rock, except it is rich in quartz as well as the feldspars.

Patented Claim: a mining claim of sufficient value that a legal process has been gone through which gives the owner not only mineral rights, but ownership of the land with all rights of use.

Period: a unit of geologic time within an era (example: Jurassic period of the Mesozoic era).

Placer: sand or gravel deposits containing gold or other valuable minerals.

Playa: a flat dry lakebed in an enclosed desert basin.

Pluvial: caused by the action of heavy rains.

Pluton: a mass of deep-seated igneous rock that intrudes the crust of the earth and slowly cools.

Potassium-argon dating: a method of dating rocks based on the decay of the potassium-40 isotope to argon-40.

Prospect: a place where an economically valuable mineral has been found, and explored for; however, no mining has (yet) taken place.

Pumice: a light-colored, lightweight frothy volcanic rock, often having enough air holes in it to permit it to float.

Pyroclastic: rock fragments formed by a volcanic explosion.

Rhyolite: a volcanic rock similar in mineral composition to granite.

Richter scale: a system for measuring the intensity of earthquakes. It is a log-rhythmic scale, meaning each numerical increase represents a tenfold increase of intensity.

Schist: a metamorphic rock, rich in mica that easily splits into plates or flakes.

Sedimentary rock: rocks formed by the accumulation of rock or organic material in the sea bottom or on top of the ground.

Seismic: earthquakes or man-made vibrations of the earth.

Stope: an underground opening above a tunnel from which ore is extracted.

Stull: large timber in a tunnel which supports the rock, thus preventing a cave-in.

Sulfide: the presence of sulfur, chemically bonded with other (metallic) minerals.

Tactite: a contact metamorphosed calcareous rock.

Tailings: A pile of waste rock at a mile tunnel or shaft. May also be finely ground ore left over after the milling process has extracted the valuable minerals.

Talc: a very soft, white mineral found in zones of some metamorphic rock.

Trilobite: a primitive and long extinct marine animal that lived on the bottom of Paleozoic seas.

Tuff: a rock formed from compacted volcanic ash.

Unconformity: a surface of erosion representing a gap in time between the older rocks below and the younger rocks above.

Vein: any mineral deposit that has filled a fissure or fracture. A relatively few contain valuable minerals, but most do not.

Volcanic ash: fine rock material ejected from a volcano.

Wave cut bench: see Marine Terrace.

Appendix B
Geologic Time Chart

Era	Period	Epoch	Years Ago (in millions)
Cenozoic	Quaternary	Holocene	
		Pleistocene	2-3
			12
	Tertiary	Pliocene	
		Miocene	26
		Oligocene	37-38
		Eocene	53-54
		Paleocene	
	Cretaceous		65
Mesozoic	Jurassic		136
	Triassic		190-195
	Permian		225
	Pennsylvanian		280
	Mississippian		310
Paleozoic	Devonian		345
	Silurian		395
	Ordovician		435
	Cambrian		500
			570
Proterozoic	Keweenawan		
	Huronian		1,000
Archeozoic	Timiskaming		
	Keewatin		1,800

Appendix C
The Plio-Pleistocene Ice Age

Epoch (Present Time)	Sierra Nevada Phase	Years Ago	Significance .
	Matthes	700 to present	
Holocene	Recess Peak	2000 to 2600	Bow & arrow replaces atlatl. Grinding stones first used. Pottery introduced. All desert lakes are now mostly dry.
Neoglacial		6,000	Ubehebe Crater blows it's top
	Hilgard	9000 to 10,500	Earliest human artifacts found in Death and Panamint Valleys.
		15,000	High water in Lakes China, Searles Panamint, Manly & Rogers. Lake Hill was a large island. Most Trona Pinnacles were formed.
	Tioga	20,000	Maximum ice in the Sierra.
	Tenaya	45,000	Maximum ice in the Sierra.
Wisconsin	Tahoe	75,000	Greatest known water depths in inland lakes. China & Searles were joined together. Lake Hill was a small island. Water poured down Wingate Wash into Lake Manly.
Pleistocene			
Illinoian	Mono Basin	130,000	
Kansan	Casa Diablo	400,000	Maximum ice in Sierra.
	Sherwin	700,000	Lake Tecopa starts to dry up.
Nebraskan	McGee	2,600,000+	Continental glaciation begins in North America.
Late Pliocene			
	Deadman Pass	2,700,000 to 3,100,000	Oldest known Plio-Pliestocene glaciation in California.

Appendix D
Ice Age Lakes in the Death Valley Area

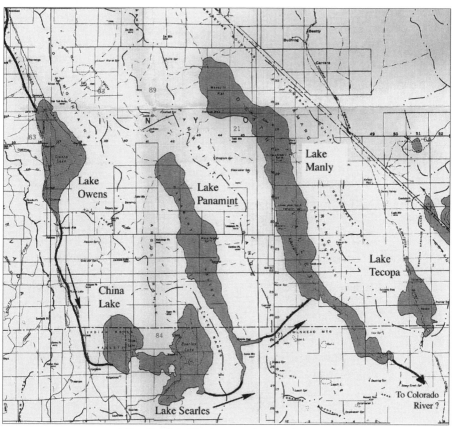

(after Snyder, Hardman and Zdenck, 1964)

Appendix E
Early Man in the Death Valley Area

Years Ago	Time Period Name	Artifacts Found	Place Found
Present day			
	Historic		
1769--			
500	*Saratoga Spring Culture*	pottery, clay figurines	Saratoga Spring
1100	Death Valley IV	pottery, fine arrowheads grinding stones pictographs & petroglyphs	sand dunes salt pans Greenwater Canyon
	Pacific		
2,000	Death Valley III	metates, manos shell beads clay figurines bows & arrows house rings petroglyphs	Amargosa River sand dunes many places
4000---			
5,000	Mesquite Flat Culture	stone circles grinding stones	
	Death Valley II	fluted points	gravel terraces
	Archaic	Fluted points, scrapers	Death Valley Lake Panamint China Lake
	Pinto Basin Tradition	Fluted points, house rings rock scrapers	Little Lake Lake Manly
	Lake Mohave Tradition		Lake Manly
9,000	*Nevares Spring Culture*	scrapers, choppers	Lake Manly
	San Dieguito Tradition		Death Valley?
11,000 ---			
	Paleo-Indian	Fluted points stone scrapers	Lake Manly Lake Panamint China Lake Owens Lake
	Death Valley I	Atlal points, house rings stone scrapers spear points	Lake Manly Lake Rogers Lake Mohave
30,000?			
40,000?		Crude stone	Calico site?
50,000?		Scrapers?	

Appendix F
Strange Happenings in Goler Wash

During the early morning hours of August 9, 1969, five people including Folger's Coffee heiress, Abigail Folger, and the very pregnant actress, Sharon Tate, were viciously murdered at a residence in the posh Benedict Canyon section of Los Angeles. Thus began a bizarre series of events that would involve dozens of people, and hundreds of crimes, drawing national attention to Goler Wash, a previously unheard of and forgotten corner of Death Valley. Within three months, the name Charles Manson was known worldwide.

Charles Manson's downfall started on September 9, 1969, with his senseless vandalizing of a National Park Service front end loader that was parked near the Race Track. This really upset the rangers, particularly one Dick Powell. A group of hippies in a red Toyota and a dune buggy had been seen in the vicinity. A couple of weeks later Powell spotted a red Toyota in Panamint Valley, complete with a band of hippies in it. By this time Powell was aware of a group of squatters living at Myers and Barker Ranches in upper Goler Wash. On September 29th, he and Jim Pursell, a CHP officer out of Bishop, made a friendly call at the Barker Ranch. Ultimately they found nine young women in their late teens and early twenties, and, very carefully camouflaged, the red Toyota and a dune buggy. No arrests were made at that time, but checks later revealed both vehicles had been stolen.

Early on the morning of October 9th, Ranger Powell and Officer Pursell returned to the Barker Ranch. This time they brought some friends with them: a small army of Park Service rangers, CHP officers, Inyo County Sheriff deputies, and even a state game warden. A pre-dawn sweep of the two ranches netted three males, ten females and two infants, along with various weapons. All were transported to Independence and booked into the Inyo County Jail on a variety of charges.

Even though thirteen members of this band had been arrested, it was thought that there were still more out there. Three days later the ranches were raided again, this time in the late afternoon. By this time Powell and Purcell were very familiar with the area and went ahead of the main force to reconnoiter. They observed four males entering the Barker Ranch house. In a lightning raid, the hippie-hunting duo burst through the door with guns drawn and arrested the four men plus three females. Still, the group's leader was not among those taken into custody.

After this second group had been cuffed and moved down canyon, Officer Pursell checked the house once again. In the darkness, he reached in a cabinet under the bathroom sink, and upon feeling a mass of greasy hair, he pulled on it.

Out tumbled Charlie Manson, the group's leader. The raid of October 12th had netted ten more suspects. The Inyo County Jail in Independence was filling up.

Conversations among some of the arrested women, overheard by deputies, suggested that some of those being held in jail might have had something to do with the murders in Los Angeles. The Inyo County Sheriff then tipped off the Los Angeles Police Department. The telephone lines between Independence and Los Angeles began smoking as officers of the two agencies began comparing notes and putting the pieces together.

Between July 27th and August 26th, Charles Manson and his gang of misfits butchered at least nine people. Gang member, Sandra Good, once bragged that the total number of murders committed by Manson's group was 35-40. That may be correct. Manson himself bragged of killing 35 people. After detective work put Manson at the Tate-LaBianca crime scene, Charles Manson was charged with the Tate-LaBianca murders on December 9, 1969. Inyo County gladly released Charlie to the Los Angeles authorities.

The same Thanksgiving weekend that the Los Angeles Police Department and the Inyo County Sheriff Department were finding they had a mutual interest in Charles Manson, some backcountry friends, Herbie and Jane Horne, Tom and Diana Jones, and Bob Boyd, and I decided to visit Barker Ranch ourselves, to check out first hand the strange doings in Goler Wash. By this time Inyo County District Attorney Frank Fowles, his Deputy Buck Gibbens and investigator Jack Gardner along with five LAPD sergeants and Los Angeles Deputy District Attorney Vincent Bugliosi had been in there to search the place thoroughly. Surely all the useful evidence had been found and our presence would cause no harm.

Nevertheless, on a hillside near the ranch house, half under a bush, but in plain sight, Herbie found a large metal can containing a marijuana pipe and a jar in which there appeared to be marijuana seed. So much for the DA's thorough search! We left the evidence where we found it, and notified the proper authorities.

On June 15, 1970, Charles Manson, Patricia Krenwinkel, Leslie Van Houton, and Susan Atkins, were all put on trial for the Tate-LaBianca murders. On March 29, 1971, the jury came in with a guilty verdict against all four defendants. The sentence was death, but later, in 1972, the death penalty was ruled to be unconstitutional by a very liberal California Supreme Court under Chief Justice Rose Bird. The quartet is still incarcerated in prison. Charles Manson has had ten parole hearings since 1978, and the next one is scheduled for the year 2007. Will Charlie ever be released? If that should ever happen, will Manson ever return to Goler Wash? Only time will tell. In the meanwhile, he still resides in Cocoran State Prison in the San Joaquin Valley.

If you want to check on Charlie's current status, one of his "family" members, Sandra Good, maintains a Charles Manson web page.

Herb Horne points to a can containing drug paraphenalia halfway hidden beneath a bush

Appendix G

Some Useful Addresses

Superintendent's Office
Death Valley National Park
Death Valley CA 92328
(760) 786-3200

Death Valley National Park
Beatty Information Office
Main Street
Beatty NV 89003
(775)553-2200

Inter Agency Visitor Center
Highway 395 and State Route 136
(P. O. Drawer "R")
Lone Pine, CA 93545
(760) 876-6222

Bureau of Land Management
Ridgecrest Resource Area
300 So. Richmond Road
Ridgecrest, CA 93555
(760) 384-5400

Bureau of Land Management
Bishop Field Office
785 No. Main Street
Bishop CA 93514
(760) 872-4881

Bureau of Land Management (Nevada areas surrounding the Park))
1553 So. Main Street
P. O. Box 911
Tonopah NV 89049
(775) 482-7800

Eastern California Museum
155 No. Grant Street
(P.O. Box 206)
Independence CA 93526
(760) 878-0258

Maturango Museum
100 E. Las Flores Ave.
Ridgecrest CA 93555
(760) 375-6900

Death Valley Natural History Association
P.O. Box 188
Death Valley CA 92328
(760) 786-3285

Searles Valley Historical Society
P.O. Box 630
Trona CA 93592
(760) 372-4800, 372-5230, or 372-5064

Historical Society of the Upper Mojave Desert
100 E. Las Flores Ave.
Ridgecrest CA 93555
(760) 375-6900

Beatty Chamber of Commerce
P.O. Box 956
Beatty NV 89003
(775) 553-2424

Death Valley Chamber of Commerce
Highway 127
Shoshone CA 92384
(760) 852-4524

Lone Pine Chamber of Commerce
126 So. Main Street
Lone Pine CA 93545
(760) 876-4444

Big Pine Chamber of Commerce
126 So. Main Street
(P.O. Box 23)
Big Pine, CA   93515
(760) 938-2114

References

Alltucker, Ken, "Nevada Mining Feels Pain from Gold's Global Decline", *Reno Gazette-Journal*, Reno NV: September 26, 1999.

Anon, *Death Valley*, American Guide Series, Boston and New York: Houghton Mifflin Co, 1939.

_____, "Geologic Map of California", *Death Valley Sheet*, San Francisco CA: California Division of Mines, 1958.

_____, "Geologic Map of California", *Mariposa Sheet*, Sacramento CA: California Division of Mines & Geology, 1967.

_____, *Romantic Heritage of Inyo-Mono*, California Interstate Telephone Company, 1966.

_____, "California Fossil Discovery Reveals New Species of Camel", *California Geology*, Sacramento CA: California Division of Mines & Geology, January/ February 2000.

Albers, J.P, and J.H. Stewart, *Geology and Mineral Deposits of Esmeralda County, Nevada*, Nevada Bureau of Mines & Geology Bulletin 78, Reno NV: Mackay School of Mines, University Of Nevada, 1972.

Ashbaugh, Don, *Nevada's Turbulent Yesterday*, Los Angeles CA: Westernlore Press, 1963.

Bailey, Edgar H. (Editor), *Geology of Northern California*, Bulletin 190, San Francisco CA: California Division of Mines & Geology, 1996.

Baldwin, Bruce G., et al, editors, *The Jepson Desert Manual, Vascular Plants of Southeastern California,* Berkeley, Los Angeles & London: University of California Press, 2002.

Belden, L. Burr, *Mines of Death Valley,* Glendale CA: La Siesta Press, 1966.

_____, *Old Stovepipe Wells*, Death Valley '49er Keepsake Publication No. 8, San Bernardino CA: Inland Printing & Engraving Co., 1968.

Betancourt, J.L., with T.R. Van Devender and P.S. Martin (eds.), *Packrat Middens: The Last 40,000 Years of Biotic Change*, Tucson AZ: University of Arizona Press, 1990.

Billeb, Emil W., *Mining Camp Days*, Berkeley CA: Howell-North Books, 1968.

Blanc, Robert P. and George B. Cleveland, "Pleistocene Lakes of Southern California" (Parts I & II), *Mineral Information Service*, San Francisco CA: California Division of Mines, April and May 1961.

Brandt, Roger G., *Titus Canyon Road Guide, A Tour Through Time*, Death Valley CA: Death Valley Natural History Association, 1992.

Brott, Clark W., Daniel F. McCarthy, Kathlyn Obendorfer-McGraw, and Mary Obendorfer, *Archaeology in Panamint Dunes, 1983,* Ridgecrest CA: prepared under contract for Bureau of Land Management, 1984.

Bryan, T. Scott, and Betty Tucker-Bryan, *The Explorer's Guide to Death Valley National Park,* Niwot CO: University Press of Colorado, 1995.

Bugliosi, Vincent, and Curt Gentry, *Helter Skelter,* Toronto, New York, London: Bantam Books, 1974.

Burchfield, B. Clark, *Geology of the Dry Mountain Quadrangle, Inyo County, California,* Special Report 99, San Francisco CA: California Division of Mines & Geology, 1969.

Caruthers, William, *Loafing Along Death Valley Trails,* Pomona CA: P.B. Press Inc., 1951.

Clark, William B., *Gold Districts of California,* Bulletin 193, Sacramento CA: California Division of Mines & Geology, 1970.

Clements, Lydia, *Death Valley Indians,* Los Angeles CA: Hollycrofters, 1954.

Clements, Thomas, *Geological Story of Death Valley,* Death Valley '49ers Publication No. 1, Palm Desert CA: Desert Magazine Press, 1954.

Chalfant, W.A., *Death Valley: The Facts,* Stanford CA: Stanford University Press, 1936.

_____, *The Story of Inyo,* Bishop CA: Piñon Book Store, 1933.

_____, *Gold, Guns & Ghost Towns,* Stanford CA: Stanford University Press, 1947.

Chartkoff, Joseph L. and Kerry Kona Chartkoff, *The Archeology of California,* Stanford CA: Stanford University Press, 1984.

Charlet, David Alan, *Atlas of Nevada Conifers,* Reno & Las Vegas NV: University of Nevada Press, 1996.

Cronkhite, Daniel, *Death Valley's Victims,* Morongo Valley CA: Sagebrush Press, 1981.

Crowe, Richard D., "Sourdough Pancakes and Fried Burro Liver", *Proceedings Fourth Death Valley Conference On History & Prehistory,* Jean Johnson, editor, Death Valley CA: Death Valley Natural History Association, 1996.

_____, "Where Is the Confidence Mine?", *Proceedings Second Death Valley Conference On History & Prehistory,* Richard Lingenfelter & James Pisarowicz, editors, Death Valley CA: Death Valley Natural History Association, 1988.

Davis, Emma Lou, and Christopher Raven, editors, *Environmental and Paleoenvironmental Studies in Panamint Valley,* San Diego CA: Great Basin Foundation, 1986.

DeDecker, Mary, "The Search For The Bullfrog Wild Pea", *Proceedings First Death Valley Conference On History & Prehistory,* Richard Lingenfelter & James Pisarowicz, editors, Death Valley CA: Death Valley Natural History Association, 1991.

Digonnet, Michel, *Hiking Death Valley,* Palo Alto CA: privately published, 1997.

Downs, Theodore, *Fossil Vertebrates of Southern California,* Berkeley & Los Angeles CA: University of California Press, 1968.

Elias, Scott A., *The Ice-Age History of Southwestern National Parks,* Washington & London: Smithsonian Institution Press, 1997.

Elliott, Russell, R., *Nevada's 20th Century Mining Boom,* Reno NV: University of Nevada Press, 1966.

Evans, James R., and Gary C. Taylor, John S. Rapp, *Mines and Mineral Deposits in Death Valley National Monument, California,* Special Report 125, Sacramento CA: California Division of Mines & Geology, 1976.

Gath, Eldon, "Quarternary Lakes of the Owens River System", *Geology And Mineral Wealth Of The Owens Valley Region*, Santa Ana CA: South Coast Geological Society, 1987.

Goodwin, J. Grant, *Lead and Zinc in California*, Volume 53, San Francisco CA: California Division of Mines, 1957.

Grant, Campbell, et al, *Rock Drawings of the Coso Range, Inyo County, California*, Maturango Museum Publication No. 4, Ridgecrest CA: Maturango Press, 1968.

Grayson, Donald K., *The Desert's Past, A Natural History of the Great Basin*, Washington & London: Smithsonian Institution Press, 1993.

Greene, Linda W., *Historic Resource Study, A History of Mining in Death Valley National Monument*, Volume I Parts 1 and 2, Denver CO: National Park Service, Western Service Center, March 1981.

Gudde, Erwin G., *1000 California Place Names*, Los Angeles & Berkeley CA: University of California Press, 2nd Revised edition, 1959.

_____, *California Gold Camps*, Berkeley & Los Angeles CA: University of California Press, 1975.

Hall, Clarence A., editor, *Natural History of the White-Inyo Range Eastern California*, Berkeley, Los Angeles, & Oxford: University of California Press, 1991.

Hall, Wayne E., with E.M. MacKevett, *Economic Geology of the Darwin Quadrangle, Inyo County, California*, Special Report 5, San Francisco CA: California Division of Mines, 1958.

Hall, Wayne E. and Hal G. Stephens, *Economic Geology of the Panamint Butte Quadrangle and Modoc District, Inyo County, California,* Special Report 73, San Francisco CA: California Division of Mines & Geology, 1963.

Hall, Wayne E., *Geology of the Panamint Butte Quadrangle, Inyo County, California*, Geological Survey Bulletin 1299, Washington DC: U.S. Geological Survey, 1971.

Henderson, Randall, *On Desert Trails,* Los Angeles CA: Westernlore Press, 1961.

Henry, Donald J., *California Gem Trails*, Long Beach CA: Lowell R. Gordon, 1957.

Hubbard, Paul B., et al, *Ballarat*, Lancaster CA: published by the author, 1965.

Hunt, Charles B., *Plant Ecology of Death Valley California*, Geological Survey Professional Paper 509, Washington DC: U.S. Geological Survey, 1966.

_____, *Death Valley: Geology, Ecology, Archaeology*, Berkeley, Los Angeles, & London: University of California Press, 1975.

Jaeger, Edmund C., *The California Deserts*, Stanford CA: Stanford University Press, Revised Edition, 1938.

_____, *The North American Deserts*, Stanford CA: Stanford University Press, 1957.

_____, "River of Bitter Waters", *Desert Magazine*, Palm Desert CA: Desert Press, Inc., July 1958.

_____, *A Naturalist's Death Valley*, Death Valley '49ers Publication No. 5, (Revised Edition) Bishop CA: Chalfant Press, 1979.

Jahns, Richard H., editor, *Geology of Southern California*, Bulletin 170, San Francisco CA: California Division of Mines, 1954.

Johnson, Leroy and Jean, *Escape From Death Valley*, Reno & Las Vegas NV: University of Nevada Press, 1987.

_____, "The Bennett-Arcan Long Camp and Manly's Sulphur Water Well", *Proceedings First Death Valley Conference on History & Prehistory*, Richard Lingenfelter & James Pisarowicz, editors, Death Valley CA: Death Valley Natural History Association, 1991.

Journigan, Russ, "The Journigan Tucki Mine", *Proceedings Sixth Death Valley Conference on History & Prehistory*, Jean Johnson, editor, Death Valley CA: Death Valley Natural History Association, 2002.

Kirk, Ruth, *Exploring Death Valley*, Stanford CA: Stanford University Press, 1965.

Johnston, Hank, *Death Valley Scotty: The Man & The Myth,* Yosemite CA: Flying Spur Press, 1972.

Kohler-Antablin, Susan, "California Non-Fuel Minerals – 1998", *California Geology*, Sacramento CA: California Division of Mines & Geology, September/October 1999.

Lanner, Robert M., *The Pinyon Pine, A Natural and Cultural History*, Reno NV: University of Nevada Press, 1981.

Larson, Peggy, and Lane Larson, *A Sierra Club Naturalist's Guide to the Deserts of the Southwest*, San Francisco CA: Sierra Club Books, 1977.

Latschar, John A., "Historic Resource Study", Volume II Parts 1 and 2, *A History of Mining in Death Valley National Monument*, Denver CO: National Park Service, Denver Service Center, 1983.

Leigh, Rufus Wood, *Nevada Place Names*, Salt Lake City UT: Deseret News Press, 1964.

Lengner, Ken & George Ross, *Remembering the Early Shoshone and Tecopa Area, Southeastern Death Valley Region*, Shoshone CA: self-published, 2004.

Lingenfelter, Richard E., *Death Valley & The Amargosa*, Berkeley and Los Angeles CA: University of California Press, 1986.

Likes, Robert C. and Glenn R. Day, *From This Mountain - Cerro Gordo*, Bishop CA: Chalfant Press, 1975.

Lofinck, Sewell "Pop", *Mojave Desert Ramblings*, Maturango Museum Publication No. 2, China Lake CA: Maturango Press, November 1966.

Long, Margaret, *The Shadow of the Arrow*, Caldwell ID: Caxton Printers, 1950.

McAllister, James F., *Rocks and Structure of the Quartz Spring Area, Northern Panamint Range, California*, Special Report 25, San Francisco CA: California Division of Mines, 1952.

_____, *Geology of the Mineral Deposits in the Ubehebe Peak Quadrangle, Inyo County, California*, Special Report 42, San Francisco CA: California Division of Mines, 1955.

McKee, Edwin H., *Geology of the Magruder Mountain Area, Nevada-California*, Geological Survey Bulletin 1251-H, Washington DC: U.S. Geological Survey, 1968.

McWhorter, Frank, "True Greasewood Is Full Of Grease", *Desert Magazine*, Palm Desert CA: Desert Magazine, January 1978.

MacKevett, Edward M., *Geology of the Santa Rosa Lead Mine, Inyo County, California,* Special Report 34, San Francisco CA: California Division of Mines, 1953.

292

Marcom, Geron, "An Introduction To Death Valley's Hidden Legacy", *Proceedings Fourth Death Valley Conference On History & Prehistory*, Jean Johnson, editor, Death Valley CA: Death Valley Natural History Association, 1996.

Maxson, John H., *Death Valley, Origin and Scenery*, Death Valley CA: Death Valley Natural History Association, 1963.

Merriam, Charles W., and Wayne E. Hall, *Pennsylvanian and Permian Rocks of the Southern Inyo Mountains, California*, U.S. Geological Survey Bulletin 1061-A, Washington DC: U.S. Government Printing Office, 1957.

Merriam, C.W., *Geology of the Cerro Gordo Mining District, Inyo County, California*, U.S. Geological Survey Professional Paper 408, Washington DC: Government Printing Office, 1963.

Miller, Julia M.G., *Geologic Map Of A Portion Of The Manly Peak Quadrangle, Southern Panamint Mountains, Inyo and San Bernardino Counties, California*, Open-File Report 85-9, Sacramento, CA: California Division of Mines &Geology, 1985.

_____, "Tectonic Evolution of the Southern Panamint Range", *California Geology*, Sacramento CA: California Division of Mines & Geology, September 1987.

Mitchell, Roger, "Saga of Cerro Gordo", *Four Wheeler Magazine*, Tarzana CA: Ames Publishing Company, September 1965.

_____, "Exploring Cottonwood Canyon", *Desert Magazine*, Palm Desert CA: Desert Magazine, November 1967.

_____, "The Legend of Lookout", *Desert Magazine*, Palm Desert CA: Desert Magazine, April 1968.

_____, "Riddle of the Racetrack", *Desert Magazine*, Palm Desert CA: Desert Magazine, November 1968.

_____, "15 Backcountry Trips", *Desert Magazine*, Palm Desert CA: Desert Magazine, November 1969.

_____, *Death Valley Jeep Trails*, Glendale CA: La Siesta Press, 1969, revised edition 1975.

_____, *Inyo-Mono Jeep Trails*, Glendale CA: La Siesta Press, 1969.

_____, "Exploring the Saline Valley", *Desert Magazine*, Palm Desert CA: Desert Magazine, November 1971.

_____, *Western Nevada Jeep Trails*, Glendale CA: La Siesta Press, 1973.

Mordy, Brooke D. & Donald McCaughey, *Nevada Historical Sites*, Special Report 88, Reno NV: Desert Research Institute, University of Nevada, 1968.

Morton, Paul K., *Geology of the Queen of Sheba Lead Mine, Death Valley, California*, San Francisco CA: California Division of Mines & Geology, 1965.

Munz, Philip A., *California Desert Wildflowers*, Berkeley and Los Angeles CA: University of California Press, 1962.

Myrick, David F., *Railroads of Nevada*, Volumes 1 & 2, Berkeley CA: Howell-North Books, 1962.

Nadeau, Remi, *City Makers*, Los Angeles CA: Trans-Anglo Books, 1965.

_____, *Ghost Towns and Mining Camps of California*, Los Angeles CA: Ward Ritchie Press, 1965.

_____, *The Silver Seekers*, Santa Barbara CA: Crest Publishers, 1999.

_____, "Nadeau's Freighting Teams In the Mojave", *Proceedings First Death Valley Conference on History & Prehistory*, Richard Lingenfelter & James Pisarowicz, editors, Death Valley CA: Death Valley Natural History Association, 1991.

Nelson, Genne, "The Personal Side of the Jayhawkers: Vignettes from the Jayhawker Collection, The Huntington Library", *Proceedings First Death Valley Conference on History & Prehistory*, Richard Lingenfelter & James Pisarowicz, editors, Death Valley CA: Death Valley Natural History Association, 1991.

Norman, L.A. & Richard M. Stewart, *Mines and Mineral Resources of Inyo County*, Volume 47 Number 1, San Francisco CA: California Division of Mines, January 1951.

Norwood, Richard H. and Charles S. Bull, *A Cultural Resource Overview of the Eureka, Saline, Panamint and Darwin Region, East Central California*, Riverside CA: prepared for California Desert Planning Staff, Eric W. Ritter, editor, under Bureau of Land Management contract, 1980.

Page, Ben M., *Talc Deposits of Steatite Grade, Inyo County, California*, Special Report 8, San Francisco CA: California Division of Mines, 1951.

Paher, Stanley W., *Nevada Ghost Towns & Mining Camps*, Berkeley CA: Howell-North Books, 1970.

Pipkin, George C., *Pete Aguereberry, Death Valley Prospector & Gold Miner*, 2nd Edition, Trona CA: Murchison Publications, 1982.

Raven, Christopher, *Landscape Evolution and Human Geography in Panamint Valley*, Contributions of the Great Basin Foundation Number 1, San Diego CA: Great Basin Foundation, 1985.

Reed, Lester, *Old-Timers of Southeastern California*, Redlands CA: Citrograph Printing Co., 1967.

Rinehart, C. Dean, and Donald C. Ross, *Economic Geology of the Casa Diablo Mountain Quadrangle California*, Special Report 48, San Francisco CA: California Division of Mines, 1956.

Romero, Miriam A., editor, with John M. Sully and Robert D. Smith, *Amargosa Canyon-Dumont Dunes Proposed Natural Area*, a report submitted to the Bureau of Land Management by the Pupfish Habitat Preservation Committee, 1972.

Ross, Donald C., *Geology of the Independence Quadrangle, Inyo County, California*, U.S. Geological Survey Bulletin 1181-O, Washington DC: Government Printing Office, 1965.

Sadovich, Maryellen V., *Your Guide to Southern Nevada*, Nevada Historical Society Guidebook Series, Carson City NV: State Printing Office, 1976.

Schumacher, Genny, *Deepest Valley*, San Francisco CA: Sierra Club, Vail Ballou Press, Inc., 1963.

Sharp, Robert P., *Geology: Field Guide to Southern California*, Regional Geology Series, Dubuque IA: Wm. C. Brown Company, 1972.

Sharp, Robert P. and Allen F. Glazner, *Geology Underfoot in Death Valley and Owens Valley*, Missoula MT: Mountain Press Publishing Co., 1997.

Smith, George C., with Bennie W. Troxel, Clifford H. Gray, and Roland von Huene, *Geologic Reconnaissance of the Slate Range, San Bernardino and Inyo Counties California*, Special Report 96, San Francisco CA: California Division of Mines & Geology, 1968.

Snyder, C.T., George Hardman, and F.F. Zdenek, *Pleistocene Lakes In The Great Basin*, Geologic Investigations Map I-416, Washington DC: U.S. Geological Survey, 1964.

Southworth, John, "The Bennett-Arcane Escape Trail Through the Panamint and Slate Ranges", *Proceedings Third Death Valley Conference On History & Prehistory*, Jean Johnson, editor, Death Valley CA: Death Valley Natural History Association, 1992.

Stinson, Melvin C., *Geology of the Keeler 15' Quadrangle, Inyo County, California*, Map Sheet 38, San Francisco CA: California Division of Mines & Geology, 1977.

Strong, Mary Francis, "Amargosa Gorge", *Desert Magazine*, Palm Desert CA: Desert Magazine, November 1975.

_____, *Desert Gem Trails*, Mentone CA: Gem Books, 1996.

Trexler, Dennis T., and Wilton N. Melhorn, "Singing and Booming Sand Dunes of California and Nevada", *California Geology*, Sacramento CA: Division of Mines & Geology, July 1986.

Troxel, Bennie W., editor, *Geologic Features, Death Valley, California*, Special Report 106, Sacramento, CA: California Division of Mines & Geology, 1976.

Tuohy, Donald R., *Nevada's Prehistoric Heritage*, Carson City NV: Nevada State Museum Popular Series, 1965.

Vredenburgh, Larry M., "Reilly: The Well Preserved Ruins Of An 1880's Mining Camp", *Proceedings First Death Valley Conference On History & Prehistory*, Richard Lingenfelter & James Pisarowicz, editors, Death Valley CA: Death Valley Natural History Association, 1991.

Von Huene, Roland, *Fossil Mammals of the Indian Wells Valley Region and How to Collect Them*, Maturango Museum Publication No. 5, Ridgecrest CA: Maturango Press, 1971.

Wagner, David L., and Eugene Y. Hsu, *Reconnaissance Geologic Map of Parts of Wingate Wash, Quail Mountains, and The Manly Peak Quadrangles, Inyo and San Bernardino Counties, Southeastern California*, Sacramento CA: California Division of Mines & Geology, 1987.

Wallace, William J. and Edith, *Ancient Peoples and Cultures of Death Valley National Monument*, Ramona CA: Acoma Books, 1978.

Weight, Harold and Lucile, Rhyolite, *The Ghost City of Golden Dreams*, 4th Edition revised, Twentynine Palms CA: Calico Press, 1953.

Weight, Harold, *Twenty Mule Team Days in Death Valley*, Twentynine Palms CA: Calico Press, 1955.

_____, *Greenwater*, Twentynine Palms CA: Calico Press, 1969.

Wheelock, Walt, *Desert Peaks Guide, Part I*, Glendale CA: La Siesta Press, 1964.

_____, *Desert Peaks Guide, Part II*, Glendale CA: La Siesta Press, 1975.

Wilson, Neill C., *Silver Stampede*, New York NY: The McMillan Company, 1937.

Wright, Lauren A., and Bennie W. Troxel, *Geology of North Confidence Hills 15' Quadrangle, Inyo County, California*, Map Sheet 34, Sacramento CA: California Division of Mines & Geology, 1984.

Yoshino, Kimi, "Manson returns to Corcoran prison after discipline", *The Fresno Bee*, Fresno CA: June 13, 1998.

Zanjani, Sally, "Jack Longstreet In The Death Valley Region", *Proceedings First Death Valley Conference On History & Prehistory*, Richard Lingenfelter & James Psarowicz, editors, Death Valley CA: Death Valley Natural History Association, 1991.

Index

Index

298

Index

Index

Index

Index

Index

Index

Index

Index

Index

Index

308

Other Guidebooks from TRACK & TRAIL PUBLICATIONS

High Sierra SUV Trails Series

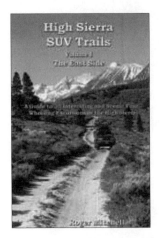

High Sierra SUV Trails Vol. I
The East Side

35 rough road adventures with excursions out of Reno, Truckee, South Lake Tahoe, Markleeville, Bridgeport, Lee Vining, Mammoth Lakes, Bishop, Big Pine, Independence, and Lone Pine.

240 pages   **$16.95**

High Sierra SUV Trails Vol. II
The Western Slope

40 rough road adventures with excursions out of Auburn, Foresthill, Placerville, Jackson, Angels Camp, Sonora, Pinecrest, Mariposa, Oakhurst, Shaver Lake, Mono Hot Springs, Kings Canyon National Park, and Kernville.

272 pages   **$18.95**

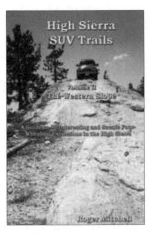

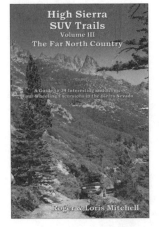

High Sierra SUV Trails Vol. III
The Far North Country

34 rough road adventures with excursions out of Auburn, Truckee, Grass Valley-Nevada City, Downieville, Sierra City, Oroville, La Porte, Quincy, Portola, Reno, and Susanville.

304 pages   **$19.95**

Look for them at your favorite bookstore or order them online at
TRACKANDTRAILPUBLICATIONS.COM

Other Guidebooks from TRACK & TRAIL PUBLICATIONS

Southern California SUV Trails
Vol. II, The Eastern Mojave Desert

34 rough road adventures with excursions out of Barstow, Baker, Shoshone, Primm, Kelso, Ludlow, Needles and Twentynine Palms,
368 pages **$21.95**

Inyo-Mono SUV Trails

40 rough road adventures with excursions out of Bridgeport, Lee Vining, Mammoth Lakes, Bishop, Big Pine, Independence, Lone Pine, and Olancha.
304 pages **$19.95**

Southern California SUV Trails Vol. I
The Western Mojave Desert

32 rough road adventures with excursions out of Ridgecrest, Randsburg, Mojave, Boron-Kramer Junction, Victorville, and Barstow.
304 pages **$19.95**

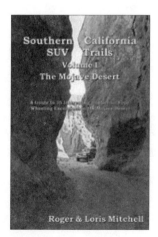

Look for them at your favorite bookstore or order them online at
TRACKANDTRAILPUBLICATIONS.COM

Other Guidebooks from TRACK & TRAIL PUBLICATIONS

Great Basin SUV Trails Series

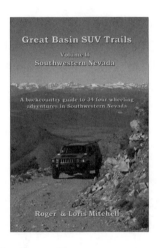

Great Basin SUV Trails Vol. I
Southern Nevada

32 rough road adventures with excursions out of Las Vegas, Boulder City, Searchlight, Laughlin, Pahrump, and Beatty.

272 pages   **$19.95**

Great Basin SUV Trails Vol. II
Southwestern Nevada

34 rough road adventures with excursions out of Beatty, Goldfield, Tonopah, Bishop, Mina, and Hawthorne.

304 pages   **$19.95**

Look for them at your favorite bookstore or order them online at
TRACKANDTRAILPUBLICATIONS.COM

These publications may also be ordered directly from the publisher. Please add appropriate sales tax (CA residents only) and Media Rate shipping of $2.75 for the first book and $1.00 for each additional book. (For Priority Mail: $4.25 for first book and $1.00 for each additional book.)

Send your check to:
TRACK AND TRAIL PUBLICATIONS
P.O. Box 1247
Oakhurst, CA 93644

Notes